The Future of Welfare

edited by

Rudolf Klein and
Michael O'Higgins

Basil Blackwell

© Rudolf Klein and Michael O'Higgins 1985

First published 1985

Basil Blackwell Ltd
108 Cowley Road, Oxford OX4 1JF, UK

Basil Blackwell Inc.
432 Park Avenue South, Suite 1505,
New York, NY 10016, USA

British Library Cataloguing in Publication Data

The Future of welfare.
  1. Great Britain – Social policy
  I. Klein, Rudolf, 1930 –   II. O'Higgins,
  Michael, 1954 –
  361.6′1′0941   HN390
  ISBN 0-631-14203-7
  ISBN 0-631-14204-5 Pbk

Library of Congress Cataloging in Publication Data

The Future of welfare.
  Bibliography: p.
  Includes index.
  1. Public welfare – Addresses, essays, lectures.
2. Social policy – Addresses, essays, lectures.
3. Great Britain – Social policy – Addresses, essays, lectures.
I. Klein, Rudolf.   II. O'Higgins, Michael, 1954 –
HV51.F88 1985   361.6   85-9054
ISBN 0-631-14203-7
ISBN 0-631-14204-5 (pbk.)

Typeset by Getset (BTS) Ltd, Eynsham, Oxford.
Printed in Great Britain by Billings Ltd, Worcester

Contents

Acknowledgements

This book is one product of a conference sponsored by the Economic and Social Research Council and organized by the Centre for the Analysis of Social Policy at the University of Bath in June 1984. The Joseph Rowntree Memorial Trust provided additional support in the preparation of the book. We would like to express our gratitude to both for their help. In particular, Raymond Illsley, the chairman of the Social Affairs Committee of the ESRC, and Nicholas Deakin, chairman of its Future of the Welfare State sub-committee, gave valuable advice and assistance. Neither the conference nor the production of the book would have been possible without the hard work, tolerance and good humour of our secretaries, Sylvia Hodges and Louise Mellerick, to whom are due our thanks and, as usual, promises to be better organized in future. Margaret Arnold provided important additional secretarial assistance and Owen Ward and Gwen Davies coped valiantly and cheerfully with the disruption that our activities caused to normal academic and administrative life in the School of Humanities and Social Sciences.

Much of the editing of this book was carried out while one of us was a visiting scholar in the Department of Sociology at Harvard University. Thanks are due to that department, and in particular to talcott and vi.

Centre for the Analysis of Social Policy   Rudolf Klein
University of Bath   Michael O'Higgins

Introduction:
Old Myths – New Challenges

RUDOLF KLEIN and MICHAEL O'HIGGINS

For about ten years now there has been a debate about the 'crisis' of the Welfare State. What is generally meant by this is that the social policy commitments taken on in the decades of optimism about economic growth have become unrealistic or unsustainable in the new era of pessimism about the prospects of continuing expansion. The language of 'crisis' provokes, in turn, the vocabulary of policy drama. If the welfare state is indeed in 'crisis' – in the sense of heading towards an inevitable collision between inherited commitments and available resources – then, clearly, there has to be a fundamental rethink of existing policies and strategies.

This book is a contribution to this debate. But it is, we hope, a contribution with a difference. For its starting point is the assumption that the whole notion of 'crisis' needs demystification, and that any attempt to rethink the functions and institutions of the welfare state must start by questioning not only inherited commitments but traditional styles of defining and thinking about social policy, including the idea that *welfare* and the Welfare State are synonymous. If we have to go back to the drawing-board, the exercise must start with our intellectual tools: the way in which we conceptualize the nature of the problems we are trying to solve.

The first aim, therefore, is to break down the notion of 'crisis', a word which, in itself, tends to prejudge the issue, into a set of specific questions amenable to analysis and to identify the policy issues which are likely to dominate the agenda of public debate for the next decade. This reflects the origins of the book: a conference at the University of Bath sponsored by the Economic and Social Research Council and designed to help in laying the foundations for what is planned to be a major research initiative. So this is emphatically not an exercise in producing instant policy prescriptions. Rather it is an exercise in thinking about the nature of the problems that are being addressed, and how these are likely to change – for there is little point in debating about how best to cope with yesterday's problems when tomorrow's are already knocking at our door.

The second aim, however, is somewhat different. It is to try to demonstrate, again in line with the ESRC's concerns in sponsoring the Bath conference, that there can be a useful dialogue between the academic community and the world of policy making. The chapters in this book therefore address themselves to issues of direct and immediate concern to policy makers, and indeed to all those interested in the development and study of social policy. But in doing so they seek to challenge, probe and test the assumptions which shape the way in which issues are defined, to extend the limits of what is thought to be feasible rather than taking existing conceptual or institutional constraints as cast in concrete for all time. For if there is to be a dialogue between the academic community and the world of policy making, it is one in which the two sides must recognize that they have different roles. The former's is to explore complexity; the latter's is to search for simplicity. The former's is to delineate the trade-offs between competing policy aims and options; the latter's is to choose between the competing options. If the academic community cannot provide blueprints for social engineering, and is wrong to try to do so, it can help the world of policy making to devise its own in the light of a fuller knowledge of its environment and the choices that are available.

The third aim shaping this book is different yet again. It is to break down traditional demarcation lines in both academic and policy discourse: it represents, as it were, a protest against restrictive practices in the universe of debate. Its starting assumption is that there is not and cannot be a sharp distinction between social and economic policy: that the two inevitably intertwine and interact. It is a point that economists have long recognized, and in pursuit of which some have sought to colonize social policy. In contrast, social policy academics – brought up in a comfortable world where Keynesian economics ruled supreme and where the growth state regularly produced the dividends required for the expansion of the welfare state – have been slow to address themselves to economic issues. The contributors to this book have therefore been deliberately chosen for their ability to engage in a cross-disciplinary dialogue and to explore the relationship between economic and social policies. In doing so, they challenge the conventional view that social policy should be seen as the dependent of economic policies: i.e. that the parameters of social policy are set inflexibly by economic circumstances. From that perspective, social policy is seen as primarily offering comfort to economic casualties (or may, indeed, even be seen to be parasitic on the wealth-creating economy). To challenge this approach is to put on the agenda for analysis, as this book tries to do, a more positive view of the nature of the relationship between social and economic policies.

Traditionally, social policy concerns are defined in terms of existing services or specific client groups. This book addresses itself, however, to issues which cut across these conventional categories (on the assumption that such conventional categories may, in themselves, determine the definition of the problem and limit the search for alternative ways of conceptualizing and tackling the issues). Thus there are no chapters specifically on the National Health Service, on the personal social services or on particular income maintenance programmes, although all of these are drawn on to provide illustrative analytical material. Instead, the chapters are organized around a number of broad themes, and it is to these that we turn next.

THEMES AND VARIATIONS

If the welfare state has historically been the residual beneficiary of the growth state, then does the converse follow? Must the welfare state become the stepchild of the stationary state? The first theme addressed in this book therefore is the relationship between economic performance and social welfare expenditure, in an attempt to answer this question. This has, in turn, two dimensions. The first is concerned with the past: much of the current debate on social policy reflects the assumption that historically the welfare state cripples the hand that feeds it – that high social spending has been at the expense of economic growth. The second is concerned with the future: much of the present alarm about the momentum of inherited commitments reflects the assumption that the demands being generated are incapable of being financed out of the dividends of economic growth.

In tackling this theme, the book starts from an international perspective to provide a context for the analysis of specifically British issues that follows. For it is all too easy to fall into the trap of thinking that Britain's problems (whatever they may be) reflect specifically local circumstances: a peculiar form of self-flagellating ethnocentricity. But, as Cameron's chapter shows, Britain's economic problems cannot easily be ascribed to excessively generous social spending since, in fact, welfare state expenditure is comparatively low. Equally, his analysis shows the need for agnosticism about the claim that high social spending is linked to poor economic performance historically: this remains a myth in search of evidence to substantiate it.

Turning to future prospects, the chapter by Gillion and Hemming is a further warning against the dramatization of the British predicament as something special or unique. Compared to other OECD countries, Britain seems better placed than the rest to accommodate the extra resource requirements of existing social policy commitments within the proportion of the national income currently devoted to welfare services. However, all such projections are vulnerable. They represent the product of two sets of scenarios. One set of scenarios is about prospects for economic growth and thus resource availability (examined in the chapter by Davies and Piachaud); the other is about the dynamics of existing policy commitments (examined by O'Higgins and Patterson). Given that the two sets of scenarios also interact with each other – that, for example, the level of social policy spending is affected by rates of unemployment – it is clear that such analytical exercises cannot predict the future. Nor are they intended to do so. Their purpose is different. It is to identify the range of uncertainty within which policy makers will be operating, to test the sensitivity of various projections to changes in the assumptions underlying them and to generate a battery of 'what if' questions: that is, to identify those factors which may be crucial if thinking about future policy is not to degenerate into a misleading exercise in mechanistically extrapolating past trends.

Such exercises, we would suggest, are not mere academic games. They have some direct practical implications. To identify uncertainty as the problem (rather than an inevitable crisis of over-spending, for which there is no evidence) is to suggest the need for a different style of policy making rather than for a dramatic reversal of existing policies. It is to indicate the need for adaptability and flexibility in planning rather than making spending projections dependent on assumptions about future growth, a point elaborated in the concluding chapter. To identify the assumptions conventionally made about efficiency in the public sector as a critical factor in determining the future resources required to deliver a particular level of services is to draw attention to the importance not only of devising conceptual tools for measuring such efficiency but also of designing a policy mix which will maximize the output of any given volume of resource inputs: a point developed in the chapter by Judge and Knapp, which addresses itself to an analysis of the relative efficiency of public and private agencies in the delivery of welfare.

While there may be no crisis of welfare in the crude sense that demands will inevitably exceed the available resources (since, in fact, both sides of the equation are subject to discretionary political decisions), there could still be a crisis in the sense of losing mass support for current social policies. Political rather than financial bankruptcy would be no less real: to argue that it stems not so much from an excess of spending but from a deficit in the willingness to pay is simply to redefine the causes of crisis. From this it follows that any analysis of the future prospects of the welfare state must take account not only of the financial statistics but also of attitudes towards social programmes and spending: a topic explored in the chapter by Taylor-Gooby. The evidence suggests that the rhetoric of 'crisis' is misleading: there appears to be no withdrawal of mass support for the basic policy aims of the welfare state, although the support varies from programme to programme and is affected, to a degree, by political ideology. And if there is disillusion with the institutions of the welfare state (as against its underlying policy aims) – as demonstrated by the widespread criticism, from both Left and Right, of its over-bureaucratization and lack of responsiveness – this may have little to do with the size of its budget. It may rather be, as the chapter by Weale suggests, because of conflicting expectations: because we expect the Welfare State to be both paternalistic and equitable in providing for needs defined by professionals, and flexible and accommodating in responding to demands defined by consumer preferences.

The political analysis, like its economic counterpart, does not yield any policy prescriptions. Nor, once again, is it intended to do so. However, the analysis offers good grounds for rejecting the kind of deterministic fatalism inherent in the use of 'crisis' rhetoric and underlines the scope for policy innovation and creativity. In a sense the seemingly muddled attitudes of the public, in that they tend to support the policy aims of the Welfare State but to sympathize with the private provision of welfare, in that they want both needs and demands satisfied, may be more rational than those of pigeon-holing academics who see the two models as being incompatible. In terms of strict logic, they may well be incompatible; but in terms of practical policy making, the challenge lies precisely in moving towards a system which will accommodate, in so far as possible, conflicting objectives. If there were no conflicting objectives there would, after all, be no need for policy makers or, indeed, for academic specialists: the job could be left to computers.

The second theme of the book is that the environment of the welfare state is changing with extraordinary rapidity and that consequently the agenda of social policy must be reshaped to take new issues on board.

The post-war welfare state in Britain, and elsewhere, rested on the Keynesian growth state, as we have stressed before. It was because Keynesian economic management had appeared to solve the problem of full employment that those concerned with social policy could afford virtually to ignore the world of work. This is no longer possible. Economic and social issues have become blurred and, to a large extent, fused as mass unemployment has once again become the central concern in Britain as in most other advanced industrialized countries. Moreover, there is widespread anxiety that paid work may itself become a scarce commodity: that we may be heading towards a society in which a large section of the population is condemned to enforced leisure.

Many of our social policies are based on particular assumptions about the role of work in the financial and social life of individuals. Some seek to train them for work; others to replace the income they lose when work is unavailable or when they are past working age. The prospect of continued high levels of unemployment, the concern about the impact on jobs of new technology, and the possibility of an economy where part-time work is more the norm than the exception, all pose challenges for the traditional framework within which social policy regards work. Yet these sets of issues have barely begun to be explored, and this book is intended to identify some of those that require further analysis and research if social policy is to address itself to this dominating problem of our time. There is not only a need to identify the dimensions of the problem, to assess the likely, emerging balance between the number of available jobs and the number of people in the labour force, which is what the chapter by Ermisch does – but there is also a need to start examining the implications for existing policies of a continuing shortage of paid employment. For example, our present social security sytem is based on the assumption that paid work is a full-time activity, and part-time work an occasional aberration. Bradshaw's chapter, therefore, examines the implications for the principles shaping our social security system if it were assumed that part-time work is a normal, usual part of economic life.

More fundamentally still, perhaps, the new environment may give social policy an opportunity to play a more active role in the economic and political management of high unemployment. This is why chapters in this book examine the scope for social policies which face head-on the question of how to distribute the shortage of jobs (Walker), and for using the welfare sector to generate more employment (Bosanquet). The conclusions drawn range from the agnostic to the pessimistic, but here clearly is yet another set of issues requiring further exploration.

The environment is changing in another important respect as well.

While the supply of jobs has declined, the demand for them is increasing as women assert their right to equal opportunities in work as in other spheres of life. It is a development with far reaching implications for social policy as the chapter by Lewis emphasizes. It is crucial to the assumptions we make about the distribution of income. It is crucial to the assumptions we make about the readiness of women to accept the (unpaid) burden of looking after the dependent in the community. It is crucial, lastly, to the assumptions we make about the structure of employment within the welfare service since this has been, as Martin Rein's chapter shows, the fastest expanding source of employment for women.

The contributions in this book are designed to be a first step in putting this new set of policy concerns on the agenda for analysis, research and debate. None is definitive or exhaustive in their discussion of the issues raised, nor is the range of topics covered comprehensive. It conspicuously lacks any discussion of the elderly and of the long-term implications of developments in information and communication technology. For the intention has not been to compile a laundry-list of specific policy problems but to try to redefine the nature of the debate about social policy: to change the focus from a narrow concern with 'crisis' seen as a problem of spending to a wider concern about 'crisis' seen as adapting both inherited ways of thinking and institutions to take account of a changing environment. This environment is uncertain, turbulent and unpredictable, where the challenge is to embody in new forms the traditional concern of social policy with the promotion of social justice – forms which are appropriate to a world in which we have to cope with discontinuity instead of merely extrapolating from the past.

1

Public Expenditure and Economic Performance in International Perspective

DAVID R. CAMERON

INTRODUCTION

During the last two decades, the economic performance of the advanced capitalist world deteriorated sharply. While the late 1950s and 1960s were marked by relatively high rates of capital formation and economic growth, and relatively low rates of unemployment and price inflation, the 1970s and early 1980s were characterized by an erosion of investment and growth rates in most countries, an acceleration in the rate of change of prices, and sharp increases in long-term rates of unemployment.

This deterioration in economic performance was accompanied by another dramatic secular change throughout the advanced capitalist world. Government, whether defined as a regulator, an investor, a producer, a consumer, or a distributor, became increasingly important. Government has always been important in capitalist economies, of course, notwithstanding the Smithian mythology that still surrounds the first industrial revolution, and such economies have always been politicized in a fundamental sense, just as are those of the socialist world. It is also true, however, that the scope of government activity and its size, relative to that of the economy as a whole, have increased in every capitalist nation in recent decades. For example, total government spending, relative to the economy as a whole, increased by about 50 per cent in the OECD nations between the mid-sixties and early 1980s. Thus, whereas Colin Clark once argued, in reference to the inter-war period, that 25 per cent of GDP seemed to represent an economic ceiling for government spending, and later scholars revised that figure upward to perhaps 50 per cent, government spending in some nations – for the most part, small European nations – has exceeded that level in recent years and in two, Sweden and the Netherlands, government spending is now equivalent to more than 60 per cent of GDP.

What makes the two trends – deterioration in economic performance and increases in government's share of the economic product – especially interesting to the political economist, of course, is the possibility that they are causally related. Given their simultaneity, is it not plausible that the disproportionately large increase in government spending may derive, in part at least, from the slowdown in economic growth, the increase in unemployment, the need to provide assistance, as well as job training and retraining to the unemployed, and the perceived need to provide funds for bail-outs and subsidies to firms in declining, labour-intensive sectors? And is it not equally plausible that the deterioration in economic performance may be a *consequence*, as well as a cause, of government's increased fiscal role? Throughout the advanced capitalist world, the simultaneity in trends has given rise to a powerful and simple political-ideological argument – that it is the growth of government that has generated and exacerbated the deterioration of the economy and, therefore, that in order to restore growth, employment, capital formation, price stability and all other economic 'goods', government's fiscal role (as well as its regulatory and producer roles) must be reduced.

The argument that the growth of government has contributed to the deterioration of the economy must be of particular concern to those who study or administer the broad set of policies and programmes defined as 'welfare' or social policy, for it is that set of policies and programmes which bears a special culpability in the new conservative orthodoxy that presumes to explain the secular decline in economic performance. And since virtually every version of that conservative orthodoxy calls for a reduction in the rate of growth, and relative importance, of social policies and programmes, any discussion of the 'future of welfare' must examine the proposition that government growth and economic deterioration are causally related.

It would be far outside the scope of this chapter to demonstrate the precise impact of the growth of government on the economy throughout the advanced capitalist world. Such an enterprise would require the specification of an enormously complex model of the economy as a whole, including the identification of all relevant sources of growth, inflation, unemployment, etc., with which the independent effects of government could be systematically compared. This chapter sets a much more modest objective for itself. It considers some of the data on economic performance – for example, rates of growth, unemployment, inflation, and capital formation – as well as those pertaining to the magnitude and growth of government spending. We shall then analyse, by comparing the levels and rates of change in these measures across some twenty nations, the extent to which economic performance is associated, in simple statistical terms, with the scope of government. Such associations say little, of course, about causal relationships. A strong statistical association may be the spurious product of unspecified factors which are the true sources of the variations in the measured variables; conversely, a weak or non-existent association may reflect the effect of unspecified factors that statistically mask or override a causal relationship. On the other hand, simple statistical associations are of *some* use, in so far as they provide empirically grounded, preliminary evidence of the likelihood that a causal relationship would be observed in a fully specified complex model of the economy. It is in this spirit that we shall examine the statistical relationships between various attributes of economic performance and the scope and increase in government spending.

ECONOMIC PERFORMANCE

Economic Growth

Table 1.1 presents a comparison of the average annual rates of change in Gross Domestic Product in constant prices between the mid-1960s and the late 1970s/early 1980s. In 1963 – 67 the average rate of growth across the advanced capitalist world was about 5 per cent, and even the low-growth nations – Ireland, Britain, Germany, Finland – experienced growth rates in that era that are enviable from the vantage point of the 1980s. In more recent years, virtually every nation has experienced a substantial reduction in the average rate of economic growth, with the overall average down to just over 2 per cent. Japan, for example, continues to lead the league in growth rates but with a much lower average rate, 4.4 per cent, in 1978 – 82 than its 10 per cent annual average during 1963 – 67; and while the 20 nations experienced a reduction of about 60 per cent in the average growth rate, several nations – most notably Spain, the Netherlands, Britain, Canada, and Greece – experienced even larger rates of decline in growth. As a result the Netherlands has joined long-time cellar-dweller Britain at the bottom of the standings in recent years with an average growth rate of less than 1 per cent per year, and Greece and Spain – recently

TABLE 1.1   ECONOMIC GROWTH, UNEMPLOYMENT RATES AND
LABOUR FORCE GROWTH IN 20 OECD COUNTRIES

	Annual economic growth (%)		*Average unemployment rate rate (%)*		*Change in total labour force (%)*
	1963–67	*1978–82*	*1965–68*	*1980–83*	*1965–81*
Japan	10.0	4.4	1.3	2.4	19.0
Finland	3.7	4.0	2.4	5.4	9.1
Portugal	6.3	3.6	na	8.1	22.5
Ireland	3.4	3.1	5.0	9.9	14.8
Norway	4.8	2.7	1.8	2.4	31.8
Australia	5.6	2.4	1.7	7.2	40.9
Italy	5.0	2.3	5.5	8.6	8.4
Greece	7.9	2.3	na	4.9	8.5
France	5.3	2.0	2.0	7.4	13.8
Austria	4.4	1.8	1.9	3.0	3.8
Belgium	4.4	1.8	2.4	11.9	12.5
Germany	3.6	1.6	0.8	5.3	1.7
Canada	5.8	1.6	3.8	9.4	64.1
Denmark	4.2	1.6	1.2	9.2	18.7
Switzerland	3.8	1.6	0.0	0.4	-0.7
United States	4.8	1.5	3.8	8.4	43.1
Sweden	4.3	1.4	1.8	2.8	15.6
Spain	6.5	1.0	2.5	14.6	7.5
Britain	3.3	0.8	2.8	10.7	2.8
Netherlands	5.0	0.7	1.1	9.9	17.1

Sources: OECD Economic Outlook, December 1983, and OECD, *Labour Force Statistics*

authoritarian and formerly the two most rapidly growing nations –
experienced simultaneously the pleasure of redemocratization and the
discomfort of low growth.

Unemployment

If the deterioration in the economic performance of the advanced
capitalist world during the last two decades is well conveyed by the
diminution in growth, the enormous human and social cost associated
with that diminution is best conveyed by the level and increase of

unemployment, data for which are also shown in Table 1.1. During 1965 – 68, the unemployed constituted, on average, slightly more than 2 per cent of the total labour force of the 18 nations for which data are available. In that period 14 nations enjoyed unemployment rates under 3 per cent and near-full employment seemed almost within reach except in a few peculiar deviant cases such as Ireland, Italy, Canada, and the United States. By the early 1980s, however, unemployment rates had increased more than three-fold and only five nations – Austria, Sweden, Japan, Norway and Switzerland – managed to keep the rate of unemployment at or below 3 per cent. In contrast to those few nations which were able to maintain their commitment to near-full employment, most economies experienced dramatic increases in the average proportion of the labour force without work. The increases were especially large in Spain (from 2.5 per cent in 1965 – 68 to 14.6 per cent in 1980 – 83), Belgium (from 2.4 per cent to 11.9 per cent), the Netherlands (from 1.1 per cent to 9.9 per cent), Denmark (from 1.2 per cent to 9.2 per cent), and Britain (from 2.8 per cent to 10.7 per cent).

Growth and Unemployment

To what extent is the secular erosion in the rate of employment associated with the erosion of long-term rates of growth? Are the two causally related, and thus two aspects of a fundamental underlying process of economic deterioration, or do they reflect distinct and possibly unrelated processes of change? One might plausibly argue that the two *are* related – that, for example, the rate of unemployment reflects the cumulative impact of growth rates in one or more preceding years and that, as a result, the countries with low rates of unemployment will be those in which high rates of growth over long periods pulled surplus labour into the production process. The German and Japanese experiences in the 1950s and 1960s would support this argument. On the other hand, one might argue that the two processes of change are distinct and quite unrelated. Thus, changes over time in the rate of unemployment and cross-national variations in those rates of change may reflect phenomena not directly related to growth – for example, political-ideological factors such as the propensity of some governments to tolerate higher rates of unemployment or demographic factors such as the variation among nations in the growth of the potential labour force (which as Table 1.1 shows is considerable).

To examine these questions we have compared the change in the rate of unemployment in each country between 1965 – 68 and 1980 – 83 with the change in the rate of economic growth between 1963 – 67 and

1978 – 82, and with the change in the total labour force between 1965 and 1982. We also compare the change in unemployment with the extent to which Leftist parties, presumably the parties most averse to unemployment, controlled government during 1965 – 82, using data set out in Cameron (1984).

The results of the analysis suggest that the secular increase in unemployment is in fact primarily a function of the long-term erosion in the growth rate, that the control of government by Leftist parties may have exerted some independent effect in dampening the rate of increase in unemployment, and – surprisingly – that the growth in unemployment had little to do with the magnitude of the increase in the labour force. To consider the latter first, variations across the advanced capitalist nations in the long-term increase in unemployment were unrelated to variations in the extent of growth in the labour force ($r = 0.02$). Thus, while it is true that Austria and Switzerland may have been able to maintain near-full employment because their total labour force increased very little or even shrank (+ 3.8 per cent in Austria, – 0.7 per cent in Switzerland), it is also true that other employment-maintaining nations – most notably Japan and Norway – experienced considerably larger increases in the number of available workers over the two decades. On the other hand, none of the nations which experienced unusually large increases in unemployment – Spain, Belgium, the Netherlands, Denmark and Britain – experienced unusually large increases in the work force, compared with the enormous increases in Canada (64.1 per cent), the United States (43.1 per cent), and Australia (40.9 per cent). And two of those nations, Spain and Britain, experienced very modest increases in the work force (7.5 per cent and 2.8 per cent respectively).

If there is little confirmation from the cross-national evidence that the secular erosion in employment was produced by an expansion of the labour force, there is some support for the proposition that nations in which Leftist parties often controlled government were somewhat more averse to rising unemployment than those in which non-Leftist parties usually governed ($r = -0.23$). Thus, Austria, Sweden, Norway, and Finland – all among the seven nations in our sample in which Leftist parties most frequently controlled government – experienced unusually small increases in unemployment between the mid-1960s and early 1980s. Conversely, Spain, Belgium, the Netherlands, France, and Australia – all with infrequent Leftist party control of government – experienced relatively large increases in unemployment. However, the relationship was far from perfect, as indicated by the modest size of the correlation coefficient, and there were several nations – especially

Britain and Denmark – in which unemployment increased considerably in spite of frequent control of government by the Labour and Social Democratic parties. And there were, in contrast, several nations – Japan, Italy and Switzerland – which experienced relatively small increases in unemployment over the two decades. Thus, in sum, while the relationship at least runs in the expected direction, its magnitude is hardly large enough to indicate the presence of a strong causal relationship between the partisan composition of government and the secular erosion of the economy.

The best predictor of the long-term increase in unemployment (from among our very small set of variables) is the erosion of the rate of growth over the long term ($r = -0.55$). There is a systematic relationship between the two: the nations with the smallest relative decreases in growth (or even, in the case of Finland, an increase) between 1963 – 67 and 1978 – 82 had unusually small increases in unemployment (although other nations – Sweden, Australia, Switzerland, and Italy – did too). Conversely, the nations with the lowest rates of growth, Britain, the Netherlands, and Spain, had relatively *large* increases in unemployment (although, again, other nations – Belgium and Denmark – did too).

Capital Formation

If the secular changes in rates of growth and unemployment are related, as the previous discussion suggests, and represent two components of a fundamental underlying process of economic change, how might we account for those processes of change? What aspect of the economy might change in such a way that growth rates erode and, in turn, rates of unemployment rise?

Many factors might be enumerated as plausible sources of the long-term erosion of growth and employment, and to answer these questions adequately one would have to elaborate a vast, complex model of the economy. That having been said, it is nevertheless possible to obtain some clues about causation from the simple statistical association of cross-national variations in aggregate economic indicators. There are of course many such indicators that might be considered but one looms as potentially more significant than any other: the level and change over time in investment – in particular capital investment in fixed assets.

In the early 1980s, as in the mid 1960s, the level of fixed capital formation varied from about 31 per cent of GDP in Japan to about 17 – 18 per cent of GDP in Britain (Table 1.2). Britain, now as then, appears to suffer – as does the United States, the other nation at the bottom of a ranking of OECD countries – from endemic underinvestment. But other countries – in particular, Germany, Belgium, Denmark, the Netherlands, Sweden, and Switzerland – have experienced unusually large decreases in investment in the recent past and several may soon come to challenge Britain and the United States for the dubious honour of being the lowest domestic investor in the advanced capitalist world.

To what extent, if at all, is the secular erosion in growth and employment associated with, and perhaps caused by, low and or declining rates of investment? Although one would be hard pressed to defend any causal inferences based on simple, bivariate, cross-national measures of association, one quite strong and consistent relationship

TABLE 1.2   GROSS FIXED CAPITAL FORMATION AS A PROPORTION OF GDP, 1965–1982

	1965–82	1963–67	1978–82
Japan	32.5	31.1	31.1
Portugal[a]	26.2	24.2	29.3
Ireland[a]	24.5	20.3	28.9
Norway	29.2	28.8	27.3
Austria	26.5	26.9	24.7
Finland	25.9	25.2	23.8
Australia	24.6	26.2	23.6
Switzerland	25.4	28.6	22.8
Greece	23.1	20.8	22.6
Canada	22.5	22.7	22.4
Germany	22.9	25.4	21.6
France	22.8	23.2	21.2
Netherlands	22.9	25.4	20.2
Belgium	21.5	22.3	19.8
Spain[a]	21.7	21.2	19.6
Sweden	21.8	24.6	19.5
Italy	20.0	20.8	19.3
Denmark	22.4	23.8	18.8
United States	18.2	18.3	18.5
Britain	18.2	18.0	16.9

Sources: OECD Economic Outlook, December 1983; OECD, *National Accounts of OECD Member Countries*

[a] The data for Ireland, Portugal, and Spain for 1980–81 are based on reported spending levels in 1980 and a conservative estimate of an increase in 1981 of 1%. The estimates for Greece and Switzerland are derived from current disbursements only.

emerges: that between investment and growth. The level of investment is closely associated with both the rate and changes in the rate of growth. The nations with the highest proportions of GDP spent on fixed capital formation in 1978 – 82 had the highest growth rates in those years ($r = 0.82$) and the largest increases (or smallest decreases) in average growth rates between the mid 1960s and early 1980s ($r = 0.69$). And, perhaps more indicative of a possible causal relationship, the nations with the highest rates of growth in the 1980s and the largest increases (or smallest decreases) in average growth rates were those such as Japan, Ireland, Portugal, Finland, and Norway, which had the largest increases (or smallest decreases) in the level of investment between the mid-1960s and early 1980s ($r = 0.72$; $r = 0.63$ respectively).

There is also a strong and consistent inverse relationship between the level and rate of change in investment and the level and rate of change in unemployment. The nations with the lowest levels of unemployment in the early 1980s were the ones which had the highest levels of capital formation throughout the two decades ($r = -0.60$) and early 1980s ($r = -0.42$), and the nations with the smallest relative increases in unemployment were those in which capital formation was highest over the two decades and in the most recent years ($r = -0.50$; $r = -0.53$). While these relationships are weaker than those between investment and growth, and while increases, or relatively small decreases in investment were only modestly associated with relatively small increases in unemployment ($r = 0.30$), they are nevertheless consistent with a model whereby employment is stimulated by growth and both employment and growth are stimulated by investment.

PUBLIC EXPENDITURE AND ECONOMIC PERFORMANCE

If it is true, as the preceding discussion suggests, that the level and rate of change in unemployment depends on the level and rate of change in growth and that both of those, but especially growth, depend in turn on levels of and rates of change in investment, then we can begin to address the new conservative orthodoxy that the deterioration of the economy derives from the growth of government. We can do this by considering whether – and, if so, to what extent – the growth in public expenditure has contributed to low and decreasing rates of investment. It is this relationship which lies at the heart of much of the recent 'supply-side' argument in favour of reducing the scope and rate of growth of government, and it is because the relationship is so often taken for granted that the future of the welfare state has so often been associated with retrenchment rather than expansion in recent years.

Public Expenditure: Levels, Rates of Change, and Composition

Table 1.3 presents data on the scope of governmental fiscal activity in recent decades in 20 OECD nations. While the data on the overall level of government spending are very useful for describing the scope of the public economy and the magnitude of its expansion in recent years, it is helpful to disaggregate the totals. It is not possible to present, from current published sources, cross-nationally comparable data for all nations over the last two decades at the ideal level of disaggregation, that of programmes and functional categories, although Gillion and Hemming's chapter, and the larger study on which it is based (OECD, 1985), mark a significant advance in this respect. However, current data can be disaggregated in one important way, between final consumption expenditures of government on the one hand, and social

TABLE 1.3   THE FISCAL SCOPE OF GOVERNMENT AS A
PERCENTAGE OF GDP IN 20 OECD NATIONS, 1964/5 AND 1980/1

	Government final consumption expenditure		Social security and social assistance benefits		Total spending	
	1964/5	*1980/1*	*1964/5*	*1980/1*	*1964/5*	*1980/1*
Sweden	17.2	29.1	9.3	19.3	35.6	63.7
Netherlands	14.8	18.0	13.3	28.0	38.3	60.6
Denmark	15.9	27.3	8.0	17.2	29.2	57.7
Ireland	13.5	21.8	8.7	15.8	32.5	55.0
Belgium	12.7	18.6	11.8	22.0	31.6	53.9
Austria	13.4	18.1	14.7	19.4	38.1	49.4
Germany	15.0	20.4	12.9	17.9	36.4	48.8
Norway	14.8	18.9	9.0	14.7	33.7	48.6
Italy	14.7	17.3	12.1	17.1	33.1	48.4
France	13.2	15.5	16.5	24.4	38.2	47.7
Britain	16.7	21.9	7.9	13.3	35.2	46.5
Canada	14.9	19.6	6.2	10.2	29.0	41.1
Portugal	12.2	14.8	3.4	11.2	20.3	39.0
Finland	13.7	18.9	7.5	10.5	30.9	38.8
Switzerland	10.5	12.6	6.7	12.4	26.7	38.2
Greece	11.7	17.0	6.8	9.8	26.3	35.2
United States	17.3	18.1	5.4	11.5	28.2	35.2
Australia	11.5	17.7	5.7	9.1	24.7	33.9
Japan	8.0	10.1	5.0	10.9	19.6	33.6
Spain	7.4	11.7	6.5	15.7	19.2	33.0

security benefits and social assistance grants, on the other. This differentiation allows one to distinguish between what government itself spends on services such as education, health and defence (the bulk of whose costs involve the salaries and wages of public employees), and what it provides to individuals for their private consumption via transfer payments.

Table 1.3 ranks the 20 nations by the proportion of GDP in 1980-81 represented by all governmental outlays, and provides also the proportions involved in final consumption by government and in social security and social assistance. This reveals several distinctions that are masked by the figures for total government outlays. For one thing, the nations which spend disproportionately large shares of their economic product on social policy are not necessarily those in which government's final consumption expenditures are largest. In terms of transfer payments for social policy, three nations spend more than one-fifth of their annual GDP. Those three – the Netherlands (28.0%), France (24.4%), and Belgium (22.0%) – pass a much larger share of the economic product through the fiscal system, essentially taking revenue from some sectors of society and redistributing to other sectors, than they consume directly in state expenditure. In contrast, the nations which top the ranking in final consumption expenditure by government – Sweden, Denmark, Britain, Ireland and Germany – consume much more directly, via public employment and services, than they pass along to individuals in the private sector.

Table 1.3 indicates also that several of the nations in which the political backlash against welfare spending and social policy has been especially acute are, paradoxically, nations in which the spending effort on social policy is relatively meagre. For example, Britain and the United States spend less than one-half the proportion of their economic product that is spent in the Netherlands and France. Yet if one were to judge by the political rhetoric surrounding the provision of welfare that emanates from the United States in the Reagan era and Britain in the Thatcher years, one might imagine that welfare spending was unusually large. One would not be inclined to believe that in fact Britain and the United States rank eleventh and thirteenth among twenty nations, just behind Ireland and Spain. This discrepancy between the levels of welfare spending effort and the political rhetoric surrounding this domain of policy suggests that welfare spending in nations such as Britain, the United States, Denmark and elsewhere provides a convenient political scapegoat for those who wish to attack the scope of government activity – activity which is, by the measure of final consumption expenditure, in fact unusually large.

Table 1.3 also compares relative spending levels in 1980/1 with those in 1964/5, and shows that in all countries spending has increased more rapidly than the economy as a whole. This is no less true for government final consumption expenditure than for social security and social assistance. Some nations – most notably Denmark, Sweden, Ireland, Belgium and Spain – experienced unusually large increases in both aspects of public expenditure; others – in particular the Netherlands and Portugal – experienced relatively large increases only in transfer payments, while in Australia and Greece the disproportionately large increases occurred in direct government consumption. In spite of these variations, however, one general pattern is evident: in *all* twenty nations, government spending on *both* social security/social assistance *and* government final consumption has increased as a share of GDP in the past two decades. The sources of this growth are examined in more detail for some of the major OECD countries in the next chapter in this volume.

Public Expenditure and Capital Formation: The Relationship

Are the simultaneous trends we have described – one involving the deterioration over time in economic performance in the advanced capitalist countries, the other the long-term secular expansion in the fiscal role of government – related? Can we observe simple cross-national statistical associations between various aspects of economic performance and the scope of public expenditure that are consistent with an unobserved causal relationship between the two? In particular, do associations exist that suggest that the expansion of public spending to the high levels witnessed in the early 1980s contributed to the deterioration in economic performance throughout the advanced capitalist world?

Table 1.4 presents the simple, bivariate correlation and regression coefficients between the two sets of variables. The data suggest a consistently inverse relationship between the scope of public expenditure and capital formation, as indicated by the negative signs accompanying most of the coefficients.

While the consistently inverse relationships presented in Table 1.4 suggest a trade-off between a large public economy and high levels of capital formation, we should note that the coefficients for the measures of *growth* in spending are actually quite negligible. Only in the case of expansion in social security and social spending is there a non-negligible impact, and even then the effect is quite modest. On the other hand, the coefficients for the several measures of *levels* of

TABLE 1.4   THE CORRELATION BETWEEN PUBLIC EXPENDITURE
AND CAPITAL FORMATION

	Gross fixed capital formation as a % of GDP	
	1978 – 82	*Change from 1963 – 67 to 1978 – 82*
Total government spending:		
as % of GDP, 1980 – 81	– 0.26	– 0.29
change, 1964/5 to 1980/1	0.00	– 0.03
Government final consumption expenditure:		
as % of GDP, 1980 – 81	– 0.39	– 0.28
change, 1964/5 to 1980/1	– 0.03	– 0.07
Social security and social assistance benefits and grants:		
as % of GDP, 1980 – 81	– 0.34	– 0.41
change, 1964/5 to 1980/1	– 0.17	– 0.18
Current receipts of government:		
as % of GDP, 1980 – 81	– 0.20	– 0.34
change, 1964/5 to 1980/1	– 0.03	– 0.13

Each element indicates the simple correlation between the relevant capital formation
variable and the government fiscal variable listed to the left-hand side.

spending are more closely associated with the investment variables, and
it would appear that relatively high levels of government spending over
a long period of time *are* associated with low and declining rates of
capital formation. Thus, for example, there is a correlation of -0.39
between the proportion of GDP in 1980 – 81 represented by the final
consumption expenditure of government and the proportion allocated
to investment in roughly the same period. And we observe a correlation
of -0.41 between the level of social spending effort (spending as a
proportion of GDP) and the change in capital formation between the
mid-1960s and the early 1980s.

The negative coefficients between the several aspects of government
spending – in particular relatively high *levels* of spending – and the
level and change in investment are not, of course, overwhelming in
magnitude; moreover, they may be spurious and reflect only the
existence of some unspecified factor that influences both social

spending and capital formation. However, we cannot escape the possibility that the public economy of advanced capitalism *has* intruded in some yet to be determined way upon the accumulation – investment – growth – job – creation process. Whether that is the case remains to be seen, and it should be the focus of systematic inquiry among those concerned about the future of welfare – if for no other reason than to defend the advances in social policy against the rhetorical attacks of those opponents of big government who, armed only with ideological clichés and a few simple bivariate correlations like those presented here, attribute the deterioration of the economy to the growth of public spending in general and social spending in particular.

2

Social Expenditure in the United Kingdom in a Comparative Context: Trends, Explanations and Projections

COLIN GILLION and RICHARD HEMMING

INTRODUCTION

Curb Spending

The relationship between countries' economic performance and the size and growth of their public sectors has been examined in David Cameron's chapter. However tenuous this relationship, most governments have been trying to restrain public expenditure in the belief that smaller government spending, lower tax burdens and reduced public sector borrowing will help restore non-inflationary growth. Because social expenditure is not only the largest component of public expenditure, but has also been the fastest growing, it is on education, health, pensions and other income maintenance programmes that discussions of public expenditure restraint inevitably focus.

The growth of social expenditure, the determinants of that growth and prospective medium-term expenditure developments are the subject of a recent OECD study (OECD, 1985). This chapter draws upon some of the material contained in that study with a view to comparing trends, explanations and projections for the United Kingdom with those for a group consisting of the major OECD countries. This comparison is the core of the chapter and forms a basis for our concluding comments on the prospects for expenditure on social programmes.

The views expressed in this paper are those of the authors; they do not necessarily reflect the views of the OECD Secretariat or Member Governments. The authors are grateful to Janice Callaghan for her assistance in preparing this paper.

TRENDS IN SOCIAL EXPENDITURE

In this chapter social expenditure refers to direct public expenditure on all social programmes with the exception of housing. Tax expenditures and private expenditures are not included. Expenditure data are either taken from or compatible with data in OECD *National Accounts*. Table 2.1 provides a summary picture of social expenditure growth in the United Kingdom and the major OECD countries since 1960. In order not to overburden this chapter with tables of statistics the three

TABLE 2.1   SOCIAL EXPENDITURE IN THE UNITED KINGDOM AND OTHER MAJOR OECD COUNTRIES 1960–81

		Annual % growth rate of:		
	Expenditure share (%)	*Expenditure in cost terms (%)*	*Real GDP (%)*	*Income elasticity (%)*
		United Kingdom		
1960	13.9			
1965	16.2			
1970	18.6		*1960–75*	
1975	22.5	5.9	2.6	2.2
1980	22.1		*1975–81*	
1981	23.7	1.8	1.0	1.8
		United States		
1960	10.9			
1965	12.3			
1970	15.7		*1960–75*	
1975	20.8	8.0	3.4	2.4
1980	20.7		*1975–81*	
1981	20.8	3.2	3.2	1.0
		OECD Europe		
1960	16.9			
1965	19.7			
1970	20.5		*1960–75*	
1975	27.5	7.3	4.5	1.6
1980	28.3		*1975–81*	
1981	30.0	4.6	3.0	1.6

Source: OECD, 1985

major continental European countries – France, Germany and Italy – are grouped together, and will be referred to as OECD Europe.

Trends in social expenditure – both in total and by programme – have been broadly similar across countries, and these can be described rather briefly. The shares of nominal social expenditure in nominal GDP (henceforth 'expenditure shares') in the United Kingdom has always been higher than in the United States and lower than in OECD Europe. Expenditure shares slightly less than doubled between 1960 and 1981, with relatively large increases between 1970 and 1975.

Table 2.1 also contains information on the growth rates of social expenditure in cost terms – nominal expenditure deflated to take account of increases in implicit GDP prices – and of real GDP. Growth rates are reported for two periods, 1960 – 75 and 1975 – 81, so that the later years of slow growth, large government deficits and expenditure restraint can be distinguished from the earlier years of growing public sectors accompanied by the economic growth and taxable capacity to support them.

Between 1960 and 1975 social expenditure in cost terms in the United Kingdom grew at about 5.9 per cent per annum on average, while real GDP grew at 2.6 per cent, implying an income elasticity of social expenditure – the ratio of the growth rate of social expenditure in cost terms to the growth rate of real GDP – for the period of 2.2. These growth rates were the lowest amongst the major OECD countries, but the income elasticity was the second highest, after the United States. The period between 1975 and 1981 saw a marked slowdown in both economic growth (real GDP) and the growth of social expenditure (in cost terms) in all countries, with the United Kingdom growth rate in both cases remaining the lowest. However, whilst the income elasticity of social expenditure dropped sharply in some countries, most notably Germany and the United States (as Table 2.1 shows, the growth rate of social expenditure in the United States fell by a remarkable amount with hardly any fall in the GDP growth rate), in the United Kingdom the income elasticity remained relatively high, and was exceeded only in France.

In all countries, education, health and pension programmes dominate social spending, accounting for about 80 per cent of the total. Between 1960 and 1981 there was a general shift, in terms of shares of total social expenditure, from education towards health expenditure, accompanied by a slight increase in the pensions share. However, the United Kingdom is the only country in which the health share of social spending has not increased over this period, small decreases in the education and health shares being compensated by a small increase in the pensions share and a larger increase in the unemployment compensation share. Although unemployment compensation is a small programme in all countries – even now only a little above 5 per cent of the total – as a consequence of rising unemployment it has recently been the fastest growing.

EXPLANATIONS FOR CHANGING SOCIAL EXPENDITURE

The growth in nominal expenditure on a particular social programme can be expressed in terms of five principal components, namely changes in (i) the GDP deflator, (ii) relative prices, (iii) demography, (iv) coverage and (v) level of service. Changes in the GDP deflator measure general inflation, and changes in relative prices reflect movements in the prices of government services as compared to the prices of goods and services in general. In education and health these are measured by the difference between changes in an education or health price deflator and changes in the GDP deflator. They therefore incorporate both a pure relative price effect – reflecting the different scope for productivity improvements as between the public and private sectors – and different rates of change of public and private sector pay. In the case of cash transfers the relative price effect compares changes in the private consumption prices and the GDP deflator. Adjusting expenditure in cost terms to take account of relative price changes produces a measure of expenditure volume, which will be referred to as real expenditure.

Changes in real expenditure are the product of what have been termed, rather loosely, demography, coverage and level of service. Changes in demography refer to changes in the number of people in the population relevant to a particular programme – the number of children of school and college age, the number of older people of retirement age, the total number of unemployed or, in the case of health care, the number of people exposed to the risk of ill-health, i.e. the total population. Changes in coverage refer to changes in the proportion of the relevant population which actually benefits from a programme. This reflects not only eligibility but also utilization (or take-up). Changes in level of service then indicate changes in real education benefits per student, real health benefits per covered person and real income per social security beneficiary.

A growth accounting exercise of this kind cannot provide what is in any sense a fundamental explanation of expenditure growth. This is to be found in the social, economic and political developments which influence the general objectives of social policy, the commitment to these objectives, and the specific means adopted to implement them. Instead, we simply decompose the changes which have taken place into a set of components which, in a purely accounting sense, identify what are likely to have been the most important sources of expenditure growth.

A decomposition of this type for the United Kingdom is shown in Table 2.2. This covers only four major programmes, the three largest – education, health and pensions – and the fastest growing – unemployment compensation. Before discussing results some further comments on method are necessary. The age categories used to define the relevant populations are 0 – 24 in the case of education and 65 or over in the case of pensions. These have been chosen fairly arbitrarily, since they are intended to be only broad categories which allow the impact of general demographic shifts to be separated from changes in eligibility and, therefore, coverage. As far as measuring coverage is concerned, the fact that there are some mismatches in the data between expenditure on a programme and the number of people who benefit from it may be a source of inaccuracy. Coverage data in health are only of a suitable quality in the case of hospital treatment; in the case of pensions, coverage data are only available for the principal state pension scheme (and sometimes refer to the number of pensions rather than the number of pensioners); and, in the case of unemployment, compensation coverage data sometimes relate only to unemployment insurance. These mismatches imply that at any point in time coverage will be inappropriately measured; however, framing the analysis in terms of medium-term growth rates should minimize any implied distortions.

Table 2.2 shows that over the period 1960 – 75 the major source of growth in real social expenditure in the United Kingdom was increases in levels of service. The average growth rate of 3.2 per cent was one percentage point greater than the growth rate of real GDP per capita. Growth was spread evenly across the four major programmes. Coverage changed very little, and while total population increased only slightly social expenditure growth did respond to a changing demographic structure, with a relative increase in the number of older people and unemployed. There was a small increase in the relative price of education and health services, partly offset by a smaller decrease in the relative price of cash benefits.

Over the period 1975 – 81 the growth of real social expenditure was modest compared to the earlier period. Levels of service grew slightly less fast than real GDP per caput (the difference was 0.3 of a percentage point), with levels of service under the education and unemployment

TABLE 2.2   THE DECOMPOSITION OF THE GROWTH RATE OF SOCIAL EXPENDITURE, 1960–1975 AND 1975–1981, IN THE UNITED KINGDOM

	Initial expenditure share	Nominal expenditure	GDP deflator	Expenditure in cost terms	Relative prices	Real expenditure	of which Demography	of which Coverage	of which Level of service	Final expenditure share
	1960									1975
	Average annual growth rates (%): 1960–75									
Education	3.7	14.5	7.1	6.9	1.8	5.0	0.6	1.1	3.2	6.8
Health	3.4	12.8	7.1	5.3	1.8	3.4	0.4	0.0	3.0	5.0
Pensions	4.1	13.1	7.1	5.6	-0.3	5.9	1.6	0.9	3.3	6.3
Unemployment compensation	0.2	17.9	7.1	10.1	-0.3	10.3	6.5	-0.8	4.4	0.7
Total of above programmes	11.4	13.5	7.1	6.0	1.0	4.9	1.0	0.7	3.2	18.8
Total social expenditure	13.9	13.4	7.1	5.9	0.9	5.0	—	—	—	22.5
	1975									1981
	Average annual growth rates (%): 1975–81									
Education	6.8	12.3	14.3	-1.7	0.3	-2.0	-0.4	-0.5	-1.1	5.8
Health	5.0	16.9	14.3	2.2	0.2	2.0	0.0	0.0	2.0	5.4
Pensions	6.3	18.3	14.3	3.5	-1.0	4.5	1.0	0.8	2.6	7.4
Unemployment compensation	0.7	29.3	14.3	13.1	-1.0	14.2	19.1	5.3	-8.9	1.4
Total of above programmes	18.8	16.2	14.3	1.6	-0.2	1.8	0.9	0.3	0.7	20.0
Total social expenditure	22.5	16.4	14.3	1.8	-0.7	2.5	—	—	—	23.7

Source: Social Expenditure: 1960–1990, Social Policy Studies, OECD, Paris, 1985

TABLE 2.3 THE DECOMPOSITION OF THE GROWTH RATE OF SOCIAL EXPENDITURE, 1960–1975 AND 1975–198_
UNITED STATES

	Initial expenditure share	Nominal expenditure	GDP deflator	Expenditure in cost terms	Relative prices	Real expenditure	of which			expenditure share
							Demography	Coverage	Level of service	
	1960									1975
	Average annual growth rates (%): 1960–75									
Education	3.6	11.8	4.2	7.4	1.2	6.1	1.1	0.9	4.0	6.3
Health	1.3	15.3	4.2	10.8	0.4	10.3	1.2	4.1	4.7	3.7
Pensions	4.2	11.3	4.2	6.9	-0.3	7.2	2.1	2.9	2.0	6.9
Unemployment compensation	0.6	12.5	4.2	7.9	-0.3	8.3	4.9	1.0	2.2	1.2
Total of above programmes	9.7	12.1	4.2	7.7	0.4	7.3	1.8	2.2	3.1	18.1
Total social expenditure	10.9	12.5	4.2	8.0	0.3	7.7	—	—	—	20.8
	1975									1981
	Average annual growth rates (%): 1975–81									
Education	6.3	8.6	7.8	0.7	0.3	0.4	-0.2	-1.3	1.9	5.5
Health	3.7	13.9	7.8	5.7	1.8	3.8	1.0	0.0	2.8	4.2
Pensions	6.9	12.5	7.8	4.5	0.0	4.4	2.5	0.7	1.1	7.4
Unemployment compensation	1.2	-2.3	7.8	-9.5	0.0	-9.5	-0.7	-4.2	-4.9	0.5
Total of above programmes	18.1	10.4	7.8	2.5	0.5	2.0	1.1	0.5	1.3	17.6
Total social expenditure	20.8	11.2	7.8	3.2	0.4	2.8	—	—	—	20.8

Source: Social Expenditure: 1960–1990, Social Policy Studies, OECD, Paris, 1985

TABLE 2.4 THE DECOMPOSITION OF THE GROWTH RATE OF SOCIAL EXPENDITURE, 1960–1975 AND 1975–1981, IN OECD EUROPE

	Initial expenditure share	Nominal expenditure	GDP deflator	Expenditure in cost terms	Relative prices	Real expenditure	of which			Final expenditure share
							Demography	Coverage	Level of service	
	1960									1975
	Average annual growth rates (%): 1960–75									
Education	3.1	14.2	5.8	8.1	2.0	5.9	0.4	2.4	2.9	5.4
Health	2.9	15.9	5.8	9.5	1.4	8.0	0.9	0.8	6.3	6.0
Pensions	7.1	13.7	5.8	7.5	-0.4	7.9	2.5	0.6	4.5	10.6
Unemployment compensation	0.2	23.2	5.8	16.5	-0.4	17.0	4.7	2.4	9.5	0.8
Total of above programmes	13.3	14.2	5.8	8.0	0.4	7.6	1.8	1.0	4.6	22.8
Total social expenditure	16.9	13.5	5.8	7.3	0.4	6.8	—	—	—	27.5
	1975									1981
	Average annual growth rates (%): 1975–81									
Education	5.4	15.0	10.5	4.1	1.9	6.6	-0.6	-0.4	2.3	5.8
Health	6.0	15.0	10.5	4.1	1.2	2.8	0.3	0.2	2.4	6.3
Pensions	10.6	17.4	10.5	6.2	0.1	6.1	1.4	0.5	4.2	12.5
Unemployment compensation	0.8	22.9	10.5	11.3	0.0	11.2	6.5	-3.2	7.9	1.3
Total of above programmes	22.8	16.3	10.5	5.2	0.8	4.4	0.8	0.2	3.3	25.9
Total social expenditure	27.5	15.5	10.5	4.6	0.7	3.9	—	—	—	30.0

Source: Social Expenditure: 1960–1990, Social Policy Studies, OECD, Paris, 1985

compensation programmes falling. Coverage was hardly expanded at all, with a decrease in the case of education. The number of young people also fell, thus yielding a decrease in real expenditure on education. The relative prices of education and health services increased only slightly, while the relative price of cash benefits decreased faster than previously.

Table 2.3, for the United States, and Table 2.4 for OECD Europe tell very similar stories to Table 2.2. The principal difference is that, on average, the growth rate of levels of service did not fall as much between the two periods in the other OECD countries as in the United Kingdom. It tended to remain above the growth rate of real GDP per caput, holding up well in France and Italy, but falling significantly in Germany and the United States. Demographic changes varied little between countries, and relative price changes displayed only modest variation. With the exception of unemployment compensation changes in coverage were also broadly similar. For unemployment compensation there was a tendency for coverage to fall in the second period, with the United Kingdom as an exception. This partly reflects changes in administrative regulations, but it also reflects the growing number of young people and married women amongst the unemployed, and the increasing importance of long-term unemployment. Young people, married women and the long-term unemployed are often excluded from unemployment insurance, which is primarily intended for the short-term unemployed with some history of previous employment. The coverage and expenditure data for the United Kingdom include these people and the benefits they receive, while the data for other countries as a rule do not.

PROJECTIONS FOR SOCIAL EXPENDITURE IN THE FUTURE

The growth of social expenditure through the 1980s, and the pressure to which this growth will give rise, are inextricably linked with parallel economic developments. There have recently been clear indications of a recovery in the United States, and the outlook is promising for Japan, but the prospects for the major European countries are difficult to assess. The OECD secretariat has forecast a continuation of recovery in the OECD area through 1984 and into the first half of 1985. The social expenditure projections presented below are based upon an informal economic scenario in which there is some further convergence of growth rates through the second half of the 1980s.[1] Towards the end of the decade growth rates are assumed to be modest throughout the OECD area, and slightly lower in Europe than elsewhere. Unemployment falls in Canada and the United States, there is little change in Japan, but Europe experiences slightly higher unemployment rates than at the beginning of the 1980s. Inflation, after some initial moderation, stabilizes.

To examine prospective social expenditure developments in the context of this rather pessimistic economic scenario it is necessary to do one of two things. Given assumptions about programme commitments through the 1980s, social expenditure projections could be made, and when compared with GDP forecasts these will indicate the pressure being exerted by social programmes on the economy as a whole. Alternatively, some assumption could be made about future levels of social expenditure relative to GDP, and the impact of this assumption on future levels of service could be investigated. From the results of either of these exercises the results of the other can be quickly inferred. We will proceed with the second, since this reflects the nature of the constraint many governments have imposed upon themselves as part of their overall medium-term budgetary stance. (For an application of the first method to the United Kingdom, see the chapter by O'Higgins and Patterson.)

It will be assumed that the objective of each government is to reach 1990 with spending as a fraction of GDP still at its 1981 level. In other words, the income elasticity of social expenditure for the period will be unity. This assumption should be compared with past experience, as summarized in Table 2.1. Since the United Kingdom has had one of the highest elasticities in the past, roughly twice that being imposed, this assumption obviously implies a marked departure from what has been achieved in the past. This is also true for France and Italy, and the imposed elasticity may be a more stringent requirement than governments in some of these countries are going to require. But Germany and the United States have achieved elasticities of one or below, and the imposed elasticity may underestimate the degree of expenditure restraint these countries themselves intend to apply.

Table 2.5 shows a decomposition of the future growth rate of social expenditure for the United Kingdom, analogous to the one Table 2.2 shows for the past. Again, only the four major programmes are considered, it being assumed that expenditure on the remaining programmes is a fixed proportion of the total. This being the case, if expenditure in cost terms on the four major programmes taken together grows at the same rate as real GDP over the period 1981-90 the expenditure share will be the same at the end of the period as at the beginning. The relative prices of education and health services are

TABLE 2.5 THE DECOMPOSITION OF THE FUTURE GROWTH RATE OF SOCIAL EXPENDITURE, 1981–1990, IN THE UNITED KINGDOM

	Initial expenditure share	Nominal expenditure	GDP deflator	Expenditure in cost terms	Relative prices	Real expenditure	of which Demography	Coverage	Level of service	Final expenditure share
	1960					Average annual growth rates (%): 1981–90				1990
Education	5.8	7.1	6.0	1.1	0.3	0.8	−1.0	0.0	1.7	5.3
Health	5.4	8.0	6.0	1.9	0.2	1.7	−0.1	0.0	1.7	5.2
Pensions	7.4	8.1	6.0	2.0	0.0	2.0	0.2	0.0	1.7	7.4
Unemployment compensation	1.4	13.4	6.0	6.9	0.0	6.9	5.1	0.0	1.7	2.1
Total of above programmes	20.0	8.1	6.0	2.0	0.1	1.9	0.2	0.0	1.7	20.0

Source: Social Expenditure: 1960–1990, Social Policy Studies, OECD, Paris, 1985

TABLE 2.6 THE DECOMPOSITION OF THE FUTURE GROWTH RATE OF SOCIAL EXPENDITURE, 1981–1990

	Initial expenditure share	Nominal expenditure	GDP deflator	Expenditure in cost terms	Relative prices	Real expenditure	of which			Final expenditure share
							Demography	Coverage	Level of service	
	1981									1990
				Average annual growth rates (%): 1981–90						
United Kingdom	20.0	8.1	6.0	2.0	0.1	1.9	0.2	0.0	1.7	20.0
United States	17.6	7.6	5.0	2.5	1.0	1.5	1.2	0.0	0.3	17.6
France	26.0	8.6	7.0	1.5	-0.1	1.6	0.3	0.0	1.4	26.0
Germany	25.6	4.6	3.0	1.5	0.6	0.9	-0.3	0.0	1.2	25.6
Italy	26.3	11.7	10.0	1.5	2.0	-0.5	0.4	0.0	-0.9	26.3
OECD Europe	25.9	9.0	6.0	1.5	0.8	0.7	0.1	0.0	0.6	25.9

Source: Social Expenditure: 1960–1990, Social Policy Studies, OECD, Paris, 1985

assumed to grow at the same rate as over the period 1975 – 81, while the growth rate of the relative price of cash benefits is implied – via changes in the GDP and private consumption deflators – by the economic scenario. Population changes are based on OECD projections up to 1990, and it is also assumed that there is no increase in programme coverage, on average, between 1981 and 1990.

Given the economic scenario outlined earlier and the above assumptions, the growth rate of levels of service across the four programmes taken together follows directly, and in Table 2.5 it has been assumed that this is the growth rate under each programme. This growth rate is 1.7 per cent, which is only slightly less than the 2.1 growth rate of real GDP per capita.

Table 2.6 contains summary projections for the United Kingdom, the United States and the major European countries. In the United States spending in cost terms is expected to rise a little more rapidly each year than in the United Kingdom, but the growth rate of levels of service is less than one fifth as large, at 0.3 per cent, compared to a growth rate of GDP per capita of 1.5 per cent. The explanation for this difference can be found in the faster growth in relative prices and more adverse demographic changes – in particular, faster growth in total population and the number of old people – in the United States than in the United Kingdom.

In France and Germany relative price and demographic changes are similar to those in the United Kingdom, so the slightly lower projected growth rates are reflected in the slower growth rates of levels of service. Italy is projected to share this slightly lower growth rate, but levels of service actually have to fall if the expenditure share is not to rise. The rapid growth in the relative prices of education and health services (which reflects the assumption that the experience of the 1975 – 81 period will continue) largely explains this outcome.

CONCLUSIONS

This analysis suggests that even fairly pessimistic economic developments do not appear to constitute a major threat to social programmes as they currently operate. In most countries, levels of service can increase, although not as fast as real GDP per capita. This picture may appear to be moderately encouraging. However, it would represent a marked break with the past, when levels of service in most countries grew faster both in absolute terms and relative to GDP per head. The average rate of increase for the OECD countries considered between 1975 and 1981 was 2.4 per cent per annum. If levels of service continued to grow at this rate between 1981 and 1990 the average expenditure share would rise from 23.1 per cent to 27.9 per cent, with particularly large increases in France and Italy.

The United Kingdom stands in stark contrast to this, since it is the only major country where the continuation of the 1975 – 81 growth rates of levels of service, 0.7 per cent, would imply a decrease in the expenditure share – from 20 per cent to 18.3 per cent – between 1981 and 1990. If the expenditure share remains at 20 per cent, levels of service in the United Kingdom can still increase faster over the period 1981 – 90 than they did over the period 1975 – 81. This is probably a surprising result. Could it, and those for other countries, misrepresent the prospects for the 1980s?

The implied growth rate of levels of service is, of course, a function of the economic scenario. Slower growth can only support slower growing levels of service. But the economic scenario is more likely to be criticized for being pessimistic rather than optimistic. Furthermore, because the analysis is couched in relative terms – how fast can levels of service grow relative to GDP per capita – the conclusions are fairly robust. Demographic changes over the remainder of the decade are predictable. And the change in the relative prices of education and health services – a historical figure from a period when their growth rates were falling – is more likely to be an overestimate than an underestimate. If there is a misleading element in the projection it is unlikely to be found in the economic scenario, or the assumed demographic and relative price changes.

The assumption that there will be no further increase in programme coverage may, however, be a source of concern. Since 1960 an increasing number of people have come to rely on the income support schemes and state welfare services. In part this reflected the expansion of programmes to meet needs that had previously gone unmet, but it also reflected the response to new needs and demands – for example, for pre-primary and higher education, for access to best-practice medical technology, for reduced pension ages. The projections described above suggest that there will be little scope for any further improvements in any one programme within the budgetary constraint without accepting slower growth and possibly lower levels of service in other programmes.

There may also be pressure on levels of service themselves. Certain programmes have increasing levels of service built into their structure. Most notable in this respect are earnings-related pension schemes which are as yet somewhat short of full maturity. If levels of service have to increase faster than allowed for in the projection in order that pension commitments can be met, this may necessitate compensating changes, either to programme coverage or to levels of service elsewhere.

Thus the result of this analysis must be a qualified one. If the welfare state is in crisis, it is not a financial crisis, at least not in the medium term. But, unless there is a major turnaround in economic fortunes, the medium-term prospects for largely unreformed social programmes are probably fairly austere. These programmes could leave the 1980s in more or less the same sort of shape in which they entered them – in terms of coverage and levels of service – without any increase in the resources devoted to them, but the general expansion and improvement which has been a feature of the past is likely to remain exactly that. To the extent that pressure for further increases in coverage and levels of service is conceded to, so room for retrenchment elsewhere within the system will have to be found, or a larger proportion of national resources must be devoted to social programmes.

Notes

1   This informal scenario, which covers the period after the second half of 1985, is not an official OECD projection. It has been prepared only as a basis for the social expenditure projections.

3

Women, Employment and Social Welfare

MARTIN REIN

INTRODUCTION

Two of the most important social changes since the Second World War are the development of the welfare state and its elaboration by systems of employer-provided social protection; and the transformation of the labour market as expressed in the growth of service sector employment, in the increase in the labour force participation rates of married women (and the accompanying decline in male labour force participation rates) and in a growing anxiety about whether the economy can generate enough jobs to meet the available supply of labour.[1]

This chapter examines the relationship between these two trends. It focuses on some aspects of the relationship between social policy and labour markets that have not been noticed and analysed. Its main argument is that those functions we associate with the provision of welfare have generated a social welfare labour market which has had as one of its consequences the integration of women, and especially married women, into paid employment. The prospects for welfare and the prospects for work are thus intimately connected, and the interaction is especially important for women.

To argue this is not to argue that these outcomes are necessarily the result of explicit policy. Indeed to begin a policy analysis in the domain of explicit purposes would be to overlook one of the major social processes whereby women have been integrated into the labour market,

The first draft of this chapter was written at the Wissenschaftzentrum, Berlin, for whose hospitality I am grateful.

namely the development of a social welfare labour market. In order to understand this social process we need a type of analysis that starts with an explicit outcome, locates the actors and resources that could have led to such an outcome, and then infers policy from action rather than from intention. Thus, 'tacit' or 'implicit' policy is a by product of a course of action pursued for reasons other than the observed behaviour.

This chapter therefore investigates changes in the pattern of employment in Germany, Sweden, the United States and Great Britain, focusing in particular on women's employment and on jobs in the Social Welfare Industry (SWI). The term SWI is used to describe employment in the health, education and social service sectors as defined in the Standard Industrial Classification, which facilitates international comparisons.[2] The four countries chosen have rather different levels of welfare state spending and a range of recent experience with respect to women's labour force participation.

WOMEN, EMPLOYMENT AND THE SOCIAL WELFARE INDUSTRY

The data presented in Table 3.1 describe the changes between 1960 and

TABLE 3.1   TOTAL LABOUR FORCE PARTICIPATION RATES (%)

Year	USA			West Germany		
	Total	Males	Females	Total	Males	Females
1960	66.8	97.1	42.6	70.3	94.4	49.2
1970	67.7	87.1	48.9	69.5	92.5	48.1
1975	69.1	85.4	53.2	67.9	87.0	49.6
1978	71.4	85.6	57.7	66.8	84.9	49.4
1981	72.7	85.1	60.7	66.1	82.3	50.1

Year	Great Britain			Sweden		
	Total	Males	Females	Total	Males	Females
1960	71.7	98.1	46.1	74.3	98.5	50.1
1970	72.4	94.3	50.8	74.3	88.8	59.4
1975	73.8	92.2	55.3	78.5	89.2	67.6
1978	74.2	91.4	57.1	79.6	87.7	71.3
1981	73.8	90.0	57.5	81.0	86.5	75.3

Source: OECD Historical Statistics, Paris 1983, Tables 2.6, 2.7, 2.8, w. 34/5
The participation rate is defined as the total labour force divided by the population aged 15 to 64.

1981 in the labour force participation of men and women in the four countries we are studying. They show that the labour force participation of women in Germany remained at about 50 per cent over the entire time period. By sharp contrast the participation rates of women in Sweden increased from 50 to 75 per cent during the same time period. The United States and Britain fall between these extremes. In the United States the increase was from 43 to 61 per cent and in Britain, starting at a somewhat higher level of 46 per cent, the rates grew more slowly to only 56 per cent. In the meantime male labour force participation declined in all countries, but most dramatically in Germany where the decline was from 94 to 82 per cent and least so in Britain where the decline was only from 98 to 90 per cent.

Changes in the Industry Structure

That modern economies have been transformed into service economies is, of course, now widely understood. But much less attention has been given to the composition of these service industries, partly because there is no widely accepted way of categorizing the service sector.[3] The research reported here starts with the Standard Industrial Classification, which groups all occupations that contribute to producing the product of a particular industry. Service industries (meaning products) are divided into the following categories: communal services (public utilities, libraries, museums etc.); business services (repair, haulage, finance etc.); consumer services (laundry and dry cleaning, retail, hotels and lodgings etc.); social services (narrowly defined as health, education and welfare); and private households (where the individual is employed directly by the household). The non-service industries are divided into agriculture and goods-producing. Between the early 1960s and 1980s in all four countries only two service industries grew substantially while the rest remained the same or declined: the two growth areas are service to business and social welfare.[4] By the 1980s the social welfare industry represented a substantial proportion of total employment in the economy of some countries. The Swedish experience is most striking – in 1983 about 26 per cent of jobs were in the social welfare industry. Germany provides a contrasting picture, with only 11 per cent of its population employed in the SWI. The United States and Britain fall between these extremes, with 18 per cent and 15 per cent of their total populations employed in social welfare.

One way to appreciate the full meaning of these figures is to compare them to the relative size of goods-producing industries (manufacturing, construction and mining). In Sweden these two industries are almost the same relative size – 26 and 29 per cent. Here too the contrast with Germany is most striking. In Germany 41 per cent of the total employed population work in the goods-producing industries and only 11 per cent work in social welfare. But even in the United States, the SWI accounts for almost as much of total employment (18 per cent) as manufacturing industry (20 per cent).

The SWI plays an even more prominent position in the service economy. Social welfare as a percentage of all service industries was almost 40 per cent in Sweden, about 25 per cent in Britain and the United States, and around 20 per cent in Germany.

Within the social welfare industry there has been an important change in the mix of health, education and social services (or social care). In most countries the relative share of education has declined and the share of health and social care has increased; Germany again is an exception because the share of education actually expanded there.

This summary has highlighted five main themes:

1   The SWI is one of the few industries whose share of employment has increased in the past 20 years in all four countries.
2   By 1983 the SWI accounted for between 11 and 26 per cent of the employment in both sexes.
3   The SWI accounted for between 20 and 40 per cent of employment in the service industries.
4   There has been a change in the product-mix within the social welfare industry in most countries with health and social service industries experiencing relative growth while education declines.
5   The variation in the experience of countries is very striking. Sweden has the largest SWI in relation to both total employment and total service employment, and Germany the smallest. Britain and the United States are in a similar position between these extremes.

When we focus on women rather than the total population the pattern we find is essentially similar to that described above. The proportions are much higher because women are much more likely to be employed in the SWI than men. Again the Swedish story stands out: by 1983 45 per cent of all employed Swedish women worked in the SWI, while 54 per cent of women employed in the service sector worked in social welfare. By contrast, only 18 per cent of women employed in Germany in 1982 worked in the SWI, with 28 per cent of working women employed in the service sector. In the United States the respective figures are 28 and 35 per cent and in Britain 26 and 28 per cent.

The SWI, therefore, accounts for almost half of all jobs that women held in Sweden and less than one-fifth of the jobs held by German women. These figures may suggest an explanation of why Sweden has such a high female labour force participation rate, while the rates in Germany are relatively low, but the structure of employment changes must be examined before such a conclusion can be accepted.

The Structure of Change in Employment

The previous section examined the growing importance of the SWI in accounting for a larger share of the jobs which women hold. This helps us answer the question of what women do when they work but takes no account of the size of the working-age population, which is necessary in order to explore the extent to which the SWI contributes to the increase in the proportion of working-age women in paid employment. Between 1960 and 1981 the non-agricultural participation of women increased by a half in Sweden, two-fifths in the United States, one-third in Britain, but only one-sixth in Germany (see Table 3.2). In all of the countries the growth of the SWI is equal to or much greater than the change in female labour force participation rates. We can conclude therefore that the SWI contributes to the inclusion of women within the labour force to some extent. However, this relationship is not simply linear, because much depends on the rates of growth of other (non-SWI) industries.

In Sweden virtually all the increase in female employment (89 per cent) was concentrated in the SWI. Since the SWI employment share doubled, Sweden experienced *both* a big increase in female labour

TABLE 3.2   SUMMARY OF EMPLOYMENT TRENDS 1960–1980 FOR FEMALE NON-AGRICULTURAL POPULATION AGES 15–64

	Change (%) 1960–80	SWI share (%) 1960	SWI share (%) 1980	Change in SWI share (%) 1960–80	SWI share of change (%) 1960–80
USA	43	8.2	16.2	98	47.6
Germany	16	4.4	8.9	102	70.3
Great Britain	32	6.6	13.8	109	56.3
Sweden	49	11.9	33.0	177	89.4

All data relate to female non-agricultural employment.

force participation rates and a near tripling of the share of employment in the SWI, so that one out of every three working-age Swedish women works in the SWI and almost half (45 per cent) of employed women work in social welfare. The role of the SWI in integrating women into the labour market is unambiguous.

In the United States the female labour force grew almost as much as it did in Sweden (43 per cent), but the role of the SWI was less dominant. None the less, almost a half of the total increase in the employment of women is accounted for by the expansion of employment opportunities in the SWI.

We can conclude that in both Sweden and the United States the SWI was an important factor in the growth of female employment between the early 1960s and the 1980s. However, its role in Sweden was decisive, because employment opportunities elsewhere did not expand, whereas in the United States, where such expansion did take place, the SWI role was important but not overriding.

The German situation requires some special comment. We saw in Table 3.1 that female labour force participation rates actually declined slightly during the 1960s, when they were rising elsewhere, so that, while higher than in Britain or the USA in 1960, they were lower in 1970. The high 1960 participation level was due to the mobilization of women, especially on farms, into the labour force during the Second World War. After the war, these now-older women gradually began to leave the farms, so that when agricultural workers are excluded, female employment shows a small increase of 16 per cent between 1960 and 1980. This is, of course, still much lower than the 32 per cent increase in Britain, the 49 per cent in Sweden and the 43 per cent in the United States.

While in Germany the participation of working women in the SWI is much lower than in Sweden – only 9 per cent as compared to 33 per cent – nevertheless, the SWI played an overwhelming role (70 per cent) in increasing female employment rates.

In Britain female employment increased by only 32 per cent between 1960 and 1980, with the role of the SWI falling somewhere between Sweden and the United States. Britain did not increase employment in the SWI as rapidly as did Sweden, nor non-SWI employment as rapidly as the USA. In Britain 14 per cent of working-age women worked in social welfare, a proportion much lower than in Sweden and slightly lower than in the United States. But even so, the SWI accounted for 56 per cent of the increase in women's employment in this period.

The importance of social welfare to female employment is even more dramatic when we focus on college-educated women. The figures are quite startling. In 1981 in the USA, 74 per cent of all women with post-graduate training and 59 per cent of college-trained women were employed in social welfare. In other countries the proportions are even higher. About 75 per cent of college-educated German women in 1971 were employed in the SWI, while in Sweden the proportion in 1981 was 66 per cent.

In summary, we conclude that the SWI has played a leading role in integrating women into the paid labour market. How dominant this role is varies from country to country. Its role is smallest in the United States (but even here it accounts for 48 per cent of the increase in female employment between 1962 and 1983). However, it is unambiguously decisive – integrating almost 90 per cent of women into paid employment – in Sweden. In Britain it contributes to more than half (56 per cent) of the increase in female employment. Even in Germany, the country with the lowest female participation rates in 1980, the smallest increase in female employment from 1960 to 1980, and the lowest proportion of females employed in the SWI, the SWI accounted for 70 per cent of such increase as there was in female employment. The SWI is, therefore, an important employer of women and the major source of the increase in female employment in the last two decades.

The Role of Welfare in State Employment

We now want to examine the state's role as employer in the SWI, i.e. the role of social welfare in the activities of the state, (defined as general government). Table 3.3 shows that two-thirds of all general government employees work for the welfare state in Sweden. The proportions are only slightly lower in Britain (62 per cent), in Germany (60 per cent) and in the United States (57 per cent).

The welfare state as employer has secondly grown in all of the countries since the 1960s, from about half of general government employment to about two-thirds. Statistics are available for the United Kingdom only between 1978 and 1981 but even in this short period social welfare grew from 61.5 per cent to 62.5 per cent as a proportion of government employment.

When we examine the welfare state as an employer for women, we find that three-quarters of all the jobs that women hold as employees of the state are in the SWI. The proportion is somewhat higher in Sweden at 79 per cent and lower in the United States at 71 per cent. When we look at trends over time the pattern is somewhat more varied. In the past 20 years SWI's share of women's state employment has remained relatively stable in the United States, increased in Sweden and Germany, and (over a much shorter period) declined slightly in Britain.

How sex segregated is the welfare state as employer? What percentage of public social welfare workers are women? Sweden and the United Kingdom show the highest patterns of sex segregation: 82 per cent and 76 per cent respectively; Germany shows the lowest proportion while the United States is somewhere in between. In Germany only 60 per cent of welfare state workers are women, and the German pattern is particularly interesting. Men are much more likely to be employed in the welfare state in Germany than in the other countries. Thus 53 per cent of all men who work for the government are.employed in the welfare industry as compared to 40 per cent or less in other countries. One clue to understanding the German pattern is to remember that, unlike other countries, the relative share of education in the social

TABLE 3.3   TRENDS IN GENERAL GOVERNMENT EMPLOYMENT

	Sector (% of total)	Female (% of total)	Female (% of sector)	Sector (% of total)	Female (% of total)	Female (% of sector)
USA 1962				1983		
Total social welfare	48.4	70.1	61.6	57.1	71.2	66.2
Health	11.4	16.5	61.7	10.4	14.0	71.4
Social service	0.3	0.5	71.0	3.5	4.7	71.0
Education	36.8	53.1	61.5	43.2	52.5	64.7
Public admin.	37.0	26.5	30.5	33.1	24.9	39.9
Other	14.6	3.4	10.0	9.7	3.9	21.7
Total numbers	7756	3302	42.6	14219	7565	53.2
Sweden 1964				1983		
Total social welfare	51.4	71.1	76.0	66.6	79.1	82.1
Health	21.2	32.4	83.9	26.0	32.0	84.8
Social Service	9.9	14.3	79.6	20.9	27.6	91.0
Education	20.3	24.4	66.1	19.7	19.6	69.0
Public admin.	20.9	12.7	33.3	13.8	8.8	44.0
Other	27.8	16.2	32.0	19.6	12.1	42.1
Total numbers	666	365	54.8	1513	1046	69.1

United Kingdom

	1978			1981		
Total social welfare	61.5	78.9	75.3	62.5	77.2	75.7
Health	23.6	30.6	76.2	32.3	35.2	79.6
Social service	6.6	9.9	87.9			
Education	31.3	38.4	72.0	30.1	35.2	71.5
Public admin.	–	–	–	–	–	–
Other	38.5	21.1	32.1	37.5	22.8	37.2
Total numbers	5010	2940	58.7	5010	3070	61.3

	Germany 1960			1982		
Total social welfare	51.3	69.0	52.7	60.1	74.2	59.6
Health	15.1	23.2	60.2	21.1	29.1	66.4
Social service	16.4	24.2	57.7	12.5	16.1	62.1
Education	19.7	21.5	42.7	26.4	29.0	53.0
Public admin.	16.3	11.8	27.6	16.5	10.3	30.1
Other	32.0	19.2	23.4	23.4	15.4	31.8
Total numbers	1814	710	39.1	3759	1813	48.2

welfare industry has been growing there. In Germany, women account for only 53 per cent of employment in education as compared to 70 per cent in Sweden and the United Kingdom and 65 per cent in the United States.

The German figures are very suggestive, since they show that the welfare state as employer can be organized so that it is not primarily a female industry. On the other hand, even in Germany, nearly three quarters of the jobs that women hold when they work for the state are in the social welfare industry. It is, therefore, not that women have more opportunities to do other things when they work for the state in Germany, but only that men have traditionally been involved in education. Even this pattern seems to be changing over time: in 1960 only 43 per cent of those employed in education were women; by 1983 the proportion had increased to 53 per cent. As the industry becomes more feminized it also provides more job opportunities for women. Does this suggest a trade-off whereby the integration of women into the labour market is accompanied by increased segregation in the industries in which they are employed? This issue is further explored in the next section, which examines a range of explanations for these data.

INTERPRETING WOMEN'S SOCIAL WELFARE EMPLOYMENT ROLE

The statistics which we have presented are very suggestive, but they do not help us understand what generates the differences within and across countries in the size and growth of social welfare employment and why social welfare employment is so highly feminized. These interpretations are not to be found in the statistics, but in a better understanding of social processes in each society. I would like to outline and explore the evidence for six different interpretations.

1   *Women's Work*

This interpretation suggests that because of traditional role stereotyping, social welfare is seen as the domain of women, so that one would expect to find a high degree of sex segregation in this industry. For example, Laura Balbo has forcefully argued that the sex role patterns growing out of traditional family organization are a useful way to describe the paid female labour of the welfare state. She uses the imagery of quilt-making to capture the essence of women's work.

> sorting out, piecing, patching and quilting suggest parallels to concepts that have been used to describe women's work in contemporary society: the servicing, the pooling and packaging of resources, self-help activities, emotional work, survival networks: how they keep at their endless tasks, how they put their vision into the planning and design of lives – their own and others – whose responsibility they carry (1981, p. 5).

This argument views women's work as piece-work, which requires skill in putting things together, especially making the most of what is available. The emphasis on quilting is somewhat different, but not inconsistent with the conventional sex stereotypes of tending and caring roles.

The empirical evidence presented in Table 3.4 clearly demonstrates the high degree of concentration of women in the SWI. If we leave aside the declining and small private household industry, we find that in almost every country social welfare is among the most sex-segregated of industries. Not surprisingly, the proportions of females in the total SWI are similar to the figures for the state's SWI presented in Table 3.3.

Sweden and Britain have the highest degree of female concentration

TABLE 3.4   SEX SEGREGATION BY INDUSTRY

	Females as percentage of total employees					
	Sweden			USA		
	1964	1973	1983	1962	1972	1983
Agriculture	25	33	25	18	19	17
Goods producing services	21	20	22	21	22	27
Communal services	31	36	40	22	25	31
Business services	31	35	38	34	38	45
Consumer services	64	59	60	41	46	49
Private household services	99	98	89	87	87	83
Social services	74	81	81	63	66	69
All industries	37	41	47	34	39	44

	Germany			Britain		
	1961	1970	1982	1961	1971	1981
Agriculture	54	49	49	12	17	25
Goods producing services	26	26	24	25	25	25
Communal services	22	26	34	20	27	38
Business services	36	39	42	27	34	37
Consumer services	64	62	65	52	56	63
Private household services	99	99	99	84	83	na
Social services	63	64	66	68	72	74
All industries	37	37	39	33	37	43

na = not available

in the SWI. Over 80 per cent of those employed in the SWI in Sweden are women as compared to 74 per cent in Britain. Germany and the United States have the least segregated SWIs, 69 per cent being women in the United States and 66 per cent in Germany. Not only does Germany have the least segregation, but it also has the lowest growth in segregation; whereas sex segregation in the SWI in the other countries increased by 6 to 7 percentage points between 1960 and 1980, in Germany it increased by only 3 percentage points.

While the SWI has become more sex segregated over time, other industries have become more integrated. This pattern of integration appears to have taken place in all countries, most rapidly in Sweden and only very marginally in Germany. In 1964, 37 per cent of the employed population were women in Sweden and by 1983 the proportion had grown to 47 per cent. In Britain and the United States the proportions increased from about 33 per cent in the early 1960s to 44 per cent in the early 1980s. In Germany the proportions remained virtually unchanged – 37 per cent in 1961 and 39 per cent in 1982.

However, this argument is much too simplistic: it does not tell us *where* in the SWI segregation is greatest. To explore this question we need to recognize that all industries are multi-occupational. If we look at the occupations within the health, education and welfare industries, we can divide them into social welfare specialists (teachers, nurses and social workers) and support workers (clerical, manual, managerial etc.). Some specialist occupations fit the sex role stereotype of women's work – day care, elementary and pre-kindergarten education, nursing, etc. – but these occupations accounted for only about 47 per cent of all social welfare specialist jobs in the United States in 1981.

When we turn to support work, the figures are equally puzzling. Women are concentrated in occupations such as cleaning, cooking, housekeeping, chambermaids and clerks, but these account for only 36 per cent of the jobs female support workers held in the US in 1981. Further, the essence of domesticity is not only 'quilting', but managing the quilt factory; but only 48 per cent of women are managers and administrators of health and educational institutions. This proportion is only slightly higher than the 44 per cent of all women in paid employment.

At best the women's work argument is only part of the story of why women are allocated to employment in social welfare.

2   The Integration of Work and Family Life: the Role of Part-Time Employment

A second argument is that social welfare uniquely makes it possible for women to integrate their work and family obligations through part-time work, which allows them the flexibility to integrate the conflicting requirements of those dual obligations. In order to examine this explanation we need to know whether the SWI provides more opportunities for part-time employment than exist elsewhere in the economy. [5]

The variation in part-time employment among women in the

different countries is most striking (see Table 3.5). In Sweden 47 per cent and in Britain 42 per cent of women work part time. In contrast, in Germany only 31 per cent work part time and in the United States only 22 per cent.[6] Thus the ranking of part-time employment across countries is very different from the ranking of employment in the SWI. Both Germany and the United States have relatively low proportions of women in part-time work, but Germany has a much smaller proportion of its population in social welfare than does the United States.

Is part-time work more likely to be found in the SWI within each country? If we look at the distribution of part-time jobs we find that in every country except Germany more people are employed part-time in social welfare than in non-social welfare jobs. In Britain and Sweden, about half of the women working in social welfare jobs work part time compared to around two-fifths of those in non-social welfare work. In the USA, the proportions are about a quarter and a fifth respectively. Except for Germany, therefore, social welfare accounts for a disproportionate share of part-time female employment.

The German situation – where fewer women work, the rate of

TABLE 3.5   FEMALE EMPLOYMENT BY INDUSTRY AND NORMAL HOURS WORKED

	Percentages of total female employment			
	USA 1983		*Sweden 1982*	
Part time	21.8		46.8	
Social welfare		36.8		48.3
Non-social welfare		63.2		51.7
Full time	78.2		53.2	
social welfare		29.9		43.8
non-social welfare		70.1		56.2
Social welfare	31.4		45.9	
part time		25.6		49.2
full time		74.4		50.8
Total	100.0		100.0	
Part time				
social welfare		8.0		22.6
non-social welfare		13.8		24.2
Full time				
social welfare		23.4		23.3
non-social welfare		54.8		29.9

TABLE 3.5   FEMALE EMPLOYMENT BY INDUSTRY AND NORMAL
HOURS WORKED – *continued*

	Percentages of total female employment			
	Germany 1982		*Great Britain 1981*	
Part time	30.7		41.6	
social welfare		16.9		32.3
non-social welfare		83.1		67.7
Full time	69.3		58.4	
social welfare		19.0		22.7
non-social welfare		81.0		77.3
Social welfare	18.4		26.7	
part time		28.2		50.4
full time		71.8		✓ 49.6
Non-social welfare	81.6		73.3	
part time		31.2		38.4
full time		68.8		61.6
Total	100.0		100.0	
Part time				
social welfare		5.2		13.5
non-social welfare		25.5		28.1
Full time				
social welfare		13.2		13.2
non-social welfare		56.1		45.2

increase in the employment of working-age women is slower than that
of other countries, and there is relatively less part-time social welfare
work – may provide us with a clue to understanding the role of part-
time employment in explaining the growth of female employment.
Perhaps part-time work is not a cause of women's employment, but a
consequence. It is not implausible to speculate that women first hold
full-time jobs, but through labour market and social policy
negotiations are able to redefine their work conditions to be more
flexible with respect to their family lives. This is consistent with the
pattern of development in Sweden.

The general conclusion is that with the exception of Germany, social
welfare employment does provide more opportunities for part-time
work than in the economy as a whole – but only marginally so. While
part-time social welfare work is strikingly important in Sweden and

Great Britain, it is much less so in the United States and in Germany, suggesting no simple link to women's work. The figures for Sweden and Britain also show that female part-time work in the economy as a whole is much higher than it is in the other two countries, but again these figures show no strong tie to female employment because Britain has a smaller proportion of its working-age women in social welfare than the United States which, however, has the lowest relative levels of female part-time work.

3 The Accommodation Argument

The third argument is that women wanted to work, but in conditions which permitted them to integrate their family, home and child-rearing responsibilities by working part time, and that the public sector accommodated to the supply of female labour because the private sector was unwilling to do so. The details of this argument and of the institutional arrangements which made the accommodation possible would need to be specified for each country if it were to be properly evaluated, but its general lines may be sketched with reference to the Swedish experience. During the 1960s efforts were made to get industry to accommodate women's interests in part-time employment. However, industry apparently preferred male foreign workers to females; as women entered the labour market, they could not find jobs. As a result, unemployment rose, not because people lost their jobs, but because women could not find employment. To avoid the political embarrassment of high unemployment, public sector jobs were found. Even the Conservative government elected in 1976 accepted the importance of expanding the public sector to absorb the increase in women seeking employment.

The general line of argument is clear. Government policy actively set out, for political and ideological reasons, to accommodate women's organized interests in part-time employment. *Jobs accommodated to workers.*

4 The Inadvertence Argument

What has driven the growth of public employment and what drives public sector expansion even when there is an explicit public policy to contain public sector growth and to expand employment in the export industries? The fourth argument – inadvertence – can be summarized as follows: the expansion of public employment in the SWI is seen not as an outgrowth of an explicit attempt to accommodate to labour supply, but rather as a consequence of a process whereby employment was an inadvertent by-product of policy initiatives designed to realize quite different objectives. The outcome was not the result of a 'policy', 'intention' or 'strategy' to realize some pre-conceived aim of integrating women into the labour market. There was no real intention to have social welfare jobs increase in order to integrate women into the labour market. Social welfare employment rose for quite different reasons: the desire to improve education and health, the commitment to the de-institutionalization of the aged and mentally ill, and so on.

Both the accommodation and the inadvertence thesis are plausible. How can we choose between them? How can we decide whether jobs are created by social, institutional and political processes of accommodation in response to the availability of women and the necessity for women to work to maintain family standards of well-being, or whether it is the requirements of the public service sectors which drive women into paid employment, perhaps by raising wages and hence increasing the relative opportunity cost of homework, or by some combination of both processes. In the real world, it is difficult to disentangle supply and demand.

5   The Reclassification Argument

Industries and the occupations employed within them are classified and reclassified by a social process. At least part of this process can be described as a process of learning by technical experts, who contribute to reshaping the classification system by the conventions they adopt when annual labour force survey and census statistics are gathered.

Every country has a system for classifying industries, generally by the products they produce; the automobile industry produces cars, the education industry produces education and so on. The name of the industry and its product are identical. But there are also anomalies. Consider the example of old people and children living in institutions. What precisely is the product of these institutions? The official answer in the United States and also in Germany was to place these institutions in the hotel and restaurant industry under the assumption that they were establishments which essentially provided places for people to eat and sleep.

However, this system of classification is not frozen. There are periodic reviews about the appropriate categories that are to be used in classifying the industrial structure: a technical committee in the United States around 1972 decided to reclassify these homes and institutions into a new category called social services. The result was that about 3 million 'new' social service jobs were created by redefinition. In Germany both systems of classification are used. The macro-census treats homes for children and aged as separate categories, while the 1970 census classified them as part of hotels and restaurants.

Reclassification is not, however, merely a technical decision by statisticians eager to improve the system of groupings. It is also a political process. In all societies the recategorization of the labour market is subject to continued political pressures. Organized groups have a very large stake in defining their job titles to higher status levels: for example, the para-professional movement of the early 1970s, which sought to reclassify support workers into para-professional workers such as welfare, health and education aides. [7]

The struggle over reclassification can, therefore, shape estimates of the size and growth of the SWI. The reclassification argument asserts that there are not more social welfare workers in society, but that they have become more visible because of the technical and political processes of renaming. The size of the welfare industry is thus, it is argued, an artefact of the system of counting.

We do not know to what extent the increase in jobs in the SWI is an outcome of reclassification − a change of occupational title rather than a change of task. One clue that such a process may be going on is the rather sharp variation across countries in the proportion of women employed in the SWI who are classified as support workers. In Sweden 74 per cent of all women employed in the SWI are specialists, whereas in Britain the proportion is only 57 per cent. (In Germany and the United States the proportions are 65 per cent). This suggests that Britain makes more use of support workers, and Sweden of specialists, but it may simply be that the process of classification is as important as alternative explanations such as differences in the industry mix or real differences in the division of labour and the system of production.

As Amartya Sen has pointed out, work has three dimensions: it confers social standing on its incumbents; it is a system of compensation; and it is the process by which labour contributes to the creation of production. All three dimensions critically enter the social process of reclassification. We can speculate that the politics of reclassification will intensify in the future, especially as the women's movement escalates its demands to have the work women do upgraded, in terms of social standing as well as of wages.

However, there are also biases of undercounting in the social welfare industry. There are many hidden categories of social welfare which are embedded in other industries. Perhaps the most obvious example is in the field of insurance. We know that in many societies private occupational fringe benefits account for as much as a third of the total labour costs of large firms. In addition, in some countries like Germany, about a third of those who are currently retired receive an occupational pension as a supplement to their social security benefits. [8] It has of course long been recognized that social protection in the public and private sectors are not only similar but also serve as substitutes. Hence they must be grouped together not only in considering expenditure but also in considering employment as well. Moreover, while life insurance and commercial insurance carriers provide these occupational pensions for firms who do not administer their own pension systems, personnel managers carry out these functions in larger firms. Thus insurance carriers and personnel managers are among the actors who are involved in the distribution of privately organized fringe benefits which parallel the activities of the welfare state. Unfortunately, none of the countries identified what precisely are the occupations that are involved in distributing private fringe benefits or private pensions. There may thus be both under- and overcounting of the growth of those engaged in the social welfare labour market.

6   *The Institutional Argument*

Finally we consider an institutional explanation which starts with the assumption that there are at least two different types of welfare states: a transfer state which distributes most of its resources in the form of cash transfers and a service state which is committed to the distribution of services. The level of aggregate spending in the welfare state may be quite similar but the employment effect of a service state will be much different from that of a transfer state.

In principle, a transfer state is guided by the income principle of distribution. Wherever possible individuals should be given income to spend as they choose, under the assumption that the indivdual knows his own utility best and that service and consumption decisions should be made directly by the individual. By contrast the service state is more guided by a principle of rehabilitation to help individuals re-integrate themselves within society. Hence the service state requires a larger number of personnel than does a transfer state. Obviously, every society has a combination of both and what is at issue is what is the ratio between government final consumption for services and income maintenance and cash transfers.

At the level of ideology the distinction is reasonably clear. Conservatives by and large are more willing to provide people with income that they cannot get in the market and to distribute this in the form of unrestricted cash transfers. They are also more eager to curtail the level of direct public employment because they do not want to expand the machinery of government and the level of public employment. Social democrats, by contrast, are more committed to broadening the scale of public sector employment as well as expanding income transfers.

Empirical evidence on the ratio of final consumption to transfers in government expenditure does not show a strong relationship between high service states and social welfare employment personnel. However, the essential idea seems useful if one distinguishes between types of service states, rather than relying on a simple service vs. transfer dichotomy. An understanding of the extent of the non-monetized service economy (relying on unpaid volunteers and family members) and of the levels of qualification required and degree of professionalization in the formal SWI would seem to be key factors in accounting for differences and changes in the size of the SWI.

CONCLUSIONS

This chapter has documented the extent to which the welfare society serves not only as a system of provision and services, but as a system of female employment. However, our understanding of the variation across countries in the level of social welfare employment and the degree that it is sex-segregated is much less adequate. Each of the theories we reviewed is plausible and some empirical evidence can be adduced in its support – but for no theory is the evidence unambiguous.

Further research will extend the statistical work and review these and other theories in more detail, but it is doubtful whether a more extensive review would lead to more definitive conclusions. The problem of interpretation lies in the twin reluctance of economists to move beyond labour market supply theory and of sociologists to enter this terrain and establish a theory of the sociology of labour markets. The puzzle we address – the allocation of women's jobs in the economy – needs to be grounded in political economy and not merely in a simplistic choice or balance between supply and demand theories.

What are some of the social policy implications of the analysis we present? Two broad policy questions emerge from this analysis: sex segregation and welfare state cutbacks.

In every country the SWI is the most sex segregated. If we are correct in arguing that the SWI is important in the inclusion of women in the labour market, then we must also ask what is the cost of integration. Our data suggest that the price for aggregate integration may be particular segregation. It is as if Sweden was able to achieve gender equalization in the overall labour market only by increasing the sex segregation within the SWI. Sweden now has almost a dual labour market, one in which half of all women are employed in the SWI, and the other in which males dominate.

We do not wish to imply that there is anything inevitable in this process. Indeed, in the United States during the economic recessions of the 1960s and early 1970s men began to enter the social welfare industries. Thus in periods of job scarcity men may crowd women out of the social welfare industry. However, if employment opportunities for women are not to be found in social welfare, then they must be found in other sectors of society, otherwise there will be an overall decline in female participation.

What is the effect of welfare state cutbacks on the employment of women? Whether to pursue a policy of expansion or contraction depends on one's theory of how industrial policy affects employment. One conception holds that the key to a dynamic and well functioning economy is an industrial policy of modernization designed to increase productivity and strengthen a country's competitive international position and hence to improve its balance of payments. Employment in the public sector should be discouraged and the expansion of private sector employment be assigned a high priority. The Swedish government has been committed to such a policy objective, but it has not been able to implement it in practice. Public employment has steadily increased and private sector employment declined.

This conception is similar to the nineteenth-century debate among the Physiocrats who believed that agriculture was the key to a well running economy. With 40 per cent of the labour market employed in agriculture it was hard to imagine a society in which only 2 to 3 per cent of the employed population would be working in the agricultural sector while producing enough to meet the food needs of the whole country. In much the same way those who favour industrial policy find it hard to imagine that 10 to 15 per cent of the population could produce all the goods needed in society. If, however, this were to happen what opportunities for gainful employment would be available for all other persons seeking work? One possible answer is the expansion of social welfare services and the adoption of a pattern of work-sharing. This requires an image of a service society that the industrial conception of productive employment finds difficult to accept.

Yet if work is to be provided for all who want it, even with work-sharing and shorter working weeks, the expansion of social welfare employment may be not only desirable but necessary.

Notes

1 These developments have generally been treated as separate domains of intellectual inquiry called social policy and labour market policy. There are, of course, a variety of attempts to link these fields. The best known efforts view the linkage as antagonistic, arguing that social protection inhibits the incentive to work and runs the risk of decreasing labour force participation by providing economic resources separately from paid work. The main intellectual task in this tradition is to try to estimate the size of these potential work disincentives in order to understand the price we pay for protection. This chapter proceeds from the different assumption that this relationship is complementary and can even be mutually reinforcing.

2 Conceptually the social welfare labour market (SWLM) includes all jobs in the social welfare industry (SWI) as well as those in social welfare occupations (SWOs) employed outside the SWI (for example, a nurse working in a first-aid station in a factory). Thus, not all jobs in the SWI are SWOs (e.g. a secretary in a school) and not all SWOs are in the SWI, but the SWLM includes both. While this chapter focuses on the SWI, a complete analysis would examine the SWLM.

3 For example, the fastest-growing service sector in the United States is the residual category of services not elsewhere classified.

4 The data summarized in this and subsequent sections are drawn from census and labour force survey material in each country.

5 It is important to measure part-time employment in terms of normal or customary hours worked; otherwise, we substantially overestimate the amount of part-time employment. For example, in the United States in January 1981, of all those who worked less than 35 hours per week, 30 per cent did so for special reasons which were outside their control, such as being placed on short work weeks during slack periods etc. The other 70 per cent represent the 'normal' part-timers. But even among those who normally work part time, about a fifth did so because they could not find a full-time job. It is only the remainder, who voluntarily work part time, who should be described as 'true' part-time workers.

6 Note that the American figure for employment in the SWI is 31.4 per cent, which is somewhat higher than that reported earlier. This is largely because for this analysis the employed population was redefined to include civilian non-agricultural workers, which had the effect of increasing the relative importance of social welfare employment in the economy.

7 For example, in France some shoemakers classified as manual workers were able to get their jobs reclassified as mechanical orthopaedists employed in

the health industry. For an interesting analysis of this process with some statistical evidence, see Thevenot, 1979.

8   See O'Higgins, 1985.

4

Work, Jobs and Social Policy

JOHN ERMISCH

INTRODUCTION: WORK AND THE ALLOCATION OF TIME

People make decisions about the allocation of their time among various direct and indirect welfare-creating uses. Participation in paid employment is but one such use, providing income to purchase goods and services, and perhaps also some investment in skill acquisition to enhance future earnings. Other uses include investment activities such as education, pure consumption such as leisure, and 'home production', which combines time and purchased goods and services in consumption activities (for example meals) and investment activities (for example the rearing of children). Thus time that is not spent in paid employment can be equally productive in creating welfare, and it can affect the quantity (through reproduction) and productivity (for example, health, education) of human time in future. Of particular importance are the inputs of parental time and other resources to a child's development. These inputs represent an investment which affects the child's subsequent earning power, health and productivity in creating welfare – his/her 'human capital'.

The extent and timing of participation in paid employment throughout one's life is a matter of choice, although often a severely constrained choice. The choice is made jointly within a family, and it reflects the other potential uses of one's time as well as market earning opportunities and other income coming into the family. This paper focuses on the numbers and characteristics of those persons seeking paid employment over the remainder of this century and their general implications for social policy. But it should be kept in mind that social policies can affect (and sometimes are implicitly responding to) the non-market uses of time noted above.

CHANGES IN THE SIZE AND DEMOGRAPHIC COMPOSITION OF THE LABOUR FORCE

The labour force consists of persons in employment or self-employment and those seeking employment. Its size and composition depends upon the size and composition of the population and the time allocation decisions made by members of the population. The latter are affected by the state of the labour market itself. In particular, when unemployment is high some people find that it is no longer worth expending time on searching for work; thus they drop out of the labour force. At progressively higher levels of unemployment more people are likely to come to such a conclusion. These potential 'discouraged workers' tend to be concentrated in particular demographic groups: among men aged under 20 and over 54 and women aged under 20 and between 25 and 44 (Ermisch, 1983, Ch. 2). While additional research would help refine the estimates of the size and nature of this 'discouraged worker effect' in each group its existence is well established. Thus while it may seem natural to consider the labour force as the 'supply of labour' (measured in persons) it is only a conditional supply, which depends on employment opportunities, as well as other factors affecting people's time allocation decisions.

Social policies are likely to affect employment opportunities. Indeed they may alter other factors influencing time allocation (for example the net wage), but their effect on employment opportunities is particularly important. Since this book is concerned with identifying changes in the environment within which social policy will operate in the future, it is not proper to make forecasts of future job availability (which partly reflect social policies) in forecasting the future supply of labour. It is preferable to forecast a potential labour force based on some low unemployment assumption.

Holding the state of the labour market constant in this way, future changes in the labour force depend upon fairly predictable changes in the age/sex composition of the population and on non-cyclical influences on time allocation decisions. The latter are reflected in labour force participation (or economic activity) rates and are primarily of two sorts: trends across birth cohorts in labour force participation and the effects of childbearing on women's participation. The former group includes trends in participation in education and in retirement age, which affect labour force participation at young and old ages, and the tendency for each cohort of women to participate in the labour market to a greater extent than its predecessors throughout its life (with the exception of those in their late teens and early twenties) (Ermisch, 1983).

In the computation of the likely changes in the potential labour force over the remainder of the century, the state of the labour market in 1979, the last cyclical peak, when unemployment was 5 per cent of the labour force, is taken as the base case. Analysis suggests that the birth rate will remain low (about 1.8 children per woman) (Ermisch, 1983), and this is assumed to sustain labour force participation rates of women of childbearing age at at least their 1979 level. In addition, the cohort trends in women's lifetime labour force attachment estimated by Joshi and Owen (1981) are applied to reflect the changing cohort composition of particular age groups. Men's age-specific participation rates are assumed to remain constant at their 1979 level. This assumption implicitly presumes that the move toward earlier retirement since 1979 is mainly due to the poor state of the labour market. When combined with projected changes in the age/sex composition of the population, the changes in labour force participation rates implied by these assumptions indicate growth in the potential labour force averaging 120,000 per year during 1979 – 91, but only 14,000 per annum during the 1990s. In the latter period the male labour force actually declines.

This forecast of the *potential* labour force is consistent with the labour force projection made by the Department of Employment (DE, 1984). The latter assumes that claimant unemployment remains slightly above its 1983 level to the end of their projection period in 1991. According to the department's estimate of the 'discouraged worker effect', the labour force would be about half a million larger in 1991 if unemployment returned to its 1979 level, and this is the amount by which our forecast of the potential labour force in 1991 exceeds the official projection.

The slowdown in labour force growth as the 1980s approach their conclusion mainly arises because the labour force entry by the large baby-boom birth cohorts of the 1960s comes to an end. The new cohorts of entrants are increasingly smaller, reflecting the steep fall in fertility in the 1970s. This also has profound effects on the age distribution of the potential labour force.

During 1973 – 81, the proportion of the potential labour force who are teenagers was increasing (see Table 4.1). The proportion under the age of 25 has also risen since 1974, and it continues to rise until 1985. Thus the proportion of young people in the labour force began rising just as the world economy began to falter. Women's proportion of the labour force had been rising throughout the post-war period and it

TABLE 4.1   SIZE AND COMPOSITION OF THE POTENTIAL LABOUR
FORCE, GREAT BRITAIN

	1973	1979	1991	2001
Number (thousands)	25,096	25,870	27,310	27,450
Percentage who are				
aged less than 20	7.7	9.4	7.4	6.5
aged less than 25	19.0	21.0	19.5	15.7
women	38.2	40.0	40.7	41.1
aged 20 – 44	19.5	21.8	23.9	22.9
aged 30 – 59	23.1	24.5	25.3	28.5
over retirement age	4.9	3.1	3.2	3.0

Source: DE, 1984, and author's calculation, explained in text. Population projection
from the Government Actuary's Department mid-1981 based projection, lower fertility
variant.

continued to do so during the 1970s. Changes in women's and in
young men's shares of the labour force are significant for the economic
prospects of one another because women are good substitutes for young
men in the productive process while both are poorer substitutes for
older men (Ermisch, 1984).

Despite these increases in the supply of young men and women
relative to older men, young men's hourly earnings rose until 1977
relative to older men's. This put the burden of labour market
adjustment on young people's ability to find a job, and young men's
unemployment rate has risen relative to that of older men (Ermisch,
1984). The rise was moderated somewhat by the decline since 1973 in
young men's hourly earnings relative to women's. Thus the rise in
young people's relative wages made the task of absorbing their growing
numbers into employment more difficult, and it was difficult enough
because of the deterioration of the world economy.

During the second half of the 1980s, young people's economic
prospects should improve as their relative numbers decline (see Table
4.1). If their relative wages remain the same, then their unemployment
rate would tend to decline relative to older men's. However, the
perverse movement in their relative wages during the 1970s suggests
that some downward adjustment in their relative wages, which could be
through wage subsidies, is still required to improve their employment
prospects significantly. The decline in young men's hourly earnings
relative to older men's since 1977 appears to have reduced their relative
unemployment rate (Ermisch, 1984). During the first half of the 1990s
the downward pressure on young people's relative earnings should

continue to abate while their relative employment prospects improve as their share of the potential labour force declines.

Women's share of the potential labour force will rise throughout the remainder of the century as more recent generations of women, with stronger labour-force attachment, move through the age distribution.

PART-TIME EMPLOYMENT

The change in the age composition of the female labour force tends, however, to change the nature of their participation in paid employment. As Table 4.1 indicates, a much larger proportion of women in the labour force will be in their childbearing years during the 1980s. This biases their participation towards part-time employment: in 1982, for example, among women aged 16 to 59, only 15 per cent of women with dependent children worked full time while 35 per cent worked part time; the comparable figures for women without dependent children are 47 per cent and 18 per cent.[1] It is these family responsibilities which help account for the fact, shown in Table 4.2, that only half of women aged between 30 and 44 work full time while much larger proportions of younger women do so. Nevertheless, women aged between 45 and 59, whose children have generally reached adolescence, work part time almost as much as younger mothers (see Table 4.2). There does not yet seem to be any growth in the proportion of women with dependent children working full time, nor any tendency for the proportion of women without dependent children who work part time to decline. However, it may be, as Lewis's chapter argues, that more recent generations of women, now in their twenties and thirties, who have a stronger lifetime attachment to the labour force than women currently over forty, will be more interested in full-time work after their children reach adolescence or maturity.

Table 4.2 also shows that except at ages above the state retirement age, only a very small proportion of men work part time. The large increase in part-time employment in the British economy since 1961 is therefore almost entirely made up of more middle-aged women working part time. The increasing proportion of women returning to work after having children (and between births) were mainly returning to part-time employment. All of the net increase in women's jobs since 1961 is accounted for by part-time jobs. Thus the growth in part-time employment opportunities was the major factor on the demand side of the labour market which underwrote the increase in women's labour force participation.

TABLE 4.2   PART-TIME EMPLOYMENT, GREAT BRITAIN, 1981

	Percentage of persons in employment working part time	
Age	Men	Women
16	3.0	7.6
17 – 20	1.4	4.5
21 – 24	1.2	9.7
25 – 29	0.9	26.7
30 – 34	0.8	49.8
35 – 39	0.8	53.5
40 – 44	0.8	49.7
45 – 49	0.8	47.3
50 – 54	1.0	47.7
55 – 59	1.6	48.9
60 – 64	4.0	65.3
65 – 69	57.3	78.9
70 and over	66.2	67.3

Source: *Economic Activity Tables*, 1981 Census, Table 2

While a shift in the structure of labour demand towards service industries contributed to growth in women's part-time employment, over 60 per cent of the growth was attributable to increases in the proportions of women working part-time within industries. The upward trend in these proportions (and the aggregate proportion) has levelled off, however, since the mid-1970s. It may be significant that the primary substitutes for part-time women workers – full-time unmarried women and young men – were becoming much less scarce after 1975 than previously. In addition, the use of part-time jobs to skirt the provisions of the 1970 Equal Pay Act would have had its main impact during the phasing-in of the Act between 1970 and 1975. Furthermore the 1975 lowering from 21 to 16 hours of the qualifying level for benefit arising from legislation concerning contracts of employment, redundancy, unfair dismissal and maternity leave reduced the incentives for employing part-timers somewhat.[2] Whatever role these changes had in causing the cessation of the rise, it does appear that there no longer is an upward trend in the use of part-timers by employers, although the shift in employment in favour of the service industries may produce a small rise in the proportion of jobs that are part time.

On the supply side, the growth over the remainder of the century in the proportion of the potential labour force who are women over 30 – the ages in which part-time employment has been important – suggests that a larger proportion of the labour force will be interested in part-time employment. If the relative scarcity of unmarried women and young men during the 1960s did indeed play a significant role in the greater use of part-timers, then the re-emergence of such a scarcity over the next ten years may again give an impetus to the use of part-timers. However, this is dependent on the state of aggregate labour demand: if this remains depressed compared to the potential labour force, then the relative scarcity of unmarried women and young men in the potential labour force may not be significant.

QUALITY OF THE LABOUR FORCE

The quality of the labour force, as measured by educational qualifications, increased sharply during the 1970s, as Table 4.3 shows. The increase was larger for men, but there were increases for both sexes. These increases in the proportions with certain qualifications have occurred because labour force entrants have higher qualifications on average than those leaving the labour force. More recent generations have higher qualifications, so that, in 1980 for example, whilst 22 per cent of men born between 1950 and 1955 had qualifications above British A-level standards, this was true of only 14 per cent of those born between 1932 and 1942, and only 7 per cent of those born from 1912 to 1922.[3] Even if generations born since 1955 only attained the same distribution of qualifications as the 1955 generation, the average qualification level of the labour force would continue to increase well into the next century because those retiring would have lower average qualifications than labour force entrants.

Some information about the qualifications which more recent generations may receive can be obtained by examining their educational activity beyond the minimum school leaving age. There was a fairly steady rise over the post-war period through 1973 – 4 in the proportion of girls staying on in full-time education beyond the minimum school leaving age and boys' staying-on rate showed a similar rise, although with a pause during 1969 – 72 (Pissarides, 1981). More recent staying-on rates are shown in Table 4.4. As the table indicates, staying-on rates for boys stagnated between 1975 – 6 and 1979 – 80, and then shot up in 1980 – 2. Except for a pause during 1976 – 9, the

TABLE 4.3   QUALIFIED PERSONS IN THE LABOUR FORCE,
GREAT BRITAIN

Highest qualification level attained	Percentage of economically active men aged 25 – 69		
	1971/72	*1975/76*	*1979/80*
Above GCE 'A' level or equivalent	11	13	17
degree or equivalent	5	7	9
higher education below degree level	5	6	8
GCE 'A' level or equivalent	4	6	7
GCE 'O' level or equivalent/			
CSE Grade 1	10	11	12
Total: at or above 'O' level	25	30	36

Highest qualification level attained	Percentage of economically active women aged 25 – 69		
	1971/72	*1975/76*	*1979/80*
Above GCE 'A' level or equivalent	9	10	12
degree or equivalent	2	3	4
higher education below degree level	7	7	8
GCE 'A' level or equivalent	1	2	2
GCE 'O' level or equivalent/			
CSE Grade 1	8	10	12
Total: at or above 'O' level	18	22	26

Source: 1980 General Household Survey, Table 6.4

rates for girls rose throughout 1973 – 82. This rise in girls' participation
in full-time education since 1973 may be related to the reduction in
employment opportunities, but there is no evidence of such an effect
for boys before 1981–82. Table 4.4 also shows participation in full-time
education by boys and girls aged 16 – 19. The trends are similar to
those for staying-on rates. It is possible that if it were not for the
deterioration in employment opportunities since 1979, there would be
no upward trend in young people's participation in full-time education
since the mid-1970s. With regard to participation in higher education
other than teacher training, there was no trend during the 1970s in the
rate of participation in higher education by qualified men (i.e. with 2
or more 'A' levels), but the comparable rate for women rose gently
during the 1970s (Ermisch, 1983, pp. 254 – 62).

TABLE 4.4   PARTICIPATION IN FULL-TIME EDUCATION BY YOUNG
PERSONS, ENGLAND AND WALES (PERCENT IN FULL-TIME
EDUCATION IN JANUARY OF ACADEMIC YEAR)

Academic year	Aged 16		Aged 16 – 19	
	Boys	Girls	Boys	Girls
1973 – 74	34	37	25	26
1975 – 76	39	43	27	29
1979 – 80	37	46	26	30
1981 – 82	43	53	29	34

Source: Department of Education and Science, *Educational and Economic Activity of
Young People Aged 16 to 19 years in England and Wales from 1973–74 to 1981–2,
Statistical Bulletin,* 2/83 (February 1983)

It appears then that the educational attainments of more recent
generations of young men may be levelling off, but women's
educational attainments are continuing to increase among more recent
generations. Over the remainder of the century, an increasing
proportion of the labour force will have achieved qualifications at each
of the levels considered here.

Training and skill acquisition do not, however, occur only through
formal education. An equally important way of acquiring skills is
through 'on-the-job training', or 'learning by doing'. This is more
important in some occupations than in others. For instance, a doctor
would still have a long learning phase after starting to practise while a
labourer may learn his job in a week. Those occupations with more skill
acquisition on the job are characterized by a steeper relation between
experience and earnings because during the period of skill acquisition
earnings are lower than in occupations with little on-the-job training,
and later when this investment in skills bears fruit (in the form of
higher productivity), earnings will be higher. Since the occupational
structure has continued to shift away from manual occupations toward
higher level non-manual occupations (see Table 4.5), on-the-job
training is probably becoming an even more important way of
acquiring marketable skills.[4] Nevertheless, entry into occupations with
a large training content does usually require particular educational
attainments above the minimum.

The growing importance of occupations with a large training
element makes youth unemployment and the discontinuity in
women's employment over their lives increasingly significant. Since
training is particularly concentrated in the early phases of a career,

TABLE 4.5   OCCUPATIONAL CHANGES DURING 1971–81

	Percentage change 1971–81	Percentage in occupation 1981
Professional: education, welfare, health	32.1	8
Professional and related supporting management	23.5	4
Literary, artistic, sport	22.2	1
Professional: science, engineering, technology	18.9	4
Security services	12.5	2
Managerial	10.8	10
Clerical	2.5	17
Personal services	1.5	11
Selling	−8.2	6
Construction and mining	−10.3	3
Processing: metal and electrical	−14.2	12
Transport and storage	−14.3	6
Processing: non-metal and non-electrical	−22.5	7
Agriculture	−24.5	1
Processing: services	−26.2	4

Source: Economic Activity Tables, 1981 Census, Table A

lengthy spells of unemployment at this time can significantly retard skill acquisition. With regard to women, earlier generations of women expected to spend less of their life in paid employment than more recent generations, with a long break for the bearing and raising of children early in their adult life. Thus they had less of an opportunity to receive on-the-job training. Also, since the returns from such training can only be received when the person works, women's prospective discontinuity in employment reduced their incentive to undertake on-the-job training. Women would tend to concentrate in 'low training' occupations as a result, although there are of course also other reasons for occupational segregation.

Recent generations of women entering the labour market are strongly attached to the labour force. It indeed appears that except for an interruption for childbearing, women born since 1960 will be in the labour force for the same number of years as men (Joshi and Owen, 1983). This stronger lifetime commitment to working should induce a larger proportion of recent generations of women to enter occupations with more skill acquisition. But the effect of the childbearing interruption on the economic rewards from skill acquisition, particularly since the return to work is often to part-time employment in a poorer job, may still discourage both women from entering and employers from offering jobs with substantial skill acquisition – good 'career prospects' in the usual sense. While motherhood is not incompatible with a long working life, it appears at present to be less compatible with a good working career. Part-time employment has reduced the length of interruptions, but at present it appears to represent almost as significant a barrier to a 'good career' as absence from the labour force.

Achievement of economic parity with men may require the availability of more skilled part-time jobs (as is the case for nurses) which allow women to use the skills they have acquired before embarking on childbearing, and provides more incentive to enter occupations which involve more skill acquisition. At present, part-time jobs are generally low skill, low paid jobs (Joshi, 1984).

These considerations help to explain why women's advance into higher level occupations and occupational desegregation have been so limited, even during the 1970s (Hakim, 1981). Another reason for the limited progress is that the expectation of a long working life has been generally held only by more recent generations of women. Older women in the labour force generally lack the qualifications or experience to move into higher level occupations. Thus changes in women's occupational distribution are bound to be slow. The extent to which the occupational distribution of younger women is changing would be a better indicator of whether gains are being made by the more recent generations who are strongly attached to the labour force.

Projections of the occupational distribution of employment by the Institute for Employment Research (IER, 1983, Table 3.5) suggest that both the expansion of jobs in higher level non-manual occupations and the contraction of manual jobs will continue at least through the 1980s. Women who become mothers will be at a competitive disadvantage for these jobs unless part-time employment is expanded in them, or unless other changes in policy or technology make childrearing and full-time employment more compatible. The re-absorption of the workers formerly in manual jobs would also appear to require policies which improve the incentives for retraining. While youth training programmes are supposed to help young unemployed people acquire skills to move into the jobs of the future, it is unclear how good a substitute such programmes are for real work experience. However, as noted earlier, young people's employment prospects should improve because of the decline in their relative numbers over the next ten years.

CONCLUSIONS

Looking to the end of the century, the considerable deceleration in labour force growth should at least make it easier to cope with an economy which does not appear to be creating a net increase in the number of jobs during the 1980s. A little under a fifth of jobs are likely to be part time on current trends, but work sharing and policies meant to encourage part-time employment in higher job levels could increase that proportion. The relatively large proportion of part-timers renders provisions like the national insurance contribution threshold and the unemployment benefit system less approporiate. At present, there is a discentive to adjust hours upward near the threshold, and the unemployed who are eligible for benefit may have high replacement ratios while many part-timers will be ineligible for any unemployment benefit because of having earnings below the threshold. This issue is more fully discussed in Bradshaw's chapter.

Other than during the years when the children are young, most conventional families (containing a married couple) among more recent generations will be two earner families; thus the proportion of two earner families in the population will continue to grow. At present, both spouses work in about three-fifths of all couples, which has implications for the income maintenance system. Among the working poor, an adjustment for the costs of employment may be necessary to compute the comparable resources of one- and two-earner families for the purposes of compensatory income support. The current unemployment benefit system is based on the one earner family and is less appropriate for two earner families with dependent children; a fully individual-based, earnings-related system may be better.[5] Other aspects of social policy also often fail to give proper recognition to the present and growing dominance of the two earner family.

Finally, the relation between social policies and the non-market uses of time, particularly parental investments in children, is an important area which needs further study. For instance, parents may respond to taxes on bequests of material wealth by investing more in the human capital of their children, or to more publicly provided schooling by reducing such investments. Or, if parents are generally observed to be investing more in their children's health and education, social policies may wish to redirect health and education expenditures. Parents may also respond to higher pensions, which entail a larger state transfer from the younger to older generation, by increasing their investment in their children. Thus the analysis of inter-generational transfers and their effect on the distribution of wealth and social mobility should not ignore the role of parental investments in children. While the nature and extent of people's participation in the labour market are important in formulating social policy, the uses of people's time outside the labour market are also significant.

Notes

1 These figures are based on General Household Survey data reported in *OPCS Monitor*, reference GHS83/2, dated 21 June 1983.
2 See Ermisch, 1983, pp. 143-5, for a discussion of the incentives for using part-time employees.
3 *General Household Survey*, 1981, table 6.5.
4 See Ermisch, 1983, pp. 137-43, for an analysis of post-war changes in the occupational distribution of employment.
5 See Ermisch, 1983, pp. 225-30, for a fuller discussion of income maintenance and two earner families.

5

The Politics of Welfare: Public Attitudes and Behaviour

PETER TAYLOR-GOOBY

Questioning is not the mode of conversation among gentlemen.

(Dr Johnson)

INTRODUCTION

In discussing public opinion surveys as guides to mass attitudes, it is wise to start with certain caveats. First, the link between attitudes to particular policy proposals and political behaviour is complex. Attitudes may incline people to particular courses of action, but many other factors may intervene between behavioural intention and overt action (Fishbein, 1967). Policy confronts an electorate through a smokescreen of propaganda and misinformation, is judged as a package and stands in relief against available alternatives.

Second, public opinion is only one among many influences on policy. A large number of studies from the twenties onwards have argued that the influence of certain pressure groups or of elite rather than mass opinion is a better guide to developments (Key, 1961).

Third, there are problems in the use of opinion survey data as a guide to public opinion. Surveys vary widely in design, method and execution; the artificiality of interviews as a mode of interaction places a constraint on the data that can be gathered; collective concepts can only be constructed by the simple aggregation of individual answers which may limit the use of the method as a guide to mass action. Many studies have shown that the same people will give different answers to the same questions when these are repeated after a lapse of time (Kavanagh, 1983, p. 14). However, the overall distribution of answers remains roughly constant, indicating that surveys are an adequate guide to general patterns of opinion.

I am grateful to Dr. Elim Papadakis for helpful comments on this chapter.

In view of these difficulties, the following account of the main features of attitudes to welfare policy is presented tentatively. The findings are strengthened by the use of evidence from studies which use different methods and by the review of conflicting work which appears to point to different conclusions.

ATTITUDES TO STATE WELFARE SPENDING

The main features of the pattern of attitudes may be grouped under five headings.

1 Beveridge not Churchill

A large number of surveys indicate strong popular support for spending on the main state welfare services. These include large random-sample national surveys (the British Election Studies, the annual Social Attitudes Study from 1983 onwards, the 1984 Attitudes to Welfare Survey); quota-sample national surveys (Gallup Polls, the BBC Election Study, 1983 (Crewe, 1983)); the Rose/Marplan Economic Issues Study of 1981 (Rose, 1983a); the Breadline Britain Survey of 1983 (Lansley and Weir, 1983); national postal surveys, such as that carried out by Hockley and Harbour (1982); and local area studies, for example Duke and Edgell (1981) in Manchester, Lansley and Gosschalk (1984) in Greenwich, Lewis (1980) in Bath, and Taylor-Gooby (1982, 1983) in Medway. In all these studies more than 60 per cent of the sample say they support current or increased levels of welfare spending. However, the pattern of support is subject to fluctuations over time, not all of which may be attributed to changes in the design of questions, and the picture of strong support for welfare spending has been challenged in four ways.

(a) Endorsing spending without offering tax to finance it is having your cake and eating it (Harris and Seldon, 1979, p. 84). This argument is reinforced by the use of the notion of 'fiscal illusion' in public choice economics. The policy-making process mirrors badly-designed surveys, it is argued, in divorcing policy manifestos from their fiscal implications. However, attempts have been made to explore how much extra income tax people would pay for services they want (Piachaud, 1974; Lansley and Weir, 1983), or to present people with choices between different spending categories to redistribute government revenues, although it is difficult to cost the implications of policy changes for individual households realistically. In the first case, most people are prepared to pay some extra tax for policies they endorse – though support for improvements declines as the cost of changes goes up. In the second, the National Health Service (NHS), pension provision and education (the major spending areas of welfare) receive strong support at the expense of defence, unemployment benefit and local authority housing (Lansley and Weir, 1983; Harris and Seldon, 1979). It is unclear to what extent these somewhat artificial techniques succeed in tapping people's willingness to commit themselves to supporting spending programmes, but in so far as surveys are appropriate instruments for tackling this issue, the evidence seems to be that people are prepared to put their money where their mouth is.

(b) Altruism and hard times: people tend to feel less generous, it is argued, when they experience a decline in their economic fortunes (Alt, 1979). Since social spending is seen as providing benefits for needy minorities it is less well supported by the mass as times grow hard. Evidence from the 1970 and two 1974 BES studies is used to demonstrate that declining altruism inclines Labour voters to defect to parties which place less stress on social programmes (1979, p. 258). This analysis focuses mainly on questions about support for 'social services and benefits' and the role of government in mitigating unemployment. More recent surveys indicate continued concern about economic decline coupled with high levels of support for the NHS and a willingness to pay taxes to support social spending. Moreover, social policy seems to be a reason for working-class Labour support (Sarlvik and Crewe, 1983, p. 274; Crewe, 1983). Perhaps altruism is on the increase, or maybe people are increasingly classing themselves among those who benefit from rather than finance the redistribution process.

(c) The watershed in public opinion: a more direct challenge claims that there was a sea change in public opinion in the mid-seventies. It is argued that a switch away from Butskellite consensus helped the 1979 Conservative election victory (for example, see Golding and Middleton, 1982; Gough, 1980). Leaving aside the contested issue of whether the policies (as opposed to the rhetoric) of the 1979 and 1983 governments represent a substantial shift to the right, this view seems to be based on only part of the evidence. Golding and Middleton, for example, generalize from attitudes to the unemployed and low-paid workers, but evidence of high levels of support for pensioners and the disabled (1982, pp. 169, 189) is given little prominence. It is difficult to demonstrate that 'economic crisis has liberated a full-scale assault on the welfare consensus' (p. 205) on this basis.

(d) Local referenda: the Coventry referendum in 1981 revealed majority support for cuts in local spending. However, the significance of this may be undermined by a number of features: the poll had a low turn-out (26 per cent); the turn-out appears to have been heavily weighted toward upper-class homeowners who might support cuts on plausible perceptions of self-interest; an opinion poll taken on the same day, which almost certainly used a more representative sample, showed that only a minority supported cuts in any single area of policy. Only 4 per cent favoured cuts in the social policy areas of primary and secondary education or social services spending (Courtenay and Jowell, 1981, p. 3).

The conclusion that there is continuing strong popular support for welfare state spending, at least on the main services, does not seem to be undermined by these counter-arguments: indeed, the level of support has probably increased in recent years. Taken by itself, this evidence suggests that the 'welfare backlash' thesis of the mid-seventies no longer applies. The psephological implications of this observation are unclear, since social spending is only one part of government policy and since the link between levels of service and of spending is not

TABLE 5.1 ATTITUDES ON TAXES AND WELFARE AS MEASURED IN GALLUP POLLS, 1978–83

Question: People have different attitudes about whether it is important to reduce taxes or keep up government spending. How about you?

	Poll date							
Preferred option	*10/78*	*5/79*	*10/79*	*2/80*	*2/81*	*2/82*	*2/83*	*10/83*
Taxes being cut, even if it means some reduction in government services such as health, education and welfare	25	34	20	22	20	21	23	17
Things left as they are	23	25	26	20	23	26	22	27
Government services such as health, education and welfare should be extended even if it means some increase in taxes	39	34	44	52	49	49	49	50
Don't know	13	7	10	6	8	5	6	6

TABLE 5.2   TAX AND WELFARE ATTITUDES

(a) *People have different views about whether it is more important to reduce taxes or keep up government services. Which of these statements comes closest to your view?* (British Election Studies, May 1979)
(b) *Which of these statements comes closest to your view? Cut taxes even if it means some reduction in government services like health, education and welfare; keep up government services even if it means taxes cannot be cut.* (BBC Election Study, June 1983)

	May 1979	June 1983
Cutting taxes	25	18
Keeping up services	61	77
It doesn't matter ((a) only)	9	–
Don't know	5	6

Choices for government policy	*British Social Attitudes, March 1983*	*Attitudes to Welfare, April 1984*
Reduce taxes and spend less on health, education and social benefits	9	5
Keep taxes and spending on these services at the same level as now	54	44
Increase taxes and spend more on health education and social benefits	32	42
Don't know	5	9

simple. Fluctuations in the level of support for spending may reflect ideas about efficiency and the scope for eliminating waste, rather than judgements on the output of services.

2 *Hayek not Keynes*

The enthusiasm for Lord Beveridge is not paralleled by endorsement of the other pillar of Butskellism, Lord Keynes. The general thrust of Keynesian planning implies that state intervention can alleviate the cyclical crises of market capitalism, ensure more or less stable growth, moderate unemployment and control inflation. Issues of wage-bargaining and industrial relations may also become the proper preserve of government. The view that official policy over the past half-century has been dominated by a concern with achieving stability (Middlemass, 1979) ties these issues together. The question of the exact nature and extent of intervention envisaged by Keynes himself can be left on one side.

Unemployment, prices and industrial relations have figured prominently on the list of important issues of the day in recent years. Public opinion appears firmly convinced that private enterprise rather than government should be left to deal with these issues. This parallels an ambiguity noted in a classic American study of political opinions (Free and Cantril, 1968). This found that strong support for a large number of interventionist programmes coexisted in a 'schizoid' manner with an equally strong approval of liberal free enterprise policies.

Election studies also show strong support for market forces against state intervention in relation to unemployment, inflation and industrial relations. The 1979 British Election Survey showed a 3:1 majority in favour of firms controlling their own profits against a policy of higher taxes and job creation as the best way to tackle unemployment, a 3:1 majority in favour of free collective bargaining and a 2:1 majority against further nationalization. In the 1983 BBC Election Survey the majority in favour of private enterprise job creation was 3:2, and the same proportions were in favour of denationalization and the view that government policy cannot create economic prosperity. The Economic Issues study provides the most detailed recent examination of these issues. Nearly 70 per cent of the sample described the British political economy as predominantly private enterprise; 80 per cent described this as their preferred system. Only 13 per cent wanted government involvement in the day-to-day planning of companies and 5 per cent further nationalization (Rose, 1983a, p. 12).

The evidence is not, however, consistent. First, in some areas there is support for the interventionist policies of particular parties, although this contradicts more general judgements about the best way to tackle the issue in question. For example, in the 1983 BBC Election Study, unemployment is identified as far and away one of the two most important issues (by 72 per cent of respondents, as against 38 per cent for defence, the next contender). Although 54 per cent of the sample thought private enterprise was the best solution to the problem in general, 34 per cent said they thought Labour had the best policies, as against 28 per cent Conservative and 16 per cent SDP/Liberal. Second, there is some evidence of support for state intervention at a local level.

Lansley and Gosschalk's Greenwich study shows that 86 per cent thought the council should be involved in job creation. Similar results are reported from a study in Camden (Lansley and Gosschalk, 1984). However, these findings are likely to be heavily influenced by the particular circumstances of the areas and the experiences of their residents.

In general it seems likely that the direction of public opinion flows strongly against Keynesianism despite the support for Beveridge's part of the post-war settlement. This may be reflected in the way in which policies of denationalization have been pursued more vigorously in the production sector of state industries than in the consumption sector of state services.

3   Pinker not Townsend

Within the overall pattern of strong (and growing) support for the welfare state, there are substantial variations in support for particular policies and services. Some services seem highly popular, pre-eminently the NHS, pensions and education. In a wide range of studies, over 80 per cent of respondents indicate approval of the NHS or willingness to pay more tax to finance it. For education and pensions the corresponding figures do not fall below 60 per cent. These services made up 38 per cent of state spending and 69 per cent of social spending in 1983 – 4. They may be regarded as the heartland of the welfare state.

Other services are less well supported. In particular, the various studies indicate much lower levels of support (one fifth of the sample or less) for increased spending on child benefits, or on benefits for the unemployed, low-paid and single parents, or on local authority housing. The 1974 and 1979 Election Studies found more people concerned about welfare benefits being excessive rather than inadequate (34 against 24 per cent in 1974, and 50 against 17 per cent in 1979). The bias seems to be against means-tested benefits which go mainly to people of working age rather than against the social insurance benefits which go mainly to the retired. This interpretation is born out by a number of small-scale surveys of attitudes to means-tested welfare (see for example, Schlackmann, 1978; Taylor-Gooby, 1976).

A similar pattern emerges in relation to policies. The British Election Study showed over 80 per cent in favour of spending more to get rid of poverty in 1974 and 1979, and over 50 per cent in favour of redistributing income towards ordinary working people in both years. However, this did not imply support for many government policies as they affect the poor: in 1979, 40 per cent thought social services and benefits should be cut back against 19 per cent who thought they should be extended.

Support for the welfare state is not a seamless web. The schism in support between favoured and unfavoured needs emerges clearly in Klein's analysis of the poll data from 1950 to 1970 where it is interpreted as 'moralism' (1974) and in Golding and Middleton's focus on 'popular contempt' for the less deserving groups (1982, p. 181). Two explanations are attractive: self-interest may lead the public to regard needs that they are unlikely to experience themselves as less worthy of support (see, for example, Alt, 1979); alternatively, cultural values associated with conceptions of stigma and desert as a 'cultural lag' from the days of the workhouse and household means-test may play a part (Pinker, 1971, ch. 4; Klein, 1974, p. 411). The second explanation is reinforced by accounts of the role and reinforcement of the work ethic in a market society. It goes hand in hand with the emphasis on a free enterprise economy in popular opinion.

The perspective presented may be challenged in two ways. There is some evidence that some of the unfavoured groups now receive more support than formerly. The Breadline Britain survey found that three quarters of its sample thought the gap between high paid and low paid too great. Similarly, less than a quarter saw poverty as due to laziness or lack of willpower – a sharp reduction on the 43 per cent in the British sub-sample for a European poverty survey in 1976. The elevation of unemployment to the most important issue influencing voting in the BBC Election Study, and the reported experience of unemployment as a problem in the family by over 40 per cent of the sample may have done something to erode the deserving/undeserving distinction in recent years.

The second problem is that it is difficult to understand why some services are repeatedly identified as not deserving of support. For example, it is not immediately clear why child benefit, which is not confined to a particular undeserving group, should be unpopular. There is some indication (Runciman, 1971, p. 266; Taylor-Gooby, 1985, p. 29) that child benefit is unpopular because it is seen as indiscriminate: it goes to the well-off as well as to the poor. However, this consideration in itself does not undermine the evidence of a pattern of attitudes that distinguishes the popular services of the heartland of welfare from the marginal services on the periphery.

4   Both Arthur Seldon and Richard Titmuss

A number of surveys show strong support for private welfare. The last in a series commissioned by the Institute of Economic Affairs (IEA) showed that roughly two-thirds of a national sample supported education and health care vouchers which could be used in the private sector and over 80 per cent thought citizens should be free to use the appropriate private sector service if they wished. The data have been repeatedly criticized (Forsyth, 1966, p. 141; Golding and Middleton, 1982, p. 181) but the Medway survey produced similar results. Surveys commissioned by the *Daily Mail* from NOP in 1977, and by the Independent Schools Information Service from MORI in 1981, show even higher degrees of support. A common interpretation of these findings is that people prefer the private sector to the state sector: state welfare spending is therefore an imposition on the taxpayer. However, the IEA and Medway data have been reanalysed and show that most of the people who want private care also strongly support the state sector. The Medway survey indicates that the same applies to pensions (Judge, Smith and Taylor-Gooby, 1983; Taylor-Gooby, 1985, p. 35). The support for private health care and education does not prevent a 4:3 majority in favour of withdrawing tax exemptions from these services in the 1983 BBC Election Study. The 1984 Attitudes to Welfare Survey supports the view that people are ambivalent in support for public and private welfare.

The peaceful coexistence of support for private and public provision is hard to explain, especially for those who claim that state and market are in contradiction for theoretical reasons. It has been accounted for in terms of popular support for a 'mixed economy of welfare' (Judge et al., 1983, p. 487), in terms of the contradictions in ideas about the state produced by the ideology of advanced capitalist society (Taylor-Gooby, 1985, ch. 6) and as a popular reaction to lack of control over bureaucratic state welfare agencies (Marsland, 1984).

5   Both Women's Interests and the Family

If the support for free enterprise and state services leads to concern that welfare may undermine the work ethic, the position in relation to the family ethic appears more complex. Feminist and other writers have pointed out that the welfare state makes assumptions about the social roles of women and men in the regulations governing social security entitlements and dependant's benefits, in the provision of support services for dependent groups and in the way in which community care policies are advanced (Land and Parker, 1978). Little work has been done so far on the relation of these policies to popular attitudes.

A major study of attitudes to the care of dependency groups carried out in Scotland in 1981 shows that people make sophisticated distinctions between the needs of different dependency groups. These distinctions lead to support for a complex mix of services to substitute for and complement informal care. 'What the public want is not care by the community, nor residential care except in specific circumstances, but a range of community-based services which best serve the interests of dependency groups and alleviate the burden on carers' (West, Illsley and Kelman, 1984). This conclusion is reinforced by evidence on attitudes to support services in the Medway Study. The implication of these findings for community care policies, especially for the increasing numbers of frail elderly, is that the direction of official policy is likely to conflict with popular attitudes. The assumption that 'care in the community must increasingly mean care by the community' (DHSS, 1981c, p. 3) runs directly counter to these findings. Further analysis of the data by West (1984) indicates that a family ethic coexists with demands for support services to alleviate family responsibilities. More work is needed in this area, but the evidence so far confirms the earlier picture of approval for a high level of state intervention in service provision for the family. Attitudes to the family ethic do not appear to run parallel to those about the work ethic: where the requirements of the work ethic conflict with a general support for state services, the work ethic is endorsed; the family ethic appears less insulated against demands for state intervention.

In summary, then, people support high levels of spending on the heartland of the welfare state. There is no evidence from attitude surveys of a 'welfare backlash'. However, this finding must be qualified in four ways: there is strong popular support for free enterprise in production alongside state intervention in consumption; people are suspicious of some services for minority needs, particularly where these appear to contradict a 'work ethic'; there is a concurrent high level of support for the private sector; and people approve of intervention in family responsibilities for the care of dependent groups.

From some perspectives this combination of attitudes implies contradiction: Beveridge saw Keynesian intervention as a precondition of the success of his plan; Seldon regards evidence of enthusiasm for the private sector as evidence of lack of support for the welfare state; Hall interprets evidence of contempt of welfare claimers as evidence of a withdrawal of support for the welfare state as a whole. These contradictions are not compelling accounts of attitudes, although they may pose problems for governments in devising acceptable policy packages. The next section considers the factors influencing opinion, with a view to discussing possible future developments in the pattern of attitudes.

EXPLANATIONS OF ATTITUDES TO STATE SPENDING

Speculating in futures is always risky. This section considers some factors that have been identified as likely to influence attitudes to welfare as a foundation for later discussion of the future development of opinion.

Attitudes, Party and Self-Interest

Survey analysts have been impressed by three features of the correlates of attitudes to welfare policies. First, support for welfare policies is related to political party identification (Whiteley, 1981), with support strongest among Labour and SDP/Liberal voters (Taylor-Gooby, 1983). There are also strong links between party and support for the less favoured services (Lewis, 1980), willingness to pay for welfare for the poor (Lansley and Weir, 1983) and opposition to cuts (Duke and Edgell 1981), and rather weaker associations with attitudes to privatization (Harris and Seldon, 1979; Judge, Smith and Taylor-Gooby, 1983, p. 474). Second, support seems to be related to factors which can plausibly be taken as proxies for self-interest: people of lower social class, living in the more deprived regions, with dependent children, in low paid work, unemployed, retired, or living in council housing are more likely to support both state spending in general and spending on the service related to their need. Similarly, women are substantially less likely than men to prefer informal and family care for dependent groups, presumably because they are forced to shoulder the greater part of the burden (West et al., 1984).

Third, while there are marked differences in support for different kinds of provision across the population, many surveys report a surprising degree of overlap in attitudes between groups with different class, sex, income, age and family compositions to particular services and issues. Thus, self-interest or political affiliation do not emerge as better predictors of attitudes to unemployment benefit (Golding and Middleton, 1982, p. 168), privatization (Harris and Seldon, 1979, p. 109), community care (West et al., 1984) and to imagery of the market (Rose, 1983a, p. 15).

If political identification shaped policy preferences, then we would expect consistency between alignment and attitudes. However, a tendency to political dealignment since the 1950s indicates a weakening of traditional loyalties (Sarlvik and Crewe, 1983, p. 333). The implication is that the public is likely to discriminate more: the influence of policy preference on party preference rather than the other way about is likely to grow, and the importance of party allegiance, as a separate factor, to decline.

The relationship between class and social attitudes has been extensively and inconclusively debated by sociologists, usually concerned with the question of why the working class is not more obviously truculent in the face of the manifest injustices of capitalism. Evidence has been advanced in recent years both to support the thesis that an individualist 'pecuniary' consciousness is becoming dominant among industrial workers (Goldthorpe et al., 1968) and to contest it. However, no conclusive statement of the links between occupational status and attitudes to welfare is available from this work (Marshall, 1984).

The increase in unemployment has also stimulated interest in production in the informal economy – including the production of welfare – and the consequent implications for self-interested support for state provision. For example, Richard Rose has argued that the coexistence of official, hidden and domestic economies offers great opportunities for the restructuring of state welfare activities because the various areas of economic life may substitute for each other. Thus 'production in the domestic economy is a significant resource for unemployed people; it can help them to get by in the face of a decline in their official economy income' (1983b, p. 33). The doctrine of substitutability has severe limits. The capacity for production in domestic and unofficial economies is limited by participation in the official economies: if you can't afford the tools it's difficult to get very far in a car repair business or to enhance your domestic production of use-values by building a home extension. 'The whole burden of our argument rests on the reality that there is only one economy and that a household's position in that is fundamental in determining its positions in other economic spheres' (Pahl and Wallace, 1984, p. 44). The implication for welfare is that people's felt need for state welfare provision is unlikely to be diminished by the experience of participation in changing economic structures of unemployment or part-time work. The imperatives of class and the structures of self-interest founded on it endure.

The general thrust of the argument so far is that occupational class, and, so far as we can tell, position in the family will continue to be important determinants of attitudes to welfare. Political allegiances are on the wane, dominant ideology requires substantiation in everyday life, the sociology of social imagery does not produce convincing alternatives, and the expansion of the black economy does not alter the basic rules of the game. The experience of welfare, however, presents a rather different picture.

THE EXPERIENCE OF WELFARE

Three features of experience of welfare suggest that influences in this area may alter the pattern of attitudes substantially. These concern consumption sector, status and use of welfare services.

Dunleavy has elaborated the influential concept of a 'consumption sector' (1979). Whereas class refers to a common employment situation, consumption sector refers to a common situation in the use of a good – for example council tenant versus home owner. Consumption sector interests can cross-cut social class. Dunleavy distinguishes private and public consumption sectors and shows that there are strong correlations between the use of privately owned or rented housing and the use of private transport, and between council tenure and reliance on public transport. Cumulative public or private sector location interacts with occupational class as an influence on political alignment in analysis of 1974 election surveys. Dunleavy argues that instrumental interests associated with sectoral location coupled with a general (albeit incorrect) belief that public consumption is heavily subsidised by progressive taxation bearing on users of the private sector go together to explain partisanship. For example, home owners are likely to believe that they pay subsidies to council tenants through tax and this tends to enhance support for Conservative policies.

The consumption sector approach is fruitful in allowing a cross-cutting interaction between everyday life experience based on occupational location and access to the means of consumption. It also makes sense of the common observation that tenure group has become a more and more significant influence on voting behaviour in the 1970s and 1980s (Rose, 1980, p. 50; Sarlvik and Crewe, 1983, pp. 107 – 8; Crewe, 1983). Tenants support Labour while home-owners do not, and this pattern cuts across traditional class alignments. The policy of heavily subsidized council house sales followed by the 1979 government therefore appears psephologically rational.

Consumption sector theories have large implications for the future development of opinion. On the one hand the state has penetrated further into the everyday life experience of many people over the last 20 years as the length of schooling, the importance of the qualifications gained from it, the role of government 'make-work' schemes in the transition to work, the numbers employed in the state sector, the proportion of the population receiving state benefits and the numbers dependent for survival on those benefits have all increased. On the other hand, private sector provision has also expanded in occupational pensions and sick pay, home ownership, private health insurance and use of private cars. In addition, state, private market and state-subsidized and/or regulated private provision intermeshes for many people in areas such as pensions, transport and housing.

However, consumption sector theories have only been thoroughly tested on a national sample in relation to transport and housing services. It is noteworthy that membership of private health insurance schemes is associated with disapproval of NHS spending, but shows no relation with opinion about other aspects of policy in the 1979 British Election Study (Taylor-Gooby, 1983, p. 648). The influence of consumption sector on attitudes may turn out to be more fragmented than Dunleavy suggests when the thesis is tested across a wide range of services. In any case access to private provision is weighted to upper social groups, so that analysis by sector may add little to class analysis.

However, it is also argued that attitudes may be influenced as much by social status, as defined by consumption patterns, as by class as defined by occupational categories (David Rose et al., 1984). The argument is that Butskellism has generated a sense of equal citizenship (in a Marshallian sense) through mass access to welfare state services, a sense that has not been seriously undermined by current rhetoric or policies. Class in the market is in perpetual conflict with status. 'Citizenship, in terms of the rights of trade unions or the continued expansion of the welfare state, is seen as the enemy of economic policy in the form of a cost which a de-industrializing economy can no longer stand' (ibid., p. 34). The experience of equal citizenship makes a re-emphasis of the market possible. Conversely, if equal citizenship is seriously attacked, the impact of unmitigated class inequalities will lead to a reassertion of the citizenship order. The experience of welfare is therefore a basis for continued support for the welfare state that is becoming more entrenched in our society.

The third issue concerns the use of welfare. Much discussion of self interest rests on the assumption that less well-off and needier people tend to derive the greatest benefit from state services. The needs associated with class position and stage in family life-cycle come to the fore. Of these, occupational class as a general determinant of chances in life is probably most important because its influence is more enduring. However, many areas of state policy in fact channel resources to better-off groups (Le Grand, 1982). This appears particularly true of education, health care and transport subsidies. The Medway study, the 1984 Attitudes to Welfare Study and the 1983 Social Attitudes Survey asked respondents whom they thought got the best value for money from the taxes they paid for state education, health care and pensions. The better-off thought the worse-off did – the conventional wisdom – but the worse-off thought the better-off derived most benefit. Further work is needed to clarify why this is. It may be the case that the impact of self-interest on attitudes differs from the simple perception of welfare as a benefit to the poor (the interpretation of Alt, 1979, for example) when the system of tax and service is considered as a whole. Recent changes in welfare provision have tended to damage the interests of the less well-off disproportionately as rents have increased faster than mortgage repayments and means-tested and short-term benefits have increased at a slower rate than pensions, while unemployment affects manual workers most severely. Coupled with a shift in the tax burden from better-off to worse-off this will exacerbate the tendency for people to experience welfare as something other than a redistributive web.

The recent expansion of the private sector is also likely to influence attitudes to the state sector. One reason for the expansion of the private sector may be the fact that state sector consumers experience bureaucratic and professional coercion within it. Lack of voice, plus opportunity, leads to exit (Hirschman, 1970). Some support for this view is provided in a survey of advertising literature for private health care. The advantages of private health care listed in brochures for BUPA CARE, WPA and PPP all range the following three attributes in order of priority: 'admission to hospital when it suits you; choice of hospital and specialist; flexible visiting hours' (BUPA CARE brochure, 1983, p. 4). The emphasis on consumer control is continued in the brochure directed at employers which mentions 'treatment might be timed to coincide with a lull in business, or during a factory's annual holidays'. The pamphlet links efficient health care, business efficiency, staff morale and recruitment, and stresses the advantages of management control of health care: 'when a busy employee has his leg in traction, you may still want to use his brain' (BUPA Company Care Brochure, 1984, p. 4). It is plausible to suggest that public provision involving bureaucratic or professional control – such as health care or education – will generate a more complex structure of opinion than other areas, such as social insurance, housing or transport. Birch (1975) argues for a more interactive model of consumer/provider relations, pointing out that the capacity of professionals to retaliate against consumers by denying or diluting service may weaken protest through fear of reprisal. The potential for such control is greatest in the areas mentioned. Disgruntlement is likely to foster further ambivalence. Such ambivalence may also be nourished by the spread of private provision, although direct experience of private bureaucracies may generate feelings similar to those resulting from use of state services.

Equally important, perhaps, recent developments in private welfare have been accelerated by a number of factors including subsidy (home ownership, occupational pension and sick pay); the vagaries of incomes policies (health care as a fringe benefit); the potential for corporate schemes; and people's judgements about the quality of state sector provision. All these factors are likely to complicate the simple pattern of belief that the user of the public sector is subsidized by the user of the private sector. People as individuals may have no serious choice about the use of occupationally based private welfare.

The general implications of this discussion are three. First, the importance of political identification as a determinant of attitudes to welfare is likely to be on the wane. Secondly, self-interest associated with occupational status and position in the family is likely to remain significant. Third, welfare is not a seamless web. The use of private services is likely to influence attitudes to the state sector as is the experience of bureaucratic or professional power in each sector. Both private and state welfare sectors are likely to be more important features of many people's lives than in the past. Perceptions of the redistributive effects of state tax and service policy may be growing more sophisticated. However, self-interested support for fiscal reliefs is likely to conflict with general support for redistribution. Since fiscal advantage is distributed on class lines this may tend to reassert the significance of class as a determinant of welfare attitudes. There are no grounds for assuming that the pattern of attitudes is liable to an abrupt change. However, the ambiguities in attitudes mean that the level of support depends on whether attention is focused mainly on services for minorities or the deserving mass, on unproductive bureaucracies or valued outputs, on the implications for economic efficiency or on personal consumption.

The next section considers the implications of the argument for some current policy proposals.

CURRENT DEVELOPMENTS IN WELFARE

The recent Green Paper on tax and spending puts forward a strategy for public policy based on constraint in service provision in order to reduce the tax burden (Treasury, 1984b). The possibility of privatizing some services is hinted at. An alternative approach to the problems of the welfare state is advanced by writers who are impressed by the achievements of corporatist economies. This section reviews the implications of public opinion for the strategies of constraint, privatization and corporatism. All three policies are likely to run counter to important strands of opinion.

The Public Sector as a Burden

The Green Paper assumes but does not argue that lower tax would lead to higher economic growth in a 'virtuous circle' (Treasury, 1984b, p. 20). Throughout, tax (and implicitly the state sector) is conceptualized as a 'burden' on the economy. Thus the argument moves from the 'inescapable connection between public spending and the taxes required to finance it' to the view that there is a choice between diverting the resources derived from growth to 'reducing the present . . . level of taxation or to further improvements in the public services or to both in some degree'. This aspect of the argument appears consonant with the strong public endorsement of free enterprise with a minimum of state interference mentioned earlier, but is inconsistent with the evidence of willingness to pay the taxes necessary to finance social services.

A dissonance between Green Paper arrangements and current opinion emerges from the reiterated point that 'on one issue there can be no doubt: the government and parliament must reach their judgement about what in total can be afforded, then contain individual programmes within that total'. People's judgements about the desirability of the favoured state programmes appear independent of their views on the resources available. More people in the 1983 Social Attitudes Survey, the 1983 BBC Election Study and the 1979 Election Study thought the country's economic position had deteriorated, yet large majorities in both surveys supported further spending. The issue of whether people are actually prepared to support tax increases that might cut their disposable income in return for social services is crucial. Opinion surveys cannot offer much guidance on this question.

The Green Paper lists a number of areas in which there is likely to be pressure for further spending. These include the commitments to earnings-related pensions which will become more pressing as the elderly population increases rapidly in the early years of the next century; the demands for a disability benefit; pressure on child benefit and provision for the unemployed; and the needs of (currently) increasing numbers of frail very old people. Public opinion is unlikely to support actions which seem to damage the position of the old or disabled. The relative unpopularity of child benefit and support for the unemployed makes these provisions more plausible targets. Again, reliance on community care for the frail elderly may encounter strong opposition from the women on whom the burden of care is placed, unless an expensive infrastructure of back-up services is provided (West et al., 1984). Perhaps the most important aspect of opinion is that the urgency of expenditure constraint which underlies Green Paper arguments is not generally accepted. The Gallup Poll data (Table 5.1) show rather that higher spending is demanded by an increasing majority over the last two years.

Privatization

The Green Paper also speculates on the policy of saving state cash by privatization. Public opinion supports both state and private provision, an ambivalence deftly echoed by the Prime Minister at the 1982 Party Conference: 'I support the growth of private health care: there's no contradiction between that and supporting the NHS.' The 1979 and 1983 governments have advanced piecemeal privatization in a large number of marginal measures: shorthold tenancy; the assisted places scheme; tax relief for employers' health care contributions; death grant insurance; local authority direct works, school cleaning and meals services; and hospital auxiliary services. Yet more major advances have only been possible through large subsidies as in the case of council house sales at reduced prices, residential care financed through the SB scheme and occupational sick pay supported by tax concessions to employers (Klein, 1984a, p. 22).

An alternative strategy might be to increase fiscal subsidies to the private sector. This would both provide an incentive to shift from the state sector and reduce the accounting figures for the size of the public sector (assuming the revenue foregone was compensated by cuts in the corresponding state services). However, areas staffed by professionals whose protests against cuts have a high degree of visibility (education and health care) or favoured state benefits (pensions) offer the greatest potential for both savings and arousing opposition. Privatization strategies in these areas seem likely to arouse a substantial public opinion backlash, but such policies may be viable at the margin of major state services, where the potential for saving is correspondingly smaller.

Corporatism

Corporatism is a complex and plastic term (Schmitter, 1977). Its relevance to welfare policy lies (like Keynesianism) in a general approach rather than a precise formulation. Mishra and Klein represent a school of authors who are impressed by the achievement of countries like Sweden and Austria in providing humane welfare services without provoking social dissensus or political concern about economic growth. Mishra (1984) argues that institutional arrangements for settling the scale and role of state and market in distribution offer a stable future to the welfare state, whether these are state-sponsored, as in the Swedish Labour Market Board, or formally independent like the Austrian Joint Commission for Wage and Price Questions. Klein concludes from a careful review of factors associated with inflation that 'public expenditure designed to maintain levels of employment may be a successful instrument for buying co-operation . . . for . . . wage restraint' (1982, p. 45). Both these arguments run counter to the assumption that social spending is a simple burden: that priorities for spending can only be considered after the output of the economy is established.

Leaving to one side the vexed question of whether such arrangements would be practicable in the UK, public opinion evidence about the likely viability of a social wage is ambiguous. While people appear to make coherent statements that link tax payment to aspirations for benefits, none the less wage settlements appear to be regarded as a matter for free enterprise solution rather than consensual negotiation. The inequalities and conflicts of class would still reign in the occupational sphere leaving rational consensus planning of welfare to the state sector. Such planning would be unlikely to produce an egalitarian outcome. The disjunction between defence of heartland services and suspicion of minority or unjustified provision might leave the vulnerable – the unemployed, the low paid or single parents – as second-class citizens. A substantial change in public attitudes would appear necessary to make corporatist debates linking what have traditionally been seen as separate economic and social issues feasible, and to make the outcome of those debates more humane.

CONCLUSIONS

The public strongly supports the heartland services of the welfare state while being equally strongly opposed to state intervention in the economy. It approves of the private sector without disapproving of the state sector, and desires state provision to mitigate the burden of family care for the elderly and other dependency groups.

Factors plausibly associated with self-interest appear to be the strongest influences on attitudes: these do not appear subject to pressures which will lead to any sudden change in the near future. The experience of the continued expansion of state intervention in everyday life may produce an undercurrent of concern at the power of service providers.

The upshot of this argument is that substantial changes in provision are unlikely to be supported if presented openly. Government policies may be able to nibble at the edges of the welfare state and attack unpopular services like child or unemployment benefit. However, the pattern of attitudes is complex. Changes may gain assent if new policies are presented in terms of their implication for some aspects of opinion but not others. In particular, welfare cuts are more likely to gain support in the context of approval of a non-interventionist state than in the context of an attack on state provision. Cuts are also more likely to be accepted if attention is focused on the damage to unfavoured groups. Privatization is more readily advanced if it is dissociated from the implications for state provision, while community care may be more marketable if it can be presented as a rolling back of the state, rather than an imposition on middle-aged women.

Politicians have been remarkably successful in recent years in promoting particular perceptions of current issues. The best example is probably the success of the 1979 Conservative government in dissociating itself from any responsibility for unemployment levels (Richardson and Moon, 1984, p. 29). Yet the structure of opinion places those who seek to rationalize or contain spending in a quandary. Support for both social interventionism and economic *laissez-faire* indicates that corporatism is unlikely to be successful. On the other hand, support for high spending irrespective of judgements on the state of the economy suggests that people are unlikely to be convinced by arguments that claim that low growth must lead to welfare cutbacks. The moral for policymakers is that they do best to work by deceit.

6

Public Expenditure on the Social Services: the Economic and Political Constraints

GAVYN DAVIES and DAVID PIACHAUD

INTRODUCTION

Despite the gloomy leaked reports before the 1983 general election about a looming fiscal crisis, more recent government analyses project scope for significant tax cuts in Britain during the rest of the decade. These prospects are based both on more optimistic forecasts of economic growth and on the assumption that the real level of public spending can be held constant until at least 1988. Whilst the chapter by O'Higgins and Patterson examines the implications of the public expenditure assumption from a disaggregate perspective by detailing the costs of possible changes in individual spending programmes, this chapter adopts the Treasury's macro-approach in order to establish the basis for their figures and their sensitivity to alternative assumptions.

It begins by analysing, on a range of assumptions about economic growth, the extent to which either real resource or financial arguments actually limit the scope for increasing public expenditure over the next five years. It then examines the Treasury's own arithmetic and the government's plans before going on to consider the consequences for public revenue and spending of modifying the Treasury's assumptions about future economic and social changes in ways that may reflect more accurately the prospects ahead.[1]

THE SCOPE FOR ADDITIONAL PUBLIC EXPENDITURE

Public Expenditure and Real Resources

In the 1960s and early 1970s, the Treasury methodology for designing medium-term public expenditure plans rested almost entirely on real resource constraints. Starting from an estimate of the underlying trend growth rate in the economy, the total resources available for public expenditure, private consumption, investment and exports were calculated. An assessment was then made of the amount of resources needed to ensure current account equilibrium, and to reach a desired ratio of gross domestic fixed capital formation to GDP. After these so called 'prior claims' had been taken into account, remaining resources were divided between public and private consumption. Apart from political considerations, the main factor determining the split between public and private consumption was the assumption that wage pressures in the economy were negatively correlated with the permitted rate of growth in consumers' expenditure (or, more accurately, with the disposable income of the employed labour force), so the control of inflation required a certain minimal growth rate (say 2 per cent a year) in private consumption. The problem of financing the level of public spending implied by this resources exercise was never specifically considered, since neither the public sector borrowing requirement nor the rate of monetary growth were considered to be even intermediate goals of macro-economic policy.

It is no longer possible to attempt to assess the scope for public expenditure in the medium term without specifically taking into account financing problems, since these now appear to be important intermediate targets for almost any possible shade of government. However, the present fashion often appears to place too much emphasis on finance, and too little on potential real resources. It is still useful to analyse the real resource scope for public expenditure, particularly since at present it suggests that there is considerable room for public spending growth in the period up to 1988/89.

The most important input into any real resources exercise is the assumed rate of real GDP growth which can be achieved over the period in question. At this stage we simply assume three different annual rates of real GDP growth between 1983 and 1988 – 1, 2 and 3 per cent – with the results shown in Table 6.1.

In order to move from the GDP figures shown in Table 6.1 to an estimate of the scope for public expenditure, we proceed as follows. First, permitted net exports (at 1980 prices) are calculated by assuming

TABLE 6.1 REAL RESOURCES AVAILABLE FOR PUBLIC EXPENDITURE, 1983 – 1988 (£bn 1980 PRICES)

	1983 level	1988 illustration assuming real GDP growth			Comments
		1% p.a.	2% p.a.	3% p.a.	
GDP (expenditure basis)	206.3	216.8	227.8	239.2	
Prior claims					
Net exports	2.7	1.1	1.1	1.1	Maintains current account balance in 1988.
Private investment	27.9	30.3	31.9	33.5	Restores share in GDP to 1979 level.
Stocks	0.7	0.7	0.7	0.7	Trend level maintained.
Other claims					
Consumers expenditure	144.8	152.2	159.9	167.9	Grows in line with GDP.
less factor cost adjust.	32.0	33.6	35.3	37.1	Taxes and subsidies unchanged.
Available for public exp.					
Total	62.2	66.1	69.5	73.1	
Public investment	11.7	12.7	13.4	14.1	Grows in line with private investment.
Public consumption	50.5	53.4	56.1	59.0	
(% growth p.a. 1983 – 88)	–	(1.2)	(2.2)	(3.3)	

Source: Authors' calculations

that the current account of the balance of payments will return to equilibrium in the last year of the period. Since the current balance was in surplus by £2 billion in 1983, this allows a shift of real resources out of net exports amounting to £1.6 billion a year at 1980 prices. On private investment, we make the assumption that the share of investment in GDP returns to the level achieved in 1979 (i.e. 14 per cent, compared to 13.5 per cent in 1983), while for stock building we simply assume that the average rate for the last ten years (£0.7 billion per annum) is maintained. After making provision for these 'prior claims', we are left with deciding how the remaining resources should be split between public and private consumption. We assume that private consumers' expenditure will grow in line with GDP, thus maintaining the relatively high share of national income achieved in 1983.

Since the move from current account surplus to current account balance frees resources for domestic use, and private consumption is assumed to grow in line with real GDP, the remaining resources would allow both public consumption and public investment to grow slightly faster than GDP. The results are shown at the bottom of Table 6.1.

There therefore seems no reason on resource grounds to hold down the rate of public expenditure growth to zero over the next few years. On the assumption of 2 per cent a year GDP growth for the economy as a whole, the permitted annual rate of growth of public expenditure would be 2.2 per cent. This conclusion, of course, is dependent on the somewhat arbitrary assumptions we have made about the split of resources between prior claims, private consumption, and public expenditure. The allocation of more resources to exports, investment or private consumption would obviously leave less for public spending, However, the scope for private consumption growth of 2 per cent a year on our central case certainly looks adequate for the purpose of holding down inflationary wage pressures, while there seems little point in diverting more resources to net exports, thus piling up further balance of payment surpluses. For these reasons, we find the case for holding down public expenditure on resource grounds extremely weak.

Public Expenditure and Public Finances

The government's own analysis of public expenditure starts not with real resource constraints, but instead with the need to hold public sector borrowing down to a policy-determined level. Table 6.2 gives projections for the public accounts in 1988/89 based on real GDP growth rates of 1, 2 and 3 per cent, and with the public expenditure growth rates which the previous analysis of real resource constraints suggested would be possible for each of the GDP growth rates – i.e. 1.1 per cent, 2.2 per cent or 3.3 per cent annually. To facilitate comparison with the most recent version of the Medium Term Financial Strategy (MTFS), we have wherever possible made the same assumptions about exogenous variables as has the government. In particular, we have allowed the rate of inflation to decline to just under 3 per cent in 1988/89, in line with government targets, and we have not varied this rate of inflation for the three different growth projections shown. Although it can plausibly be argued that a higher rate of inflation would be likely on the higher growth assumption, this in fact makes little different to the PSBR figures shown, unless inflation proceeds at different rates in the public and private sectors.

Our projections for government receipts (lines 4 to 8 of Table 6.2) are based on the following methodology. For oil taxation, interest receipts and miscellaneous receipts, we simply take the government's central assumption published in the MTFS, on the grounds that these categories of revenue will not be much affected by variations in GDP growth rates. For other taxation and for national insurance contributions, we assume that all tax rates are left unchanged in the period up to 1988/89 from the 1983/84 starting point. The result of this procedure (assuming that all specific duties and income tax allowances are up-rated in line with the inflationary element in their tax bases each year) is that tax revenues grow broadly in line with relevant tax bases (wages and salaries, consumers' expenditure etc.). If each tax base retains its share in GDP achieved in the initial year, then *total* tax revenues will grow simply in line with nominal GDP. (This is broadly the procedure followed by the Government in drawing up the MTFS each year).

Moving to general government expenditure (lines 10 – 15 of Table 6.2), we have adopted a similar approach. For asset sales, interest payments and miscellaneous expenditure, we have simply taken the MTFS projections. For social security, we assume that payments grow at the same rate as the number of recipients, with the annual up-rating being in line with price inflation. (Our unemployment assumptions obviously vary according to the real GDP growth rate chosen. These are shown in line 18 of the table, and are discussed further below.) Finally, for programme expenditure, we allow volume growth in line with the rates derived from the real resource calculations outlined above, while the price deflator for public spending is assumed to grow simply in line with the GDP deflator.

TABLE 6.2   GOVERNMENT ACCOUNTS ON VARIOUS ASSUMPTIONS
FOR GDP GROWTH AND PUBLIC EXPENDITURE, 1983/84–1988/89

	1983/84	1988/89 assuming real GDP Growth		
		1% p.a.	2% p.a.	3% p.a.
Assumptions				
1 Nominal GDP (£bn)	304.0	387.2	406.8	427.0
2 Real GDP*	100.0	105.1	110.4	115.9
3 GDP deflator*	100.0	121.2	121.2	121.2
Gen. govt. receipts (£bn)				
4 Oil	9.0	9.0	9.0	9.0
5 Other taxation	87.5	111.4	117.1	122.9
6 Nat. ins. contns.	21.5	27.4	28.8	30.2
7 Interest & misc.	10.5	11.0	11.0	11.0
8 Total receipts	128.5	158.8	165.9	173.1
9 Volume of programme expenditure*	100.0	105.6	111.5	117.6
Gen. govt. expenditure (£bn)				
10 Asset sales	−1.0	−2.0	−2.0	−2.0
11 Social security	35.3	47.7	46.2	44.7
12 Other programmes	86.2	110.3	116.5	122.9
13 Planning total	120.5	156.0	160.7	165.6
14 Interest & Misc.	18.5	20.0	20.0	20.0
15 Total expenditure	139.0	176.0	180.7	185.6
16 PSBR (£bn)	9.8	16.7	14.3	12.0
17 PSBR (% of GDP)	3.2	4.3	3.5	2.8
Memorandum				
18 Unemployment (000)	2969	4158	3464	2769

Source: Authors' calculations
* indicates 1983/84 = 100

On all these assumptions, we derive public borrowing figures as
shown in lines 16 – 17 in Table 6.2. On the central case, with 2 per cent
annual real growth in GDP, our 2.2 per cent assumed growth in real
public expenditure on goods and services results in a very slight rise in

from 3.2 per cent of GDP in 1983/84 to 3.5 per cent in
This small increase reflects both the fact that public
is permitted on resource grounds to grow slightly more
rapidly than nominal GDP and the impact of the projected rise in
unemployment over the period. On the 3 per cent annual growth case,
the slight decline assumed in unemployment brings down social
security payments enough to permit 3.3 per cent growth in public
spending on goods and services *and* a reduction in the PSBR to only 2.8
per cent of GDP by the end of the period. On neither the 2 nor the 3
per cent growth cases is there consequently any serious financing
difficulty involved with the public expenditure growth rates suggested
by the real resource constraints examined above. It is only on the 1 per
cent GDP growth rate case (which we consider to be the least likely) that
a problem emerges. In this case, higher unemployment results in an
additional financing burden for the public sector, taking the PSBR up
to 4.3 per cent of GDP by the end of the period. Even this, however,
would be substantially less than the average borrowing requirement
recorded over the last ten years.

There is, therefore, little need, either on finance or on real resource
grounds, for a real freeze on public expenditure over the next five years.
On the most likely growth rate assumptions for real GDP (2 to 3 per
cent), a slightly faster growth of real public expenditure would be
permitted on real resource grounds, and could be financed without any
sizeable increase in the PSBR. As the next section demonstrates, the
government's efforts to persuade the electorate of the need to hold
public expenditure down reflect the over-riding political priority it has
given to the objective of reducing taxation during its second term of
office.

THE GOVERNMENT'S PLANS

The 1984 budget spelled out the government's tax and expenditure
plans for the medium-term in very considerable detail. Table 6.3 sets
out these plans and summarizes the economic assumptions which lie
behind the MTFS. The Treasury believes that real GDP growth of 2.25
per cent per annum on average over the next five years (implying
roughly 2.5 per cent in non-oil GDP) will be consistent with a
continuing decline in the rate of inflation.

If the Treasury's economic projections are right, then government
receipts might develop as shown in lines 6 – 10 of Table 6.3. Oil taxes
are expected to stay roughly stable in nominal terms from now on, with

a decline in production in the second half of the period being offset by increases in the nominal oil price in line with world inflation. On unchanged policies, other taxes and national insurance contributions are expected to grow more or less in line with nominal GDP, following the path outlined in line 10. On the expenditure side, the key assumption is of stable levels of real spending. This results in a rise only in line with the price increase element of nominal GDP. As a result, the share of general government spending in GDP drops by about 4.5 per cent over the next five years. These figures are summarized in lines 11 – 16 of Table 6.3.

If these 'unchanged policy' assumptions were fulfilled, tax revenue would rise roughly in line with nominal GDP, while public expenditure would decline sharply as a proportion of national income. As a result, the PSBR would, on unchanged policies, also decline sharply, from £7 billion in 1984/85 to a negative £6.5 billion (i.e. net repayment) in 1988/89. The MTFS does not, however, envisage any further reduction in the nominal level of the PSBR – it is projected to be £7 billion a year until 1988. There is therefore a substantial and growing difference between the 'unchanged policy' PSBR and the target PSBR, and this difference creates room for what the Treasury calls a 'fiscal adjustment' – which means either tax cuts or spending increases. Since the government plans to hold spending constant, we assume it intends to devote all of the 'fiscal adjustment' to tax cuts. The magnitude of such cuts is indicated in line 19 of Table 3, which suggests that compared to current policies there is scope for tax cuts worth £13.5 billion in 1988/89 alone, and amounting to £32 billion over the four years from 1985/86 to 1988/89. If implemented, these cuts would cause the overall tax burden to drop from 38.9 per cent of GDP in 1984/85 to under 36 per cent in 1988/89 – still somewhat higher than the level which the government inherited in 1978/79, but a major reduction, especially for the employed labour force, on the 1983/84 level.

A tax cut of £13.5 billion in 1988/89 at nominal prices is equivalent to a cut of £11.1 billion at 1983 prices. This figure is strikingly close to the increase in public expenditure of £11.2 billion which O'Higgins and Patterson's central scenario C suggests will be necessary by 1988/89 if the government is to fulfil its particular spending commitments and meet the demographic pressures on public expenditure. Even their scenario D, the most optimistic from the government's viewpoint, suggests that an additional £6.6 billion will have to be spent in 1988/89 – and that scenario assumes that most public sector wages will only increase at half the rate of those in the private sector in the intervening

TABLE 6.3 THE GOVERNMENT'S MEDIUM-TERM STRATEGY

	1984/85	1985/86	1986/87	1987/88	1988/89
Economic assumptions					
1 Nominal GDP (£bn)	328.0	350.0	371.0	392.0	412.0
2 Real GDP (1983/84 = 100)	103.0	105.3	107.3	109.5	111.8
3 GDP deflator (1983/84 = 100)	104.8	109.3	113.7	117.8	121.2
4 Real GDP growth (%)	3.0	2.2	1.9	2.1	2.1
5 Inflation (%)	4.8	4.3	4.0	3.6	2.9
Government receipts (unchanged policy, £bn)					
6 Oil taxes	10.0	9.5	9.5	9.5	9.0
7 Other taxes	94.5	102.0	110.0	116.5	123.0
8 Nat. ins. contributions	23.0	24.5	26.0	27.5	29.0
9 Interest and misc.	11.0	10.5	11.0	11.0	11.0
10 Total receipts	138.5	146.5	156.5	164.5	172.0
Government expenditure (unchanged policy, £bn)					
11 Asset sales	-2.0	-2.0	-2.0	-2.0	-2.0
12 Social security	37.2	39.5	41.6	43.5	45.2
13 Other programmes	91.3	94.5	96.9	100.0	102.8

14 Planning total	126.5	132.0	136.5	141.5	146.0
15 Interest & misc.	19.5	20.0	21.5	20.0	19.5
16 Total expenditure	146.0	152.0	158.0	161.5	165.5
Borrowing requirements (£bn)					
17 PSBR (unchanged policy)	7.0	5.0	0.5	-3.0	-6.5
18 Target PSBR	7.0	7.0	7.0	7.0	7.0
Tax cuts (£bn)					
19 Permitted tax cuts from 1984/85 base	0.0	2.0	6.5	10.0	13.5
Tax burden (% of GDP)					
20 Total taxation	38.9	38.3	37.5	36.6	35.8
21 Non-oil taxation	35.8	35.6	34.9	34.1	33.6

These figures represent our best estimates of the Treasury projections underlying the MTFS. In some cases, lack of information has forced us to make rough guesstimates. Some figures differ from those in the MTFS by up to £0.5bn, reflecting the Treasury habit of rounding their estimates to the nearest £0.5bn.

years and makes no provision for any increases in the value of social security benefits.

This analysis of the government's plans therefore suggests that if their underlying assumptions are correct, there will indeed be scope for significant 'fiscal adjustments' during the rest of the decade, but this can only be translated into major tax cuts at the expense of the spending increases needed to maintain current levels of provision in social and other government programmes. The next section investigates the sensitivity of these assumptions.

THE ECONOMIC CONTEXT AND ASSUMPTIONS

Earlier sections have used the government's assumptions about future changes and assessed their implications. As Table 6.3 indicated, those assumptions allowed a 'fiscal adjustment' (tax cuts or public spending increases) totalling £13.5 billion in 1988/9 at nominal prices. This section examines the reliability of those assumptions and the effects on the size of the possible fiscal adjustment of alternative assumptions.

Future Growth of Gross Domestic Product

The Treasury's MTFS assumption is of 2.25 per cent per annum growth. This may seem optimistic since periods of real GDP growth of more than 2.5 per cent a year are fairly rare in British history, and the average annual growth rates in 1973 – 7.9 and 1979 – 83 were 1.3 per cent and 0.1 per cent respectively (Treasury, 1984b, tables A.3 and A.4). However, the past few years have seen a strong policy of disinflation being pursued in the UK and in most other developed economies, and it is almost certain that UK real GDP in 1984 remains considerably below trend; for example, CBI Industrial Trend Surveys still show that more than half of British industrial companies are working below capacity. For these reasons, the very low rate of growth achieved in the last five years is unlikely to be reproduced in the next five, and the present degree of slack in the economy should be reduced over the next half-decade, leading to a rate of output growth which is above the underlying trend.

The main determinants of the underlying trend rate of growth in the economy are the rate of change in the labour force and in productivity, and the likely rate of change of oil production. On the labour force, as Ermisch has discussed, Department of Employment projections show expected growth of 0.4 per cent a year in the labour force from now until 1988, with little change thereafter. On labour productivity, the 1979 – 83 period saw average annual growth of 1.4 per cent a year, somewhat better than had been achieved in the previous six years, but not as good as the underlying rate in the early post-war period.[2] The Treasury's official assumption is that productivity growth in the medium term will lie somewhere between the low rate observed since 1973 and the much higher rates achieved in the 1950s and 1960s. This line of argument appears reasonable and, if valid, would point to a trend rate of productivity growth of around 2 per cent a year. This, plus the assumed rate of growth in the labour force, would lead to an *underlying* rate of GDP growth of 2.5 per cent a year in the non-oil sectors, or (making allowance for a forecast reduction in oil output) very slightly less in the economy as a whole.[3]

As things now stand the Treasury's assumption of 2.25 per cent a year growth therefore seems reasonable. But in the past reasonable forecasts have often come to grief due to unforeseen setbacks – pessimism in a UK forecaster is normally no vice. We have estimated the impact of assuming that annual growth will, on average, be 1 per cent per annum below this Treasury estimate. This has major impacts on both sides of the government accounts. First, though resulting in a higher level of unemployment, the level of social security payments is increased by amounts varying from £0.2 billion in 1985/86 to £1.0 billion in 1988/89. (As in all the other cases outlined below, we assume that the 1984/85 outturn is fixed.) In addition, the reduction in GDP growth makes the 'unchanged policy' level of taxation considerably less buoyant, so that tax rates need to be higher in order to raise the same amount of total revenue. This, taken together with higher public expenditure, reduces the scope for a 'fiscal adjustment' in 1988 by about half, from £13.5 billion to about £6.6 billion in nominal terms, or from £11.1 billion to £5.4 billion at current price levels.

Future Changes in the Labour Force

John Ermisch's chapter discusses in some detail recent and prospective changes in the size and composition of the labour force. Such changes can have important implications for taxation and social expenditure, and may therefore affect the size of the 'fiscal adjustment' which is possible. For example, recent changes in the labour force and the working population have increased spending on pensions and unemployment benefits. The rise in women's employment has reduced the amount of time available for domestic care of disabled and elderly people. (This development was, of course, both a cause and an effect of increased social expenditure since, as Martin Rein's chapter demonstrates, employment in the paid social services was the major location of women's increased labour market participation.) Furthemore, the rise in female employment has led to more two-earner households, whose higher relative incomes has added to pressures to increase social security benefits in order to maintain the relative living standards of households without earners.

The main prospective changes which may be important are related to the effects of unemployment and the retirement age on the size of the labour force, and to the extent of female participation in the labour force. Although a significant fall in unemployment would obviously decrease the pressure on spending, it would also be likely to increase the size of the labour force as 'discouraged workers' and others saw prospects of a job. If unemployment fell to around one million, there might be around 150,000 more men and over half a million more women in the labour force – with both direct and indirect effects on social expenditure. Even without a change in unemployment, women's activity rates may continue to rise. Although many of these new entrants would be married women currently without independent rights to benefits, their entry would displace others with such entitlements. An entry of one-third of a million women might increase the number of benefit-claiming unemployed by a quarter of a million (since some of the new entrants would be in part-time jobs) which would increase social expenditure by about £450 million.

Alan Walker's chapter considers a range of options which would reduce unemployment by reducing the size of the labour force. Earlier retirement and a lower pension age is one of the most commonly suggested remedies, but, apart from the problems Walker mentions, it would probably lead to higher social spending. Average benefit spending per head for both the retired and unemployed is now similar, so a one-for-one trade-off between jobs and retirement would have little effect on spending; however, not all the retired would necessarily be replaced (Walker cites non-replacement rates of 25 per cent and 50 per cent) and the new young pensioners might be more likely to seek part-time employment, thus further reducing the jobs available to younger groups. Reducing unemployment by contracting the labour force is likely to increase rather than decrease social expenditure.

Future Changes in Productivity

Our central case is based on an annual growth in productivity of 2 per cent which is exceptionally high in historical terms, having been sustained over a lengthy period only from 1951 – 73. It could be that new information technology, altered industrial relations or other factors will result in very high productivity growth in the future, although there is no strong evidence to support this view. However, what is desirable in order to reduce unemployment is low productivity growth accompanied by high growth in output.

TABLE 6.4   PRODUCTIVITY, OUTPUT AND UNEMPLOYMENT, BEGINNING OF 1988

	Estimated unemployment for output growth of		
	1% p.a.	*2% p.a.*	*3% p.a.*
Productivity growth			
1% p.a.	3300	2510	1810
2% p.a.	3900	3300	2510
3% p.a.	4590	3900	3300
	Extra cost of unemployment *(£million 1983 prices)*		
Productivity growth			
1% p.a.	–	– 1460	– 2760
2% p.a.	+ 1110	–	– 1460
3% p.a.	+ 2390	+ 1110	–

Source: Authors' calculations
The unemployment data are based on labour force growth of 0.4% per annum.

The effects of different combinations of productivity and output growth on the level of unemployment and of expenditure on the unemployed are shown in Table 6.4. If productivity grows 1 per cent faster than output this adds £1.1 billion to social expenditure in 1988. If productivity grows 1 per cent more slowly than output this reduces social expenditure in 1988 by £1.5 billion (at 1983 prices). If output grew by 3 per cent a year and productivity by 1 per cent this would allow a fiscal adjustment of £2.8 billion which could either allow extra public expenditure of this amount or a reduction in the tax burden amounting to 0.8 per cent of GDP. We are inclined to expect a rapid rise in productivity with little if any more rise in output – and consequently we expect unemployment to be at least as high in 1988 as it is now.

Higher Inflation

We have considered the possibility that inflation will prove higher than the government currently expects, and estimated the impact of an increase of 1 per cent a year in the rate of inflation compared to the government's projections over the period. (This would still allow the annual rate of inflation to drop to under 4 per cent by the end of the parliament.) The impact of this change is highly dependent on whether increased prices are allowed to flow through to higher public expenditure. We distinguish two cases – in the first, we allow cash limits to move up in line with higher price inflation, while in the second we hold cash limits unchanged allowing only social security benefits to be increased in line with higher prices.

There is a substantial difference between the two cases in the scope available for tax cuts. If cash limits are increased in line with inflation, then the scope for tax cuts is left virtually unchanged from the government's main case. While public expenditure rises by roughly 1 per cent a year compared with the main case, the higher level of nominal GDP raises the underlying tax receipts on unchanged tax rates. Since these two effects are almost exactly offsetting, there is very little impact on the 'unchanged policy' PSBR, and virtually no curtailment of the scope for tax cuts. If, on the other hand, cash limits are not increased in line with higher price inflation, the impact on the government accounts is different. In this case, the increase in nominal GDP flows through to higher tax revenues, but there is no matching increase in public expenditure (except in the social security bill). In consequence, the gap between 'unchanged policy' tax revenue and the level of public expenditure actually increases, creating additional room for tax reductions.

Our estimates suggest that the scope for tax reductions increases by £1 billion a year if inflation is 1 per cent higher than the government's projection, so that the fiscal adjustment in 1988/89 could be more than £4 billion greater. It is therefore possible for inflation actually to have a beneficial impact on the Chancellor's tax-cutting arithmetic, provided that cash limits are non-accommodative; and, even if they are accommodative, inflation has little or no detrimental impact on the prospect for tax reductions. The only exception to this, of course, would be if economic growth were choked off to reduce the inflation rate.

Less Optimistic Oil Projections

The Treasury has assumed that oil production will peak in the next year or two, and then decline gradually over the next three years. The centre of the Department of Energy's oil production range shows output of 120 million tonnes in 1984/85 dropping to slightly under 100 million tonnes in 1988/89. On oil prices, the official forecast assumes that the nominal price is unchanged in the next two years, and thereafter rises in line with world inflation. For our less optimistic oil case we have made two changes to these assumptions. First, we allow no increase in the nominal price of oil at any time over the period. Second, we take the bottom end of the Department of Energy's production range, instead of the middle. By the end of the period, this results in oil prices around 15 per cent lower than the Treasury expects, with output some 20 per cent lower. If the percentage tax-take is left unchanged from the main case, tax revenue will drop roughly in line with the combined cut in oil production and oil prices. As a result, the loss of oil revenue rises from £0.8 billion in 1985/86 to £2.8 billion in 1988/89. All of this needs to be made up by higher taxation on the non-oil economy. [4]

The overall effect on the Chancellor's margin for tax cuts is not drastic; it reduces the cumulative total from £13.5 billion over four years to £10.7 billion, which is well within the margin of error of this type of projection. However, from 1988/89 onwards, the continued scope for tax reductions does become more dependent on the Treasury's assumption of a steady rise in the real oil price – something which must be judged, to say the least, highly questionable.

CONCLUSIONS

All the variant assumptions discussed in the last section are summarized in Table 6.5. The most important assumption is, of course, the rate of economic growth. With growth over five years averaging 1 per cent rather than 2.25 per cent the government would be unable to reduce the share of non-oil taxation in GDP even with level public spending. Variations in productivity and oil revenue projections are quantitatively much more important than possible variations in labour force projections – although the latter could affect social expenditure by something of the order of £500 million. Non-accommodating cash limits would in effect represent further public expenditure cuts and thus allow more scope for tax cuts.

TABLE 6.5 SUMMARY OF VARYING ASSUMPTIONS

	Fiscal Adjustment 1988/89		Non-oil tax (as % of GDP)
	At 1983 prices (£bn)	At nominal prices (£bn)	
Central government case	11.1	13.5	33.6 (35.8 in 1984/85)
Effect of:			
1 1% p.a. lower economic growth	− 5.7	− 6.9	+ 1.7
2 Increased women's economic activity	− 0.5	− 0.6	+ 0.15
3 Extra 1% productivity growth over output	− 1.1	− 1.3	+ 0.3
4 1% higher inflation			
cash limits accommodating	+ 0.1	+ 0.1	− 0.02
cash limits non-accommodating	+ 3.4	+ 4.1	− 1.0
5 Less optimistic oil projections	− 2.6	− 3.2	+ 0.8

Most of the changes in the Treasury's arithmetic which we have explored are in the direction of greater pessimism from the point of view of achieving tax cuts: lower growth, higher inflation, future growth of the labour force, higher productivity growth and a less optimistic oil profile. It is quite legitimate to argue that we should also have explored the possibility of other, more optimistic outturns than those contained in the Treasury's main case. We have avoided this course because past experience suggests that the combination of economic assumptions made by Treasury may prove to be on the optimistic side. However, even taking this less optimistic approach, the scope for fiscal adjustment in the medium term does look reasonably robust. Provided the economy manages to attain an annual growth rate of 1 to 2 per cent at worst then there will be room for tax cuts. The government's non-aggressive approach to reductions in the PSBR guarantees this.

Of course, this conclusion has a clear corollary: if the scope for a fiscal adjustment looks reasonably robust, then part or all of this scope could be absorbed by public expenditure increases, rather than tax reductions. In fact, the government's own central case suggests that, if tax rates were left unchanged in the next five years, there would be scope within the Chancellor's PSBR targets for real public spending to grow by about 2 per cent annually. The government's case for zero growth in public expenditure is therefore based neither on real resource grounds, nor on finance grounds: it is based simply on the desire to create room to reduce taxation.

While the economic case for zero growth in public expenditure is not convincing this does not mean that social expenditure poses no problems. As O'Higgins and Patterson demonstrate, making even modest real improvements in pensions, together with the costs of demographic changes and of the government's commitments on defence and law and order would use up all of the £11.1 billion (at 1983 prices) available for fiscal adjustment on the government's central case. More pessimistic assumptions about GDP growth would leave less scope for fiscal adjustment. Increased social expenditure could of course be off-set by reductions in other public expenditure programmes but this seems unlikely given the priority the government has attached to other large programmes, such as defence and law and order, and the inflexibility of other programmes, such as payments to the European Community. Increased social expenditure in practice probably means higher overall public expenditure: this is possible but it seems likely that it would absorb most or all of the available fiscal adjustment. The government, within its self-imposed PSBR targets, could well be faced by a situation in which the maintenance of social provisions leaves no scope for any tax cuts and could require taxation to rise as a proportion of GDP.

Thus we conclude that the case for *zero* growth in public expenditure is not based on economic constraints but rather on a political desire to give absolute priority to tax cuts. Some growth in public expenditure is possible while still achieving significant tax cuts. Within the Government's own financial constraints the pressures on public expenditure and the likely economic constraints over the next five years may in effect mean that the maintenance of existing social provisions and the achievement of *any* overall tax cuts are irreconcilable objectives.

Notes

1   This chapter was written in May 1984 and is based on information available then.
2   While it is true that productivity growth has improved in the last two years to over 3 per cent per annum, this has probably been due to a one-off period of labour shedding which cannot be expected to continue indefinitely.
3   The *actual* rate of growth in real GDP could be higher or lower than the underlying rate, reflecting a change in the degree of capacity utilization in the economy. It is difficult to be certain whether a sustained increase in capacity utilization will be possible over the medium term without triggering an increase in the rate of inflation unacceptable to the government.
4   We do not allow for the possibility that lower oil prices will produce a different profile for UK inflation and output from that shown in the main case.

7

The Prospects for Public Expenditure: a Disaggregate Analysis

MICHAEL O'HIGGINS and ALAN PATTERSON

INTRODUCTION

The eternal debate about the appropriate level of public expenditure acquired new salience both with the slow down of economic growth since the mid-1970s and with the election in 1979 of a Conservative government committed to rolling back the frontiers of the state, and in particular to reducing the level of public expenditure in order to cut both taxation and public borrowing. The most recent surge of interest in this issue reflects the growing realization that despite the efforts of a government volubly determined to cut it, public expenditure has continued to grow in real terms.

Over the first term of office of the Conservative government, public expenditure in cost terms rose by more than 6 per cent, at a time when economic growth was negligible; further real growth of 1.5 per cent occurred during the first year of its second term. This growth was due to a mixture of the effects of political commitments and of the recession, not matched by programme reductions of equivalent magnitude. The defence and law and order programmes which took about 14.5 per cent of public expenditure in 1978/79 accounted for around 17 per cent in 1983/84. These increases were not matched by corresponding reductions in social expenditure shares. Whilst the relative importance of the education budget declined slightly that of

The research on which this paper is based was supported by grants from the Economic and Social Research Council and the Joseph Rowntree Memorial Trust. We are grateful for comments and assistance from a range of our colleagues, including Sara Horrell, John Hudson, Stephen Jenkins and Rudolf Klein.

the health and social services programme increased by slightly more. More importantly, the social security budget, which accounted for only just over 20 per cent of public expenditure in the mid 1970s and 25 per cent in 1978/79, took up almost 30 per cent of public spending by 1983/84. Reflecting the impact of part of the political response to the recession, the employment services budget (defined as including redundancy and maternity fund, special employment and Manpower Services Commission expenditure) grew very rapidly, although from a very small base. The major drops in budget shares were in the overseas aid, trade and industry, and housing programmes; the housing cut was quantitatively the most important, its share coming down from about 5.5 per cent in 1978/79 to less than 2.5 per cent by 1983/84. The share of total social expenditure (defined as education, health and social services, social security, housing and employment services) therefore increased from about 55 per cent of public expenditure in 1978/79 to 57 per cent in 1983/84 (O'Higgins and Ruggles, 1985, Table 2). Faced with the diverse pressures for expenditure growth in both the protective and the social programmes, the government therefore allowed real total public expenditure to rise during its first term in office.

Given the government's commitment to cut public sector borrowing, this spending growth led to tax increases. In fact if both the GDP and the tax revenues derived from North Sea oil and gas are excluded from the calculations, the share of GDP taken in taxes reached 39 per cent in 1981/82, and although this was reduced to 38 per cent in 1983/84 (Treasury, 1984b, p. 10), that level was still higher than any experienced in the post-war period prior to 1979.

The resulting concern about the level of taxation and government borrowing required to pay for public expenditure is clearly shown in the Treasury's Green Paper, *The Next Ten Years: Public Expenditure and Taxation into the 1990s*. Although heralded as the official launching of a debate about public expenditure in the medium term, the Green Paper is primarily concerned with how to achieve aggregate levels of public expenditure which would allow a reduction in the overall level of personal taxation. In this respect, it is a further stage of the government's argument 'that finance must determine expenditure, not expenditure finance' (Treasury 1984b, p. 21).

The Green Paper assumes that public expenditure will be kept constant in real terms until 1988/89 and then examines the effect on the tax burden of two different public expenditure assumptions for the five years thereafter – unchanged real public expenditure and real spending growth of 1 per cent annually. On the economic growth scenarios which the Green Paper adopts (2.25 per cent economic growth annually until 1988/89, 1.5 per cent or 2 per cent thereafter) these levels of public expenditure would lead to a tax burden in 1993/94 which would be below 1978/79 levels. These spending policies and growth scenarios would, in other words, allow taxation to be reduced below the levels at which it stood when the government took office in 1979.

The Green Paper contains a four-page discussion of the expenditure pressures on particular programmes, but the various pressures are generally unquantified and there is no attempt to examine their combined impact over a period of years. Overall, therefore, it has two major weaknesses with respect to any discussion about public expenditure in the medium term:

1   Its assumption that public expenditure can be kept constant until 1988/89 bears no relation to recent experience, and we are given no indication of why such recent experience might not be repeated;
2   No detailed attempt is made to show how the different pressures on individual expenditure programmes might be accommodated within the aggregate assumptions about the level of public expenditure. In other words, although we are told the answer to the arithmetic of the various public expenditure programmes, we are not told *how* the arithmetic is going to add up.

Whilst Davies and Piachaud's chapter examines the Green Paper's assumptions from a macro-perspective, this chapter adopts a disaggregate approach to examining the prospects for public expenditure. It details the factors which affect pressures on the cost or level of service in particular spending programmes and examines the aggregate level of public expenditure which would be produced by particular sets of cost and pressure assumptions. The analysis does not seek to predict the level of public expenditure, or the magnitude of particular economic or political variables: it is concerned with an examination of scenarios – that is, with a series of 'What if?' questions. The scenarios allow the examination of the degree of variation between the results of different packages of assumptions, and the identification of the assumptions which are especially important in causing such variation. This then permits an analysis both of the feasibility of the government's target and the scope for new spending developments or initiatives.

The chapter proceeds by outlining the particular variables which affect public expenditure and are taken into account in the model on which the analysis is based. It then goes on to describe the range of scenarios, reflecting different economic and political variables, within which the development of public expenditure is examined. The results under the various scenarios are then outlined and their implications considered.

MODELLING THE DEVELOPMENT OF PUBLIC EXPENDITURE

The analysis begins with the 17 public expenditure programmes identified in the government's annual White Paper setting out its expenditure plans for future years (e.g. Treasury 1984a). We define programme expenditure as the total of these 17 programmes; in contrast to the usual public expenditure planning total, this concept excludes the proceeds of asset sales and makes no provision for a contingency reserve fund.

In seeking to construct scenarios for the development of this spending, four factors – explicit political decisions, economic performance, demographic changes and cost pressures – may be isolated.

Political Decisions

The technically ideal type of baseline projection model might be described as one which calculated simply the effects of continuing the programmes and standards required by current legislation over a period of years. Since it is clearly impossible to guess and combine in packages every possible political decision, this solution might seem the best way of setting out a benchmark from which political decisions may cause deviations. For a scenario-setting exercise it suffers, however, from the weakness that it requires that the current set of legislative commitments allow a unique assessment of their expenditure implications. This is often not the case. Although the level or value of, for example, a particular social security benefit may be explicitly stated in legislation, the quantity and standard of health care, education and defence to which an individual or community may be entitled is not usually so stated. Scenario-building therefore requires the construction of assumptions about the political response, in spending terms, to, for example, demographic changes which affect the pressure on public services. Therefore, while the scenarios set out below as far as possible avoid predicting future political decisions (as distinct from projecting the implications of past and current decisions) clear assumptions are made in particular scenarios about political responses to economic, demographic and cost changes.

Economic Performance

Economic factors will affect both the resources available to public expenditure (and the public expenditure/national income ratio) and also the cost pressures on particular parts of public expenditure. Factors such as the relative price effect, the rate of increase of public sector wages, the level of unemployment, and perhaps the real value of some social security benefits may all vary with wider assumptions about the state of the economy. This analysis does not attempt to create a model in which such outcomes are fully specified by endogenous economic or political relationships: it simply sets out assumptions which try to capture the range of what is reasonably possible.

Unemployment levels depend both on the size of the labour force (discussed by Ermisch) and the differential between the growth rates of GDP and of productivity: as Davies and Piachaud note, if high GDP growth is a result of rapid productivity gains there may be few job gains. Changes in unemployment from the average 1983/84 level are, therefore, calculated by adding labour force size changes and the employment changes which would follow from particular differentials in the growth rates of GDP and productivity. The resulting social security costs or savings are then calculated by assuming that a variation of 100,000 in the number of unemployed changes costs by £185 million (Treasury, 1984a, Volume 2, p. 90).

The analysis operates in 1983/84 prices: while relative price and cost effects are taken into account, the general level of inflation is not. There are no formal assumptions about the effects of high or low rates of inflation on other aspects of or inputs to the analysis, though the magnitudes of the assumed relative price and cost effects are more consistent with the continuation of relatively low rates of inflation.

Demographic Factors

The demographic changes, concentrated at the bottom and top of the age range, which Ermisch's chapter discussed, have clear implications for public expenditure on social provision. Table 7.1 sets out data which show the expenditure increases which would be required to meet the demographic pressure on health and social services – that is to allow current levels of provision to be maintained in the face of a client population of changing age-composition. It is worth noting that it shows the major pressure occurring during the 1980s with much lower pressures likely in the 1990s. In this analysis the baseline assumption has been that spending on health and personal social services will be increased in line with these demographic pressures, in order to allow current standards of service provision to continue. The effects of demographic changes have also been taken into account in the assessment of the numbers likely to be eligible for child benefit and retirement pensions.

TABLE 7.1   ANNUAL REAL EXPENDITURE GROWTH (%) REQUIRED TO MEET DEMOGRAPHIC PRESSURE ON THE HEALTH AND PERSONAL SOCIAL SERVICES PROGRAMME

1983/84	+ 0.3	1989/90	+ 0.7
1984/85	+ 0.6	1990/91	+ 0.6
1985/86	+ 1.0	1991/92	+ 0.4
1986/87	+ 0.8	1992/93	+ 0.1
1987/88	+ 0.9	1993/94	0.0
1988/89	+ 0.7	1994/95	+ 0.2

Source: Application of mid-1981 based OPCS principal population projections to 1984 public expenditure white paper (Treasury, 1984a) data on the relative cost of health and pesonal social services for different age groups

Cost Pressures

The final set of public expenditure pressures and the area where the impact of economic, political and demographic factors can also be included is that of cost pressures on public expenditure. As these are the proximate determinants of the eventual level of spending both on particular programmes and on general government as a whole, the analysis allows considerable flexibility in the data inputs at this stage.

The costs of social security transfer expenditure are distinguished from other public expenditure. In each scenario assumptions are made about changes in the real value of child benefit, of retirement pensions and of other benefits and also about the numbers in receipt of other benefits. The costs of changes in the level of unemployment are taken into account in the manner described above and, as already noted, the numbers receiving child benefits and retirement pensions are endogeneously calculated.

With respect to public expenditure other than social security transfers, the analysis uses separate assumptions about changes, from a 1983/84 base-line, to six different factors. These are changes in:

1. The numbers employed in the public sector.

2. Real public sector wage rates.

3. The relative price effect for non-wage current expenditure.

4. Volume changes in non-wage current expenditure.

5. The relative price effect for capital expenditure.

6. Volume changes in capital expenditure.

The particular assumptions chosen are described and discussed below in the light of the six scenarios with which the model is illustrated.

ASSUMPTIONS ABOUT PUBLIC EXPENDITURE PRESSURES

Tables 7.2 and 7.3 detail the assumptions which are made in order to arrive at the modelled results about the prospects for public expenditure. Two broad sets of assumptions are made: those which vary depending upon the economic scenario chosen, and those which are assumed to apply regardless of the particular scenario. The reasoning behind the various assumptions is briefly summarized in what follows.

Six different scenarios are developed in Table 7.2, encompassing four different assumptions about future levels of economic growth. The low and high assumptions assume 1 per cent and 3 per cent real annual growth in GDP; these are respectively less than and greater than the average rates which would occur if previous trends were to repeat themselves. Two more central assumptions about economic growth are each applied to two scenarios; the higher of these, growth of 2.25 per cent a year, is what the Green Paper assumes over the next five years, whilst the lower rate, 1.5 per cent, is the lower of the two assumptions which the Green Paper makes for the first five-year period spanning the turn of the decade.

The assumptions about productivity growth cover a range which allows productivity to rise both more rapidly and more slowly than GDP, whilst broadly having higher productivity growth at the higher

TABLE 7.2 PROJECTING PROGRAMME EXPENDITURE: ASSUMPTIONS UNDER DIFFERENT SCENARIOS

Real changes measured annually to 1993/94 unless otherwise stated	Annual percentage change under scenario					
	A	B	C	D	E	F
GDP	1.0	1.5	1.5	2.25	2.25	3.0
Productivity per employee	1.5	1.8	2.2	1.80	2.2	2.2
Value of retirement pensions	0	0	1.0	0	1.5	1.5
Public sector wages:						
Defence and law and order	1.5	2.0	3.0	2.5	3.5	3.5
Health and social services:						
to 1985/86	1.5	2.0	3.0	2.5	3.5	3.5
1986/87 to 1993/94	0.8	1.0	1.8	1.25	2.5	2.5
All other programmes	0.8	1.0	1.8	1.25	2.5	2.5
Capital expenditure – volume: transport, housing and other environmental services	1.0	1.0	2.0	1.5	3.0	3.0
Capital expenditure – relative price effect: all programmes	-0.5	0	0.25	0	0.5	0.5
Unemployment (calculated endogenously) 1983/84 = 3.0m						
1988/89	4.1m	3.9m	4.4m	3.0m	3.5m	2.6m
1993/94	4.6m	4.2m	5.1m	2.4m	3.4m	1.6m

GDP growth levels. Within the relatively narrow range of 1.5 to 2.2 per cent annual growth in productivity, the two central economic growth assumptions each have alternative productivity assumptions of 1.8 per cent and 2.2 per cent annual growth. As indicated by Davies and Piachaud, this GDP/productivity growth differential influences the change assumed in the level of employment, hence the use of alternative differentials for given GDP growth levels.

In general it is assumed that the real value of social security benefits will be increased only in line with inflation, and therefore (since the exercise is carried out in real terms) there are no assumptions about social security value increases. However, it is plausible to argue that in the event of a resumption of economic growth the political pressures for some benefit increases will be relatively strong, so in three of the economic growth scenarios – one each of the two central assumptions and the high growth assumption – the real value of retirement pensions is increased somewhat. The choice of pensions is not difficult to explain in political terms: pensioners are clearly one of the politically more popular groups of social security beneficiaries (as Taylor-Gooby's chapter demonstrates). The fact that none of the levels of increase in the real value of retirement pensions are as great as the rates of increase in GDP, or in wages, reflects a judgement that even the popularity of pensioners may not exempt them from some relative constraint in coming years. Apart from the demographically determined increases in the number of pension and child benefit recipients, and the endogenously determined changes in the level of unemployment, no changes are assumed in the number of recipients of other social security benefits.

The assumptions about the rates at which public sector wages will grow differentiate between those sectors where recent experience demonstrates a government commitment to maintain wages and salaries broadly in line with those in the private sector, and those where wages in recent years have tended to grow less rapidly than in the private sector. In the former category, we place the defence and law and order wage budget and therefore assume annual rates of real wage increases which vary from 1.5 to 3.5 per cent depending upon the scenario. These rates reflect our assumptions about the approximate rates at which average private sector earnings might grow given the different productivity assumptions. We do not assume that earnings in the remainder of the public sector will be kept absolutely constant in real terms: with any resumption of economic growth it seems highly unlikely that there would not be at least some real wage increases in the rest of the public sector. The rates we have assumed are, broadly

TABLE 7.3   PROJECTING PROGRAMME EXPENDITURE:
ASSUMPTIONS COMMON TO ALL SCENARIOS

Social security
It is assumed that the real value of social security benefits – except
retirement pensions (see Table 7.2) – is kept constant. The
numbers receiving retirement pensions and child benefits are
assumed to vary in line with demographic changes.

No. of employees	
Defence	0%
Law and order	1% to 1987/88
Health and social services	0.5% to 1987/88
	0% 1988/89 to 1993/94
All other programmes	1% to 1987/88

Non-wage current expenditure: relative price effect	
Defence	2% to 1987/88
	1.5% 1988/89 to 1993/94
Health and social services	1%

Non-wage current expenditure: volume	
Defence	3% to 1985/86
	1.5% 1986/87 to 1993/94
Law and order	1%
Health and social services	0.5%
Education and science	– 0.5%
Trade, industry, energy and employment	– 5% to 1986/87
Northern Ireland	1% to 1984/85
Other public and common services	9% to 1984/85

Capital expenditure: volume	
Defence	3% to 1985/86
	1% to 1993/94
Health and social services	0.5%
Education and science	– 2% to 1988/89
Trade, industry etc.	– 5% to 1986/87
Other public and common services	50% to 1984/85

(1) The basis for the major assumptions is explained and discussed in the text.
(2) The assumptions on Northern Ireland, trade and industry, and other public and
common services are consistent with the 1984 Public Expenditure Plans (Cmnd. 9143 II).
(3) The 0.5% annual increase in the volume of health and social services non-wage
current expenditure is in addition to any changes required to meet demographic
pressures.

speaking, about half the rates at which we project private sector and defence and law and order earnings to grow, with a somewhat higher ratio on two of the higher growth scenarios. Because of the higher pay settlements which have been agreed for some groups of workers in the health service during the 1984/85 and 1985/86 financial years, we allow health and social service earnings to grow in line with defence earnings for these two years, after which they revert to the rates of increase projected for the remainder of the public sector.

The only other sets of assumptions which vary with the scenarios concern capital expenditure. We assume a slight relative price effect for capital expenditure across all programmes; at the low growth rate assumption this relative price effect is marginally negative, reflecting the effects of competitive tendering, whilst as the growth rates increase it becomes slightly positive. We also assume that the next few years will see some growth in the volume of capital expenditure on transport, housing and other environmental services, not least because of their relative neglect in recent years. We assume greater willingness to fund such provision at the higher growth rates.

Table 7.3 lists the assumptions which apply regardless of the particular economic scenario chosen. With respect to public sector manpower, we base our assumptions upon the plans indicated in the 1984 public expenditure White Paper (Treasury 1984a). We assume no change in defence programme manpower because although the defence civil service is due to decrease over the White Paper period, this is counteracted by a slight expected increase in the numbers of the armed forces. We assume that the manpower decline in the health and social services will be somewhat less than in the other non-protective programmes, despite the considerable pressure for efficiency savings in the NHS , both because of the political popularity and salience of these services (as Taylor-Gooby has shown) and because of the staffing implications of the sharp impact of demographic pressure on these services over the next few years.

We assume relative price effects for non-wage current expenditure in the two programmes where such effects have been most obvious over a period of years, defence and health and social services. Recent declines in the magnitude of the health service relative price effect would suggest that our assumption of 1 per cent is on the high side, but it is consistent with the longer-term experience in health costs. The defence relative price effect assumption of 2 per cent is in line with current experience; we assume a slight decline to 1.5 per cent from 1988 onwards as the pressures for better cost control begin to have some effect after the NATO commitment to real defence expenditure growth expires. This may however be unduly optimistic, given the continuing cost escalation of the Trident programme.

Our assumptions about the volume expenditure on both capital and non-wage current items are broadly in line with the pattern so far. After the expiry of the NATO commitment to 3 per cent real annual growth in defence expenditure in 1985/86, we assume a continued priority to real increases in defence expenditure, though at a lower rate. The plausibility of this rests on assumptions both about the current government's defence posture, and about the likely priority given by the opposition parties to strengthening conventional defence systems. The slight positive health and negative education changes reflect the demographic pressures in each sector. The assumption of 5 per cent annual real reductions in the trade, industry, energy and employment programme represents the outcome of assumptions of larger cuts in the trade and industry part of this programme item; this reflects both the experience of the last few years and the government's clear stance on both privatization and the external financing limits of public sector industries.

Our sets of assumptions, then, are relatively conservative. They assume neither major increases nor swingeing cuts in programme expenditure. This is a deliberate part of our approach to scenario-building. We are not seeking to predict any major changes of policy which governments may choose to make, merely to capture the range of likely pressures on public expenditure within a broadly unchanged policy stance. It may of course be the case that a review of the implications of these conventional pressures would lead to radical policy changes in order to achieve different outcomes: that is one of the purposes of scenario-gazing.

SCENARIOS FOR PUBLIC EXPENDITURE OVER THE NEXT DECADE

The general results of the exercise in terms of public expenditure magnitudes are set out in Table 7.4. In Scenario A, the low growth scenario, programme expenditure grows by 6 per cent up to 1988/89 and 11 per cent up to 1993/94 from its 1983/84 base, representing real spending increases of £7 billion and £13.7 billion, respectively. However, it rises only very marginally as a percentage of national income, from the 1983/84 share of 40 per cent to a 1993/94 share of 40.3 per cent.[1] In the highest growth scenario – F – real public expenditure increases only slightly faster, by 8 per cent (£9.3 billion) in the first five years and 16 per cent (£19 billion) over the complete decade. The impact of the higher level of GDP growth is reflected in the programme expenditure/GDP ratio which drops by around half a percentage point annually to under 35 per cent by 1993/94. In this scenario, therefore, the relative size of the public sector would be cut by almost one-seventh over the decade.

In the central scenarios – B to E – a similar range of results emerges. In the two scenarios where a more restrained budgetary position is adopted by the government, scenarios B and D, public expenditure grows by around 6 per cent and 11 per cent to 12 per cent over the shorter and longer periods respectively, while on the slightly less restrained scenarios, C and E, the corresponding figures are 9.5 per cent and 19 per cent to 20 per cent. These figures are equivalent to spending growth of around £7 billion and £14 billion on the restrained scenarios, and over £11 billion and around £23 billion on scenarios C and E. However, only in Scenario C – the less restrained, lower-growth central scenario – does the programme expenditure/GDP ratio rise and even then it does so by less than one percentage point over the decade. Whilst the main reason for declines in this ratio in other scenarios is GDP growth, the government's budgetary position is not unimportant. This is illustrated by the differences between scenarios D and E which have a common economic growth rate but different productivity and expenditure restraint assumptions. By 1993/94 the programme expenditure/GDP ratios in the two scenarios differ by three percentage points.

TABLE 7.4   PROGRAMME EXPENDITURE GROWTH IN THE UK
UNDER VARIOUS SCENARIOS, 1983/4–1993/4

		Scenario					
		A	B	C	D	E	F
1988/9	1	105.8	106.2	109.2	105.5	109.7	107.7
	2	40.3	39.5	40.6	37.8	39.3	37.2
	3	7.1	7.5	11.2	6.7	11.8	9.4
1993/4	1	111.3	112.2	118.7	110.9	120.1	115.9
	2	40.3	38.7	40.9	35.5	38.5	34.5
	3	13.8	14.9	22.8	13.3	24.5	19.4

1 = Index of growth in total constant price programme expenditure; 1983/84 = 100
2 = Total programme expenditure as a percentage of GDP; 1983/84 = 40
33 = Increase (in £billion) of constant price programme expenditure over 1983/84 total
(£121,728 bn)

Table 7.5 summarizes the implications of the various scenarios for the expenditure shares of selected programmes. Since the main assumptions are generally based on the continuation of recent policies, it is not surprising that the pattern of changes since 1978/79 is projected to continue. The combined defence and law and order budget share would rise to around 19 per cent in 1988/89, and to over 20 per cent by the early 1990s. Housing and education continue to decline, with education below 10 per cent in 1993/94, whilst health and social services grow steadily in response to demographic pressures. The greatest variation is in the social security programme, showing the importance of the range of assumptions on the level of unemployment and the real value of pensions. By 1993/94, these amount to a spread of over three percentage points in the projected programme share.

When the results are examined across all the scenarios then, it is clear that on these relatively conventional assumptions about expenditure pressures and changes at the detailed level, public spending is going to rise in real terms over the next decade. The magnitude of the rise ranges between 5 per cent and 9 per cent (£6.5 billion to £11.5 billion) by 1988/89, and 11 per cent and 20 per cent (£13 billion to £24 billion) by 1993/94. From a starting-point of 40 per cent in 1983/84, the scenarios show the programme expenditure/GDP ratio between 37 and 40.5 per cent by 1988/89 and 34.5 and 41 per cent by 1993/94.

TABLE 7.5   SELECTED PROGRAMME EXPENDITURE SHARES, 1978/79, 1983/84, 1988/89 AND 1993/94

| | percentage of total programme expenditure | | | |
| | Actual | | Range on scenarios A to F | |
Programme	1978/79	1983/84	1988/89	1993/94
Defence	11.4	12.9	14.7−15.1	16.1−16.9
Law and order	3.1	3.8	4.1−4.4	4.4−4.9
Housing	5.4	2.8	2.2−2.3	2.1−2.5
Education	11.8	11.0	10.1−10.3	9.6−9.9
Health and social services	11.3	12.1	12.6−12.9	13.0−13.5
Social security	25.0	29.0	27.6−29.3	25.4−28.7

The central prospects for public expenditure are therefore for slow real growth, accompanied by a decline in the share of GDP for which it accounts. This suggests that it is unlikely that the government's stated target of zero real growth in public expenditure during its current term of office can be met on current policies. It also indicates that this failure should not be a matter of concern, even for this government, since with a reasonable level of economic growth these real increases in public expenditure are consistent with its having a declining share of GDP. This detailed, disaggregate analysis therefore suggests that there is no 'public expenditure crisis' – or at least that the crisis is not one of economics.

The Growth of Public and Private Sector Wages

The assumption that most public sector wages can continue to be held to lower rates of increases than corresponding private sector wages is not entirely plausible, despite the experience of recent years. Even if the type of catch-up settlement familiar over the last two decades were not to return in the next decade, it may be argued that at some point the government will have achieved its objective of shifting wage relativities between the public and private sectors, so that patterns of comparable increases may return. To examine how sensitive the results are to the nature of the assumption about wage comparability, Scenario D – the higher, central growth scenario with budgetary restraint – was re-run assuming that all public sector wages go up at the real rate of 2.5 per cent annually, the same rate at which it is assumed private sector wages will increase. The results in Table 7.6 indicate an effect which is

TABLE 7.6   THE EFFECT OF WAGE COMPARABILITY AND AN EFFICIENCY GAINS ASSUMPTION ON PUBLIC EXPENDITURE IN SCENARIO D

	Index of total programme spending (1983/84 = 100)		*Programme expenditure as percentage of GDP*	
Scenario D with:	*1988/89*	*1993/94*	*1988/89*	*1993/94*
Conventional assumptions (as stated in Tables 7.2 & 7.3)	105.5	110.9	37.8	35.5
Wage comparability – i.e. all public and private sector wages rise at 2.5% p.a.	106.9	114.2	38.3	36.6
Annual efficiency gains (cost savings) of 1%	102.1	103.8	36.6	33.3

The procedures and assumptions underlying the data and scenarios are explained in the text and in Tables 7.2 and 7.3.

perhaps slighter than might have been expected. As compared to the conventional Scenario D assumptions, real public spending would rise by about 1.5 per cent faster to 1988/89 and over 3 per cent faster by 1993/94. This slows down the rate at which the programme expenditure/GDP ratio declines but by 1993/94 the ratio declines to 36.6 per cent assuming full wage comparability, as against the previous result of 35.5 per cent on the standard assumptions. Since the standard assumptions about public sector wage increases seem as low as is plausible, this would appear to be a good measure of the sensitivity of the results to wage comparability assumptions. Of course, if public sector wages rose more rapidly than those in the private sector the effect would be correspondingly greater.

EFFICIENCY AND PUBLIC SECTOR COSTS

The relative efficiency of the public sector has acquired a particular salience for the debate on public expenditure because of the arguments sometimes referred to as Hague's Law (Hague, 1980).

The key feature of this set of arguments concerns productivity levels in the public sector. As treated by national accounts statisticians, public services do not show any efficiency gains: their value in the national accounts is simply the cost of their inputs. This may be taken to represent either an assumption that there are no productivity gains in the public sector or an acceptance that such gains cannot be measured until we can measure input – output relationships in the public sector.

In practice it is an uneasy mixture of the two. Hague's arguments are based partly on this national accounts convention and partly on a view that even if there are some productivity gains in the public sector, these are likely to be less than the corresponding gains in the private sector. The argument then has three aspects.

First, Hague argues that to ensure pay comparability between public and private sectors when productivity is rising, or is measured as rising, only in the private sector implies higher rises in measured public sector unit costs. In principle, this type of relative price effect applies not simply to comparisons of public and private sectors, but to any comparison of sectors where productivity rises at different rates. In particular, it is often applicable to comparisons of the manufacturing and service sectors, since productivity typically rises more slowly in the latter. The fact that most social policies are of a service rather than a manufacturing character might lead one to expect lower productivity rises in them regardless of their public sector character.

The second feature of Hague's Law is what might be called output equality. This essentially argues that rising private affluence is likely to lead to pressure for matching public affluence, that is, for parallel output increases in both the public and private sectors. If there is no measured rise in public sector productivity, this implies shifting inputs from the private to the public sector in order to keep measured outputs in each sector rising in line with each other.

The third aspect of Hague's Law is output elasticity, which suggests that increased affluence leads to a relative increase in the demand for the output of services such as health and education which are predominantly publicly-provided and, therefore, generates cost, output and public expenditure increases even beyond those implied by the two previous aspects of the Law.

The three aspects of Hague's Law therefore relate to two phenomena:

1   The absence of measured productivity increases in the public sector; and
2   the argument that people may want more health and education services as they become more affluent.

The statistical and substantive parts of this argument need to be distinguished. If the problem exists only because of curious national accounts measurement conventions, then we may not be too concerned: even if public and private sector productivity increased at the same rates the arithmetical phenomenon of measured resources being transferred from the private to the public sector would still occur if people's perceptions and demands were guided only by the data appearing in the national accounts statistics. In so far as the problem is a statistical one, our answer obviously should be to seek to improve our statistical methods. This immediately, however, leads to substantive questions about the extent to which there are productivity rises in the public sector and how they can be measured.

In the absence of clear answers to these questions, we can still usefully consider the possible implications of alternative responses. If there are few or no productivity gains in the public sector, then the broad thrust of Hague's Law is correct. However, before considering any consequent policy recommendations we might wish to examine the extent to which there could be productivity gains in health and education provision even in private hands. It may be that the decision we would face would be to what extent are we prepared to see an increasing proportion of resources devoted to health and education (whether in the public or private sector) rather than the more common question as to what extent we are willing to see increasing amounts of resources going to state education and state health care provision.

Conversely, if Hague's Law is rejected on the basis of the argument that there are productivity gains in the public sector then the question arises of how and to what extent we take the achievement of such productivity gains into account in either our expenditure or policy planning. It is certainly the case that social policy analysis and planning has not normally devoted much attention to the implications of efficiency improvements for service provision or for expenditure needs. Do such improvements mean that we can release resources from one service area, either for service improvements elsewhere or for government to use in such other ways as it may wish? Hague's Law in other words is important for social policy: if it is correct it poses serious questions about how we can fund services at an adequate level of quality; if it is incorrect, then the output of public social services has been increasing even faster over recent years than the measured inputs, which have themselves increased faster than national income in general. If we believe efficiency gains to exist, then perhaps demographic pressures on the health and social services can be met not by increased funding but by increased efficiency.

Because of the importance of the relative efficiency argument to the economic and political debate about public expenditure and social policy, the analysis also investigates the implications for expenditure of assuming that specified levels of programme outputs can be attained because of efficiency improvements which yield a 1 per cent annual reduction in the cost of inputs (excluding social security transfers). This can also be interpreted as measuring the dimensions of the resources which would be released for other uses if public service productivity increased by 1 per cent annually. The effects are fairly large. Whilst real public expenditure increases by more than 5 and 10 per cent over the five and ten year periods respectively on the conventional assumptions, the addition of the efficiency gain assumption reduces the growth to 2 per cent and less than 4 per cent over the comparable periods. Similarly, it leads to the programme expenditures/GDP ratio dropping half as fast again as on the conventional assumptions, so that it is down to 33.3 per cent by 1993/94. This efficiency gain assumption therefore has twice as great an impact on the results as the change in the wage comparability assumption. The size of this impact reinforces the argument presented by Judge and Knapp that the efficiency issue deserves urgent attention in social policy analysis.

CONCLUSIONS AND IMPLICATIONS

This exercise has set out and examined a range of assumptions, broadly consistent with current policies, about the many dimensions of changes in particular components of public expenditure. When the consequent public expenditure aggregates are examined, it is clear that, provided economic growth is of the order of 1 per cent or more annually, there is no public expenditure crisis. At these levels of economic growth a restrictive budgetary stance, which none the less maintained the general standards of public services, ought to see programme expenditure growing at about the rate of GDP. At higher rates of economic growth (which seem more likely) a relaxation in the degree of budgetary restrictiveness is still compatible with a decline in programme expenditure relative to GDP. Unless the government seeks absolute cuts in the level of public expenditure, very sharp cuts in its relative share of GDP or is concerned that public revenues will or should grow more slowly than GDP, these data do not suggest any need for more radical policies to cut public spending.

Interpreted from a different perspective, the data suggest that within the likely range of economic growth levels there is scope for matching changes in social need and indeed for some increases in the real level of social policy expenditures, without increasing the overall share of programme expenditure within GDP. Obviously if that latter share is increased the scope for improvement is correspondingly greater.

Such extra resources might be allocated in the traditional way through annual arguments and decisions about small real increases in expenditure or service levels across a wide range of public programmes. However, we would argue that there is merit in maintaining, for planning purposes, a broad assumption that input levels into services will remain roughly constant, apart from increases to meet demographic pressures, during the next decade. One reason for this suggestion is that it would force the efficiency and productivity question more firmly onto the agenda: rather than being a grudging response to a harsh government, an attempt to ensure and utilize increased efficiency in the public sector should be a priority for anyone who wishes to see better provision for those who use social welfare services. There is another, and more important, reason for our suggestion, however, and it is one which ties in with the arguments about social policy making in Klein and O'Higgins' concluding chapter, and in particular their advocacy of purposeful opportunism as a policy-making approach.

An assumption of broad constancy in current input levels would create the scope for longer-term decisions identifying fewer but more significant areas in which the resources available for future development could be channelled – restraining ourselves on a broad front in order to be able to make a smaller number of more significant changes. It is not hard to think of areas where such major policy initiatives are desirable. The debate on the need for a major tax and social security reform package rumbles on, for example, with general agreement on the need for some type of reform but most proposals stymied by the apparently high costs of making the transition to a new system without inflicting large losses on some groups within the population.[2] The development of effective social policies with broad support might be much better served by financing such a package (including tax cuts as well as benefits improvements) than by a more conventional series of minor improvements across the range of programmes. Other examples are not hard to find. We might develop an effective programme (including both cash and service provisions) of education and training for 16- to 18-year-olds; we might in a particular year decide to increase funds for the NHS in such a way as to eliminate regional inequalities in funding – that would at least mean that each region could thereafter be treated in a similar fashion from year to year, as compared to the current situation where the over-resourced regions are having to pay for the sins of the past in a long series of debilitating erosions of their relative funding. We might even consider a broader programme to aim at dealing with inequalities in health, and so on.

The existing systems of social policy planning encourage the incremental development of the status quo whilst making it more difficult to effect significant policy transformations. Although our exercise suggests that the next decade will allow extra resources to be devoted to social expenditure, the extra is unlikely to be sufficient to allow *both* incremental improvements in most programmes and major developments in particular programme areas. The forces of incrementalism are inherently strong – what is needed therefore is a planning mechanism which considers short-term changes in the light of their contribution to long-term objectives.

NOTES

1   It should be emphasized that the ratio concept we are using is total programme expenditure as a percentage of GDP, not total public expenditure. This explains the ratio of 40 per cent in 1983/84 which is lower than the conventionally quoted figure.

2   For a review of recent contributions to this debate, see Jenkins, 1985.

8

Efficiency in the Production of Welfare: the Public and the Private Sectors Compared

KEN JUDGE and MARTIN KNAPP

INTRODUCTION

The persistent fiscal pressure facing modern welfare states places a considerable premium on the search for efficiency gains. One of the most urgent questions in domestic public policy debate is whether the organization and production of social services can be modified in ways which promote policy goals at lower costs. Perhaps the most common response to this problem is to advocate the wholesale privatization of public services. Minford, for example, makes no bones about it: 'The rule should be: *no* state production' (1984, p. vii).

The normative arguments in support of the claim that for-profit enterprises are more efficient than public agencies fall into four distinct categories: they are more economic, offer greater flexibility and consumer choice, provide more scope for innovation and specialization, and improve management and evaluation. However, such beliefs are frequently supported by ideology and colourful references to the alleged weaknesses of public services rather than by unambiguous evidence about the superior performance of private companies. Savas, for example, writes that the public sector

is very inefficient in delivering services, due to a host of factors,

We would like to thank Robin Darton and Jill Smith for their advice and assistance, and participants at the Bath conference for their comments on an earlier version of this chapter. The research reported here was supported by the Department of Health and Social Security general grant to the PSSRU. We alone bear responsibility for the contents of this chapter.

including absence of management skills, lack of motivation, political interference, patronage, rigid civil service systems, public employee unionism . . . lack of agreement on goals of government programs, the difficulty of measuring performance (particularly in many of the 'softer' services), and the monopoly structure . . . of many public services. (1977, p. 2)

These assertions have considerable popular appeal but too often they are based on over-simplistic distinctions between the 'public' and 'private' sectors which hide more than they reveal. What is needed is a clear and objective conceptual framework to evaluate the performance of different agencies in varying circumstances. In the first part of this chapter, therefore, we introduce a theory of the production of welfare which can be used for making these kinds of efficiency judgements. We then show how this theory can be used in empirical work to investigate inter-sectoral cost comparisons in one area of British social care. Given the results we obtain – which are consistent with similar results in the USA – the next section seeks to explain why, in certain circumstances, the private sector might be more efficient than public agencies in producing social services. A final section briefly considers some of the obstacles to the efficiency-improving innovations which we advocate.

The policy relevance of our conclusions should not, however, be misinterpreted. We certainly take the pluralist view that services can be produced and delivered in a variety of ways and that the most efficient mix should be chosen on the basis of evidence rather than rhetoric. But useful policy guidance has to acknowledge a wide range of considerations, and we believe a flexible approach to questions of public-private mix is highly desirable. For example, a radical reshaping of public sector production to embrace critical lessons learnt from the more efficient parts of the private sector might be just as conceivable a rational policy response as, say, contracting-out service delivery to non-statutory agencies. The context is crucial and so lessons for policy in one area may not be applicable to another. At the very least, though, our examples provide food for thought for those struggling to maximize the achievement of social policy goals.

CONCEPTUAL FRAMEWORK

In the social care sector, as in most areas of social policy, the 'public versus private' dichotomy is over-simplistic. There exists a multiplicity of production agencies and financial arrangements which together define a broad range of policy alternatives. Most care needs are recognized and tackled 'informally' by relatives and neighbours, whilst 'formal' care interventions can involve a number of different public agencies, voluntary (non-profit) organizations and private (for-profit) producers. Some of these social interventions will be financed collectively out of local and central taxation, others will be financed privately, either collectively (by co-operatives or charitable contributions) or personally. Once again, however, the majority of care interventions are 'informal' and will involve no financial exchange whatsoever. This variety of agents of production and sources of finance can be simplified with the help of Figure 8.1.

The resultant matrix of social care arrangements within the mixed economy raises a host of policy issues and associated research questions. In this chapter we focus on one set of policy issues fundamental to the development of the social care sector: starting from an assumption of public finance, what is the most efficient means of production? This

Figure 8.1   The mixed economy of social care

Finance	Production			
	Public	*Private*	*Voluntary*	*Informal*
Public	Social work	Private residential homes	Special residential accommodation for the handicapped	Public foster care
Private-collective		Co-operative residential homes	National Society for the Prevention of Cruelty to Children	
Private-personal	Charges for local authority services	Private domestic help	WRVS meals-on-wheels	Private foster care
No exchange				Neighbourhood and family mutual aid

Source: adapted from Judge (1982)

concentration on the issue of productive efficiency is not meant to imply the dominance of this criterion over all others, particularly allocative efficiency and distributive justice, nor to draw attention from the crucial policy issues thrown up by the alternative sources of finance. However, assumptions about the relative productive efficiencies of the public, voluntary and private sectors (and, in some cases, of the informal care sector) are crucial data in almost all decisions about the role and scope of government, and are the subject of a great deal of rhetoric but little evidence. It is our contention, therefore, that arguments about the public and private *production* of welfare should be resolved empirically and, in contrast to justifications for collective financing, largely removed from the realm of political theory and moral philosophy.

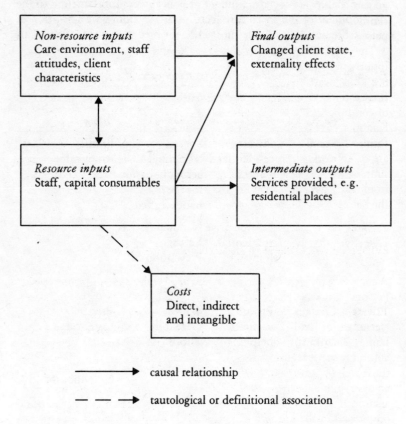

Figure 8.2   The production of welfare (from Knapp (1984))

To talk about productive efficiency is to make a statement about the relationship between inputs (or costs) and outputs. In a social care context it is both unhelpful and dangerous to attempt to define productive efficiency without regard for the objectives of services and the well-being of clients. Average cost differences between sectors tell us little of relevance for policy on their own, for such average cost figures merely measure identifiable expenditure averaged over a measure (of dubious relevance) of the number of clients served. They ignore, *inter alia*, the fact that social care services do not attempt merely to provide shelter and sustenance for clients but to enhance their levels of well-being. We thus need to have regard for *final outputs*. We must also be careful not to neglect the important influences of non-resource inputs – the influences on the production of final output which are generally neither tangible nor marketable. They include aspects of the caring environment, the attitudes of staff, the personalities and personal histories of clients, and so on.

The set of complex relationships between resources, non-resource inputs, outputs and costs we term *the production of welfare* (Figure 8.2). Briefly stated, the production of welfare approach argues that final and intermediate outputs are determined by the level and modes of combination of the resource and non-resource inputs (Davies and Knapp, 1981; Knapp, 1984). This perspective serves to emphasize that forms of organization and variations in the technology of production are of greater importance in the explanation of such differences than simplistic public versus private comparisons. This is clear, for example, from an earlier study of public and voluntary providers of day care for the elderly (Knapp and Missiakoulis, 1982).

EVIDENCE : RESIDENTIAL HOMES FOR THE ELDERLY

A survey of residential provision for the elderly was conducted by the Personal Social Services Research Unit (PSSRU) in a stratified sample of 12 local authority areas in England and Wales in the autumn of 1981 (see Darton, 1984). Information was collected *inter alia* about 456 homes and more than 14,000 residents in the public, private and voluntary sectors. Unfortunately, we were not able to collect data about the psychological well-being and quality of life of residents. In an analysis of inter-sectoral cost differences, therefore, we had to make the assumption that *in general* the private sector produces similar final outputs to local authority provision. Having visited many homes, we are confident that this is a reasonable assumption, but it should be borne in mind when interpreting our results. In fact, despite popular disquiet about private sector provision, those who have examined private old people's homes in detail have come to a similar conclusion. Table 8.1 reports the subjective assessments of homes produced by teams from the National Corporation for the Care of Old People (NCCOP) in 1964 – 65 and the PSSRU in 1982 – 83, whilst Table 8.2 shows registration officer's assessments of the standards of physical care and social environment in *all* private homes in a PSSRU sample of local authority areas in 1982.

TABLE 8.1   SUBJECTIVE ASSESSMENTS OF PRIVATE HOMES FOR THE ELDERLY

Assessment	NCCOP, 1964 – 65 (%)	PSSRU, 1982 – 83 (%)
Very good	22.2	23.5
Good	37.8	49.0
Average	31.1	21.6
Bad	8.9	5.9
Very bad	–	–
	(N = 45)	(N = 51)

Sources: NCCOP (1965); Judge (1984)

Theory suggests that there are many factors which explain intersectoral cost differences. Even when the final outputs of public and private homes are similar it is quite possible that the 'technology' employed in each sector is different. Different production functions, therefore, will mean different cost functions. However, it is worth emphasizing that in the private sector we have to estimate *charging* functions. In principle, these should be decomposed into two

TABLE 8.2   REGISTRATION OFFICERS' ASSESSMENTS OF PRIVATE HOMES FOR THE ELDERLY

Assessment (N = 201)	Quality of physical care (%)	Quality of Social Environment (%)
Good	64.2	56.7
Satisfactory	29.9	34.3
Poor	5.9	9.0

Source: Smith (1984)

elements: the cost of providing the service, and a 'mark-up' for profit. With the data at our disposal, this was not possible, and so for practical purposes the distinction is blurred.

The results are based upon two equations which predict private charges and public costs respectively. In each case, five broad groupings of factors (and interactions between them) were examined:

1 Characteristics of homes (size, occupancy level, distribution of beds on different floors, whether beds above the ground floor were accessible by lift, the proportions of single and shared bedrooms, whether the home was purpose-built, whether the home was organized around a group living design, and whether staff accommodation was provided);

2 characteristics of staff (proportions of staff with nursing and social work qualifications, whether or not additional volunteer staff were used, and whether there were any students working in the home);

3 non-residential services provided (whether day care was provided from within the home or in an associated day centre used by residents, whether there was sheltered housing sharing staff or facilities of the home, and whether meals were prepared for meals-on-wheels services);

4 characteristics of residents (dependency characteristics including mobility, incontinence, self-care capacity, confusion, behavioural problems and depression, admission and discharge rates, the proportion of short stay residents, and whether the home was used for clients of one or two sexes); and

5 characteristics of local areas (a general labour cost index, unemployment rate, female economic activity rate, population sparsity, indicators of the ease or difficulty of recruiting staff and census indicators reflecting the socio-economic characteristics of areas).

The 'best' charges function for private homes 'explained' 52 per cent of the observed variation in average charge per resident around a mean charge of £78.15 per week (Judge, Knapp and Smith, 1983). The estimated cost function for local authority homes 'explained' 76 per cent of the observed variation around the mean average cost per resident week of £83.46 (Darton and Knapp, 1984). The functions were fitted to data for 140 and 218 homes respectively. Differences between the two functions in the explanatory power and statistical significance of the hypothesized cost-raising factors confirm that the two sectors employ quite different technologies of care. By adding a capital component to predicted operating costs in the public sector – based on average capital costs in the survey areas – the average *total* cost per resident week in local authority homes becomes £91.81, which is 17 per cent higher than the average private sector charge of £78.15. After accounting for differences in resident characteristics (which were few anyway), home design, occupancy, area factors and so on, private home charges are clearly lower than local authority costs.

Comparisons of charges in private homes with local authority costs are fraught with difficulties. But given that the dependency of the residents in the two sectors is very similar, the apparent cost advantage in the private sector is striking. However, cost comparisons between sectors are complicated by two factors: the presence of different production technologies, which we now examine; and the possibility of differences in output which we are unable to examine with existing data.

Given the known sensitivity of costs and charges to the characteristics of residents, homes and areas, do these intersectoral differences merely reflect different care services or circumstances? If private homes *do* have a cost advantage, that is if good quality care for residents with a range of dependency characteristics could have been purchased more cheaply, then we would expect a particular pattern of cross-sector predictions. First, we would anticipate that actual charges in private homes would be lower than predicted costs in these same homes, using the local authority cost function to make the predictions. The reverse should be expected for local authority homes: predicted average charges in such homes should be lower than actual average total costs.

The results (presented in Table 8.3) are not as unambiguous as might at first be expected, although there is a simple explanation for this. The effect of imposing a 'foreign technology' in an unfavourable environment might be expected to inflate costs/charges. This proved to be the case. It is not surprising, therefore, that the cost advantage to the private sector should appear to fluctuate. Whereas the application of private technology to the public sector stabilizes costs, the opposite situation results in very inflated charges. However, even the most cautious interpretation of these results suggests that, after taking account of differences between sectors and differences in the circumstances in which care is provided, private homes were no more expensive than local authority homes. We believe the evidence suggests a stronger conclusion. This is buttressed by a closer examination of Table 8.3 where it can be seen that the ratio of costs to charges *increases* when each sector's technology is applied to the other.

TABLE 8.3   COMPARISONS OF THE APPLICATION OF DIFFERENT
TECHNOLOGIES OF CARE IN RESIDENTIAL HOMES FOR THE
ELDERLY TO PRIVATE CHARGES AND LOCAL AUTHORITY COSTS

Sector	Actual (£)	Cross-sector predictions (£)	Proportionate change (%)
Private charges	78.15	115.89	+ 48.3
Local authority costs	91.81	91.41	− 0.4
Cost Ratios of Public to Private Technology	1.175	1.268	

Source: Derived from Judge, Knapp and Smith (1983)

EXPLANATIONS OF COST DIFFERENCES

Although there are few data about the comparative efficiency of the
public and private sectors in the production of welfare, the evidence
presented above does suggest that private residential homes in England
and Wales are less costly and might represent better value for money
than their non-profit counterparts in the public and voluntary sectors.
The most recent review of intersectoral differences in American nursing
home costs argues forcefully for further research on the topic (O'Brien,
Saxberg and Smith, 1983), but there is a growing body of research
which suggests that proprietary homes are more efficient than non-
profits.

   For example, Birnbaum et al. (1981) report 'the results of 11 distinct
econometric cost analyses conducted by the authors on 20 sets of
nursing home data' (p. 1095). Having standardized for such factors as
the range of services offered, the characteristics of patients, scale of
occupancy rate, and where possible, data about quality of care, the 'cost
studies consistently found that facilities operated by non-profit
voluntary and governmental organizations have higher costs than for-
profit nursing homes, by at least several dollars per day' (p. 1097).
Koetting (1980) found that public and voluntary non-profit facilities
had daily operating costs which were on average 25 per cent greater
than those in the for-profit sector, and his fairly comprehensive cost
function could only explain a fraction of the difference. Leaving aside
such exogenous complexities as regulatory costs for more detailed
consideration below, how can these differences, common to both
Britain and America, be explained?

The most important of a wide range of factors which could account for cost differences are summarized in Figure 8.3 (Judge and Darton, 1985; Knapp, 1984, ch.10; Millward, 1982). There are those factors – such as home size and occupancy, the dependency characteristics of residents, input prices and resident throughput – which have been found to be associated with cost or charge variations *within* sectors and which could therefore account for variations *between* sectors. For example, we found a scale effect in the private sector: large homes have higher charges. This probably reflects a higher proportion of paid staff (the 'free' proprietorial input may be no smaller, but proportionately is less important) and the broader range of facilities offered in larger homes. This contrasts with the scale effect in the public sector: larger homes have lower costs. Private old people's homes tend to be smaller than their public counterparts and this scale difference, combined with

Figure 8.3   The sources of intersectoral cost differences in the production of welfare

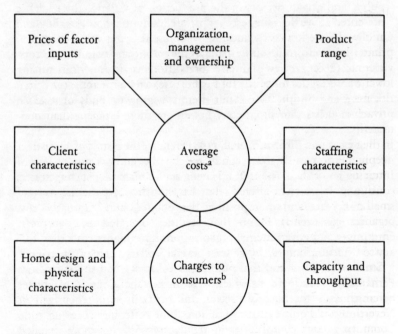

[a] Assumes standard treatment of VAT, overheads etc.
[b] Differences between charges and costs are due to subsidization, the use of volunteer staff and profit margins.

the observed effects on charges and cost, could in principle account for part of the intersectoral cost difference.

Second, there are differences in product range, in part associated with the dependency of residents and the physical characteristics of buildings, and in part reflected in the pursuit of different care objectives. Third, it has been argued that managerial efficiency is lower in the public than in the private sector, stemming from the monopoly position of public enterprises and from the pursuit of objectives other than profit maximization or cost minimization. The categories 'public' and 'private' are theoretically weak and imprecise, but differences in managerial style, type of ownership and motivational forces can reasonably be hypothesized to exert an influence on cost. Differences in the style of management and the nature of ownership, for example, are likely to translate into differences in proprietorial involvement, the returns on capital investment, the trade-off between long hours and the satisfaction gained from self-employment and the need to establish a market niche in a growing industry.

Management Incentives

On the basis of our continuing research, there appear to be five principal reasons to account for the British results: the traditional virtues of small business enterprise; low returns on capital investment; lower wage rates for employees; a less ultra-cautious approach to client risk management; and the lower proportion of single rooms in the private sector. However, the further we proceed with our analyses the more it appears that the single most important reason is the first one. In the vast majority of homes the proprietors live on the premises or are deeply involved in the running of the home in other ways. Interestingly, this is consistent with one of Koetting's (1980) main conclusions in which he emphasizes the greater productive efficiency of small owner-managed enterprises when compared with larger, 'chain' organizations. Indeed, it seems that the characteristics of small business enterprises, as distinct from the more generic 'private sector' hold the key to understanding the major differences in comparative efficiency.

Small businesses in modern economies are remarkably diverse. Perhaps the one safe thing to emphasize about them is their heterogeneity: there is no unambiguous definition of a 'small firm'. Nevertheless, inquiries by the Bolton (1971) and Wilson (1979) Committees have identified certain common characteristics. Small businesses, especially in the service industries, are relatively young; employ few people; place very little reliance on external loan finance; have little experience of unionization, although participation in employers' associations is more extensive; pay lower than average wages; and are closely controlled by their owners. These are precisely the characteristics which describe most private residential homes for the elderly.

More important than these general characteristics of small businesses, however, are the attitudes and motivations of the entrepreneurs who own and manage them. It is commonly suggested that such people are ruthless profit-maximizers, a breed apart. An entrepreneur, however, is simply the owner of a business enterprise, who combines investment with personal effort in pursuit of a return on the risk capital and labour involved. Unfortunately, the media emphasis on a small minority of businessmen perpetuates a false ideology of entrepreneurship which paints a distorted picture of the realities of business life. In fact, Scase and Goffee report that 'many proprietors are motivated by a wide range of social and non-economic factors of the sort that are often neglected in general discussions of entrepreneurial types' (1982, pp. 32-3).

Almost all studies of small businesses which are firmly based on empirical evidence emphasize that the desire for independence is the critical motivating factor. The Wilson Committee reported that the 'main advantages of being a small firm are felt to be the independence and freedom offered' (1979, p. 55), and the Bolton Committee claimed that the 'desire for independence appears to be over-riding and indeed may on occasions even operate against their own economic interest' (1971, p. 24). The personal satisfaction of working for oneself is probably the strongest motivation for establishing a small business, but there are other non-economic factors at work. There is the desire to be sufficiently closely involved with all aspects of a firm's operation to really appreciate what is being done. Regular personal contact with day to day problems provides its own source of satisfaction. Golby and Johns emphasized that the 'essential point seemed to be the feeling of mastery provided by being in personal control of an enterprise small enough to be supervised in detail' (1971, p. 7). The crucial point is that small businessmen expect a reasonable return for the risks they take with their capital investment and the efforts they put into their firms, but that as Scase and Goffee emphasize the typical entrepreneur is not solely motivated by a desire for profit maximization (1982, p. 161).

The result is that many small businesses represent excellent value for money and it should come as no surprise to discover that they are regularly more efficient than larger organizations in *both* the private and public sectors. Moreover, if we turn from these general statements to a particularly topical social policy example, we can illustrate the importance of entrepreneurial qualities in the rapidly growing private residential care industry. We have shown elsewhere the extent to which private residential homes for the elderly are quintessentially small business enterprises (Judge, 1984). Nevertheless, two particular characteristics are worth emphasizing and illustrating: the degree of proprietorial involvement in the running of homes; and the diversity of non-economic circumstances and motivations which prompted the owners to establish these businesses in the first place.

There were very few homes in our sample where the proprietors did not take some kind of active role in its operation: only five out of 153 respondent homes did not appear to have some level of proprietorial involvement. Table 8.4 illustrates the distribution of homes by categories of proprietorial involvement for both the main and the interviewed samples of homes.

TABLE 8.4   PROPRIETORIAL INVOLVEMENT IN PRIVATE RESIDENTIAL HOMES FOR THE ELDERLY

Types of proprietorial involvement	Main sample		Interviewed sample	
	Number of homes	Proportion of total	Number of homes	Proportion of total
No direct proprietorial involvement	6	4.2	1	2.0
Part-time involvement only	7	4.9	3	5.9
One full-time only	50	35.2	18	35.3
One full time *and* one part time	17	12.0	6	11.8
Two full time	55	38.7	20	39.2
Three or more full and/or part time	7	4.9	3	5.9
Total[a]	142	100.0	51	100.0

[a] Ten homes have been omitted because detailed information about proprietorial involvement is missing and another home has been excluded because despite its formal registration it is clearly a voluntary home.
Source: Judge (1984)

The extent to which these homes are traditional family enterprises in which husbands and wives share substantial responsibilities is clearly suggested by the fact that more than 50 per cent of homes have two proprietors, of whom at least one works full time. Such proprietors worked an average of 99 hours per week. Indeed most full-time proprietors report themselves as working very long hours – not far short of 70 per week in most cases. When we visited a sub-sample of homes we were able to confirm that they are predominantly family enterprises: 70 per cent of them are owned by two or more members of the same family. The second critical fact is that 90 per cent of the proprietors have an interest in only one home; the remainder control either two or three homes. Broadly speaking the homes in the sub-sample can be separated into four main categories:

1 *Husband and wife teams* (60 per cent) – which can be sub-divided into those where both partners work full time (36 per cent), and those where one of them (the wife in every case except one) works full time and the spouse provides some form of tangible support whether or not it is formally recorded as part-time employment (24 per cent).
2 *Women entrepreneurs* owning and managing the homes on their own (18 per cent).
3 More complex *partnerships*, often some form of two-generation family organization.
4 A *miscellaneous* category mainly consisting of 'absentee' or 'low profile' proprietors who rely to a considerable extent on 'managers'.

Another illustration of the importance of proprietorial involvement is the relatively limited reliance on employees. In our sample, the average number of non-proprietorial staff employed in private homes was 11.2. Only two very small homes in the sample managed without employing additional help. The seemingly high level of employment is not typical of small business in the service sector of the economy, but the phenomenon is explained by two factors. First, caring for long-term care groups such as the frail elderly is a highly labour-intensive activity. Second, many of the people employed in private homes work part-time; the average number of whole-time equivalent staff was only 6.1. As a result, in the largest group of homes in the sample, proprietors themselves provide 45 per cent of the total labour input.

At least as important as the degree of proprietorial involvement, however, are owners' attitudes and motivations. The reasons given by proprietors to account for their decision to acquire a private home are almost as numerous as the number of homes, but the evidence certainly supports the contention by Scase and Goffee (1982) that small business entrepreneurship is principally motivated by non-economic factors. An attempt has been made to summarize the primary motivations

TABLE 8.5   MOTIVATIONS OF PROPRIETORS

Reasons	Mentions by proprietor[a] (%)
Personal satisfaction	24
Close to retirement	9
Influence of friends or relatives	16
Chance/Opportunistic	18
Health or stress related	16
Business reasons	20
Female employment	11
Elderly relatives	7
Redundancy	4
Congenial employment	29

N = 45, but excludes 'inherited' homes.
[a] some proprietors cited more than one reason.
Source: Judge (1984)

expressed by proprietors, and this is shown in Table 8.5, but it is essential to emphasize both the idiosyncratic and multiple nature of the factors which influence the decision to become an entrepreneur. Nevertheless, certain characteristics of the ownership of homes do seem to be associated with particular motivations.

Women seem particularly motivated by the need for employment compatible with family responsibilities, by a desire for personal satisfaction and by the influence of friends and relatives. Full-time husband and wife teams are most closely associated with the search for congenial joint employment and personal satisfaction in pleasant surroundings. Part-time proprietors are motivated chiefly by purely business factors, and those owners with previous employment experience in private homes seem most likely to have responded to opportunistic chances. The evidence described in more detail by Judge (1984) strongly suggests that, in almost all cases, factors other than the search for substantial financial gain account for their business activities.

There are a number of reasons why private residential homes for the elderly might represent good value for money. These include the willingness of many proprietors to forego current market rates of return on their investment in favour of future capital gains, and an ability to recruit staff at or below market clearance wage rates in return for very flexible conditions of work. Overall, though, we believe that the very substantial degree of proprietorial commitment to their homes provides a critically important part of the explanation for the high degree of efficiency with which owner-managed residential homes seem to operate.

OBSTACLES TO GREATER PRODUCTIVE EFFICIENCY

Totally convincing proof of the greater productive efficiency of certain kinds of for-profit enterprise requires further research which includes the collection of substantial output data. It used to be suggested that output measurement was too imprecise, but this is no longer a convincing argument. Conceptual and empirical developments in the multi-dimensional measurement of well-being and health status, for example, facilitate the careful design of research instruments to collect data with which to model sophisticated simulations of the production of welfare (Challis and Davies, 1984; Rosser, 1983). In the meantime, therefore, our conclusions are inevitably provisional, although the central message is clear enough: the greater use of small business enterprises to *produce* social services would reap rich efficiency gains. But, if this is true, why do not public agencies contract-out more of their services?

One familiar set of explanations is centred on the intransigence of public sector unions and the use of industrial and political muscle to maintain their quasi-monopolies. It is not our intention to minimize the importance of such factors, but we believe they represent essentially transitional problems. We are also aware of, although we do not share, the view that there are moral objections to welfare for profit (see Gilbert, 1984; Watson, 1984). In contrast, we prefer to focus attention on a different reason for the failure to achieve optimum levels of efficiency in the mixed economy of welfare: the belief that the public production of social welfare is in itself a public good.

Public Goods and Regulatory Costs

Even if it is the case that for-profit enterprises are always and without exception more efficient in producing services and client well-being than public agencies, it does not necessarily follow that public production can be ruled out. There will be occasions when goals other than productive efficiency are paramount. Even Patrick Minford recognizes this and allows certain exceptions to his 'No State Production' rule:

on 'security' grounds, as with police, armed forces, judges and part of the civil service. Even though there would no doubt be gains in efficiency from having private companies offering policing to the state as consumer, and tendering for the 'police contract' for an area such as Merseyside for, say, five years, it is obvious enough that the public prefer to trade any such gains in efficiency for the sake of political security and control. Suppose, for example, that the private security company's employees broke the law or took bribes; who would police them? The public prefer instead that carefully selected representatives be given the task of building up a force with standards of public morality and service especially inculcated. What I am saying here is that public production of these goods is itself a 'public good' - i.e. the public security cannot by itself be provided privately (1984, p. vii).

The problem facing Minford is that he breaches his own defences by deploying such an argument; he cannot logically deny the possibility that the public production of other services displays such public good characteristics. In fact, this very argument is employed by many who favour the total nationalization of the production of education and health services. In our view there are very few social services which display public good characteristics similar in degree to internal and external security services, and perhaps this explains why in almost every sphere of social welfare some kind of private enterprise can be found. But there is a more cunning variant of the public good argument. This perspective posits and advances the case for asymmetric distrust of the different sectors stemming in part from a belief that the traditions of public administration ensure quality control in the public sector, and which is further fuelled by the disproportionate publicity given to any examples of reprehensible behaviour in the private sector. This is then used as evidence to support the revealed preferences of many risk-averse customers for publicly provided services, and the more extensive regulation of the private than the public sector. Once these differential regulatory costs are incurred they will partly or wholly offset any productivity gains in the private sector. However, such an argument neglects two important considerations.

First, the system of quality control by government agencies is itself costly, although this cost is rarely taken into account in making intersectoral comparisons. It was not, for example, included in our own comparisons of public and private old people's homes. By definition, the small business model of the private home has no direct equivalent to these local authority overheads, except that it contributes to them in a small way through the registration procedure. Pursuing consistency between the sectors may well tip the balance back in favour of private productive efficiency.

Second, and more important, the case for regulating the private sector is mirrored in the public sector. Those who are most enthusiastic about the desirability of *public* social services should examine their actual performance more closely. We must emphasize that we are not sanguine about and do not wish to deny the existence of examples of bad practice in the private social care sector, but it would be naïve and foolish to presume that significant changes in care practices cannot be achieved within the public sector. It is quite clear from studies of local authority old people's homes that marked improvements in the production of intermediate and final outputs could be realized without an increase in the resources employed (Darton and Knapp, 1984; Willcocks et al., 1982). For example, anyone who is complacent about the standards of care in such homes should read the highly critical report prepared by the Social Work Service of the DHSS about public residential provision for the elderly in London in the late 1970s (DHSS, 1979). The record of the public sector is no better in other areas. Bebbington and Davies (1983) found marked 'target inefficiencies' in the allocation of home help services, and inspections of boarding-out practice by the Social Work Service led them to conclude that

> there is no room for complacency; almost every aspect of practice is criticised. Visits to children who were boarded-out were either delayed or missed, statutory requirements for medical examinations were neglected, schooling did not feature as important and reports and reviews were not made as they should have been. There was widespread disregard of the Boarding-Out of Children Regulations which prescribe minimum standards of practice that must be adhered to in the selection of foster parents, the placement and visiting of children, the reviewing of their situation and the writing of reports. . . . [These Regulations] prescribe only minimum standards of safeguard for a vulnerable group of children, but even these minimum requirements were neglected and, in some places, seemed unknown. (DHSS, 1981a, p. 25)

In our opinion there is an urgent need for tightening the regulation of *all* sectors, and there is no rational basis for asymmetric distrust based on the actual practices of the different sectors.

CONCLUSION

One of the main aims of this chapter has been to suggest that there is more rhetoric than evidence available about the comparative efficiency of the public and the private sectors in the production of welfare. As in so many other areas, there is a considerable need for further empirical research. But new investigations must improve on their precursors by collecting final output data and ought to be guided by production of welfare theory.

Notwithstanding the above remarks, there is some evidence to suggest that private enterprises can be more efficient than public organizations, but simplistic references to the profit motive are insufficient to account for this. A review of the performance and characteristics of small owner-managed enterprises suggests that various behavioural and organizational factors are critically important in promoting greater efficiency. We conclude therefore that small businesses are often more efficient than larger organizations in the private, public and voluntary sectors.

This message should not be misinterpreted. We emphatically do not mean to suggest that all service delivery agencies in the public domain – be they district general hospitals or large secondary schools – should be handed over to small businessmen. It is quite possible that in many instances public services could be produced more efficiently if they were contracted out to small private enterprises, but it is equally likely that in other instances this will be impractical. The crucial point, whether or not privatization is possible or desirable, is that all agencies which assume responsibility for the production of welfare should adopt as far as possible what appear to be the critical efficiency-generating characteristics of small owner-managed enterprises. These include substantially decentralized managerial responsibility for the deployment of resources, combined with comprehensive cost-consciousness through shadow pricing where necessary and the use of appropriate incentive reimbursement mechanisms. It is beyond the scope of this chapter to explore such possibilities, but they clearly exist. They can be applied in the public sector as well as anywhere else, as experiments with health maintenance organizations, clinician budgeting and community care programmes for the frail elderly have shown.

9

Why Are We Waiting?
the Problem of Unresponsiveness in
the Public Social Services

ALBERT WEALE

INTRODUCTION

The modern welfare agency is, of necessity, a large-scale, bureaucratic organization. Such organizations are often, from the point of view of those who have to depend upon their services, slow, cumbersome and high-handed. They suffer, as it is sometimes put, from bureaucratic unresponsiveness. How serious is this charge when considering the future of welfare services?

This chapter approaches the question with three objectives:

1 to clarify the nature of the problem that is captured in the buzzwords 'bureaucratic unresponsiveness';
2 to discuss the extent of this problem in modern welfare services; and
3 to speculate on whether there are developments within those services that could reduce the problem.

To anticipate my conclusion, there is naught for our comfort in available solutions to the problem. Indeed it will be one of my themes that attempts to solve the problem of bureaucratic unresponsiveness in some respects will make it worse in others. Even if we can agree on what

I should like to thank Lyn Harrison, Rudolf Klein and Stein Ringen for written comments on an earlier version of this chapter, and participants in the discussion at the Bath conference. I am grateful to Norma Chin and Sal Cuthbert for secretarial services. This chapter was completed while I was a Visiting Fellow at the Social Justice Project, Australian National University, and I should like to acknowledge the Project's support.

the problem is, there are no obvious and easy solutions to the difficulties it presents, only a series of piecemeal measures that might have some effect.

THE PROBLEM DEFINED

What do we mean when we say that the public services are unresponsive? To answer this question we need to do a little logic-chopping. In the most general case, A responds to B if some action of A appropriately matches some condition of B, and if a change in the condition of B would induce an appropriate change in the actions of A. For example, a politician might respond to the concern of her constituents about video nasties by proposing legislation, asking for a government inquiry or putting down a parliamentary question. I leave aside the complicated questions involved in determining how a response might be appropriate to note simply that responsiveness requires some matching of A's actions to B's condition. Lack of responsiveness would therefore involve a failure on the part of A to match his or her actions to B's condition. Whenever lack of responsiveness is alleged, it is always sensible – though it may sometimes be tedious or otiose – to ask: who is being unresponsive to whom in respect of what? On occasions, as we shall see, the answer to this question is not always straightforward.

It follows from this analysis that responsiveness is not always a desirable feature of a system. This can be easily seen by noting that one sort of responsiveness can conflict with another sort of responsiveness. For example, if policy-makers are responsive to tax payers they may be unresponsive to social service clients. If teachers are responsive to parents they may be unresponsive to children. And if doctors respond to medical needs, they may not respond to expressed patient wants. It further follows that before we judge how best to remedy the problem of unresponsiveness, we must first judge whether the successful application of the remedy will not create a more serious problem elsewhere.

In what follows, I shall consider three specific versions of the charge that the public services are unresponsive. Each of these three versions correspond to some view about the objects to which the public services should be responsive. The three charges are:

1   Public services are unresponsive to the preferences of their consumers.

2   Public services are unresponsive to the needs of their consumers.
3   Public services are unresponsive to the preferences of citizens.

In discussing these claims I shall be more than a little vague about what is intended by the term 'public services'. I shall assume that the relevant public services in the welfare state have the following characteristics: there is no price mechanism linking the supplier of the service to the consumer; there is no profit motive on the part of suppliers; the financing of the services comes in the main from tax revenues; allocation to consumers is made by public officials or professionals within the public services; the overall development of the services is decided either by elected politicians or by high-level civil servants. In discussing such features in a general way I am, of course, doing great violence to some important distinctions, for example the differences between allocation by public officials and allocation by professionals. My plea in mitigation is that public discussion of the future of the welfare state, say over issues of privatization, often concerns itself with the question of how far the whole set of characteristics that define the public welfare services should be allowed to continue in their present form. I hope, by taking a broad view of the nature of the public services, to bring together the various reasons that people have held for thinking that they are unresponsive.

PUBLIC SERVICES AND CONSUMER PREFERENCES

One version of the charge that public services are unresponsive to the preferences of their consumers can be so framed that it is true almost by definition. According to this argument the public services cannot achieve allocative efficiency in the use of their resources because lacking information about the relative strengths of consumers' preferences, they have no rational basis on which they can make an allocation satisfying competing consumer wants. Allocative efficiency in this context has a precise meaning: it is the principle that resources are efficiently deployed when there is no feasible reorganization of their use such that some consumers can be made better off without making others worse off.[1] The origin of the present problem, it is alleged, stems from the absence in the public services of the price mechanism which in market-provided services both signals to producers the uses to which resources should be put and provides an incentive to them to make the appropriate switch of resources. Remove the price mechanism and, it is claimed, public services cannot be responsive to the preferences of their consumers.

Consider a well-known example. At any one time there are a large number of middle-aged men who are waiting in queues for hernia operations in the NHS (Klein, 1983, p. 155). They are waiting in this way because of a series of policy and professional decisions in the service to give low priority to non-urgent surgery. The evidence from what we know of those who use private practice is that a number of people in this situation are willing to pay for a private service. The absence of a price mechanism within the NHS means that patients in NHS queues have no way of signalling to providers the strength of their preference, and of course the taxation levied on them to pay for the NHS means that patients on average have less ability to enter the private market. The system of allocating health care resources is clearly unresponsive to these people. And, if we may be allowed to generalize, the relatively low proportion of national income that we spend on health care in the United Kingdom – a matter of some collective patting on the back by the Royal Commission on the National Health Service (1979, p. 22) – might be interpreted by others as a criticism. Consider how much more people would spend, it might be argued, if they could register their preferences by a more extensive use of the price mechanism. Similar points can be made about the educational service and also about National Insurance benefits. In each case the absence of a price mechanism means that the service provided does not reflect the preferences of consumers,

What merit is there in this criticism? The fundamental question this criticism raises is how far the public services should be responsive solely to the preferences of their consumers. The services with which we are concerned are not pure public goods in the technical sense; they do not provide indivisible benefits to a body of consumers all of whom must have the benefit if any do. Instead the benefits are quite divisible and exclusive: an operation is performed on one individual and not another. With pure public goods there is an argument for state supply purely in terms of giving people what they want, but when we come to services like health and education we may wish to ignore wants that would be expressed in an open market

1 because we are worried by the distribution of the resources required to satisfy them;
2 because we believe that consumers are not the best judges of their own welfare in complex areas of medical, educational or insurance practice; or
3 because we wish to preserve a plural value system in our society and are worried by the prospect of everything being reduced to a common money measure.

If taking the service out of the market stems from an attempt to act on any of these motives, then it would seem inconsistent to complain that the public services do not reflect preferences, since part of the point of allocating them outside of the normal price mechanism is to restrict the extent of consumer sovereignty.

The upshot of this argument is that it is difficult to make much of the point that the public services should respond to preferences in order to increase allocative efficiency. However, there is another sense of efficiency that is more deeply embedded in popular sentiment, and more relevant to the present case. This is the sense of efficiency in which we say that an organization is efficient if it performs to standards that a reasonable and qualified person would expect of such an agency. Organizations are inefficient, in this sense, if they fail to answer letters in reasonable time, make inconsistent or wrong decisions on claims, provide services below an adequate professional standard and consistently refuse or are unable to rectify a wrong. Organizational inefficiencies of this sort (which Leibenstein (1966) termed X-inefficiency) probably constitute the plain person's understanding of inefficiency in the public services, and do provide a legitimate ground for complaint if they involve lack of responsiveness to consumer preferences. We may wish to restrain peoples' willingness to pay for certain services from a concern with social welfare, but it would be difficult to argue for the positive benefits of high-handedness and incompetence.

There is no obvious source from which we might obtain a reliable estimate of the extent to which these inefficiencies are perceived to exist within the public services. Such sources as the Parliamentary Commissioner reports (e.g. 1979) would suggest that the usual causes of grievance are delay and incompetence. Public services can either take a long time in coming to a decision or adopting a course of action, or when they do act they sometimes persist in the wrong course of action despite the clear existence of reasons why they should not. These complaints can be fairly general across the public services, and apply as much to a nurse who fails to provide adequate care, as to a social security office which wrongly refuses somebody benefit.

Clearly the complaints that are dealt with by official bodies like the Parliamentary Commissioner are only the tip of the iceberg, although there is some evidence to suggest that the volume of the submerged portion may be rather small. Consumer surveys of the NHS have for a long time shown a high level of satisfaction with the services that patients receive. Swedish evidence covering the period 1968 to 1981 shows that only small proportions of the population feel that they have been treated wrongly or unfairly by public agencies ranging from child care services to social insurance. In most cases the proportion of people saying that they had been badly treated was less than 5 per cent, and the only agency to show a higher rate than this was, perhaps not surprisingly, in the area of property taxation.[2] Of course, one could argue that consumers *ought* to be more dissatisfied, but that is a quite separate matter from saying that welfare agencies are unresponsive to problems and complaints as things stand at present.

The problem of inefficiencies within the public service is only a special case of inefficiencies within all those organizations which supply services. It can always be argued that consumers of the services of private organizations have an alternative more readily open to them than consumers of public services, for unless the private organization is a monopoly the consumers can always switch their purchasing power to another private organization. However, as Hirschman (1970) has pointed out, the extent to which the power to exit provides a signal and incentive to private organizations within a market to be more responsive to consumer preferences is strictly limited. When consumers switch their purchases this may be interpreted by a private firm as a signal that the quality of their product is falling. Equally it may be taken to mean that there is a change in relative prices in the economy or that some new consumer product has been introduced. Anyone observing the phenomenon of consumers switching their purchases has considerable difficulty in identifying from that fact alone what has motivated the switch. (Analogously, the sharp rise in private medical insurance during the early 1980s cannot easily be interpreted as consumer response to a decline in the quality of the NHS; nor can the increase in private education be attributed simply to the spread of comprehensive schools.) The problems of identifying the motives of behaviour bedevil attempts to judge how responsive suppliers are to changes in choice by consumers.

There is little evidence about how responsive private firms are to the voiced complaints of citizens, although clearly this is the sort of information we should need in order to make a fair appraisal of the public sector. However, such evidence as there is does not support the claim that private organizations are more responsive to complaints that public sector bodies. Indeed, in a reported study by the National Consumer Council, the conclusion was that private firms showed 'appalling' indifference, rudeness and ignorance when consumers complained about faulty goods.[3] There is little comfort in this for the view that market discipline makes private organizations more responsive to consumers.

What conclusions can we draw about the responsiveness of the public services to consumer preferences? I should like to suggest that where there is a problem of lack of responsiveness this more often takes the form of X-inefficiency rather than allocative inefficiency. More importantly, however, we have no way of knowing how far this form of inefficiency is a special problem for the public services rather than for large scale organizations, including private firms, operating in a modern economy.

PUBLIC SERVICES AND CONSUMER NEEDS

Much of the criticism levelled against the welfare state stems from the fact that public service institutions have not been as successful in meeting needs as was originally hoped. Ignorance, disease, squalor and want may not be quite riding across the land like the Four Horsemen of the Apocalypse, but there is sufficient evidence of the failure of the welfare state to eliminate deprivation to be worrying. How far is this due to the fact that the public services are not adequately responsive to the needs of consumers?

Again, we may begin with one of the characteristic features of the public services, but this time consider the implications of their being tax-financed. Bureaucrats and professionals have leeway in such a system to pursue their own preferences rather than the needs of their clients. There is no reason to be cynical in holding this view. The claim is not that civil servants are more interested in increasing their own empires at the expense of those who use their services. It is simply that any professional ethos is bound to encourage the development of certain attitudes and practices which run contrary to the needs of consumers. Let me pick out three features of a professional ethos that can lead to this result: professionals will prefer the interesting to the mundane; they will prefer the prestigious to the ordinary; and they will prefer the fashionable to the unfashionable.

A preference for the interesting is well documented in several areas of the welfare services. Thus, social workers have been shown to prefer dealing with families with children rather than the elderly, and the NHS still finds it more difficult to recruit to the geriatric and mental health services than other branches.[4] The preference of the prestigious is shown in pressure for CAT scanners, in the teeth of much scepticism from those who have looked at costs and benefits, or in the attention given to open heart surgery. Occupational and preventive health care, which probably hold out more prospect for an improvement in the health status of modern populations, are correspondingly ignored by professionals. Examples of fashion include the introduction of the Initial Teaching Alphabet without serious appraisal beforehand, the craze for tonsillectomies that swept through children's wards in the 1950s and the post-Robbins expansion of higher education followed by a contemporary fashion for its contraction.

What these examples show is that the supply of services through bureaucratic and professional decision-makers will not always lead to an appropriate response to the *needs* of consumers. There is, however, another aspect of needs that the public services may be in danger of ignoring, and this is what I shall call the need for self-respect. Courtesy and consideration in service should figure prominently in the objectives of public bureaucracies. In this regard there are some examples of good departmental practice – I have in mind for example the work the DHSS has done on redesigning its claim forms – but the point of Sir Ernest Gowers, that communication as with equals is an essential element in a modern bureaucracy, should not be forgotten.

In appraising the lack of responsiveness of the public services to the needs of consumers, the crucial question to ask is how far the problem springs from the intrinsic features of public bureaucracies or how far it is a more widespread difficulty. Clearly some of the problems are not unique to public services. Cost escalation is a well-known and serious problem in US medical care, so there is some evidence at least that professional groups within private organizations will distort the allocation of resources away from the needs of consumers. The problem arises because professional and bureaucratic access to information and expertise means that they must necessarily be given discretion within an organization: organization means discretion as well as oligarchy. Moreover, it should be clear that the restriction of discretion cannot be accomplished by laying down rules and guidelines for public servants to follow. The 1980 reforms in supplementary benefit attempted a wholesale restriction on the discretion of public officials, but evidence on the effects of this reform suggests that from the viewpoint of the client there has effectively been no change. To restrict discretion requires the knowledgeable participation of clients, but professionals and officials have the position they do because no one is thought to be in a better position than they are to make a judgement of need.

PUBLIC SERVICES AND CITIZEN PREFERENCES

At first sight the charge that public services are unresponsive to the preferences of citizens may appear strange. As Peter Taylor-Gooby has shown in chapter 5, the public welfare services enjoy by and large a high degree of popularity. It would appear that the evolution of the welfare state has broadly followed the contours of popular sentiment. And yet on closer inspection the picture is not as clear as this suggests.

First, although the public services in general enjoy a high level of public esteem, there are variations within this pattern, as Taylor-Gooby has shown. Unemployment benefit or child benefits are less popular, for example, than retirement benefits. Second, the increasing restrictions placed upon local government mean that the opportunities for the expression of local citizen preferences are correspondingly limited. Third, despite the moves towards increased public participation in the planning of services, the trend is to create forms of participation that are consultative rather than authoritative: there has been no reversal of the policy which replaced directly elected Poor Law Guardians by centrally appointed public officials (Hadley and Hatch, 1981, p. 12).

The mechanism by which citizen preferences are expressed in an authoritative way is essentially the general election and the associated processes of party competition. As a device for reflecting citizen preferences on public services, party competition suffers from two defects. The first, and most obvious, is that political parties do not offer discrete policies to the electorate on different items of policy; instead they offer policy packages in which the elector is forced to choose between packages each of which has to be taken as a whole. Welfare issues have had a high degree of salience among electors since the war, but it cannot be said that in choosing a party of government the electorate has delivered a judgement on any particular policy item. Only politicians short of arguments at the despatch box suppose they have a mandate for the policies they introduce.

The second problem with elections in determining citizen preferences is that the process of party competition not only reflects preferences, it also shapes them (compare Klein, 1974, pp. 406 – 7). In bidding for votes politicians have an incentive to persuade the electorate that more rather than less is possible in the public services. Election manifestos provide a guide to the form which this competitive bidding takes. Suppose we look at election manifestos since 1974 – the first year of the end of economic growth as it was experienced in the

1950s and 1960s. The general pattern is for all parties to promise to improve retirement incomes, help first-time home buyers, improve nursery school facilities and increase the incomes of the disabled. There is rarely any prominent mention of the tax changes that would be consequent upon these improvements and no mention at all of the tax expenditures that many of them involve.

I do not want to over-emphasize the role of election manifestos. (I once heard Richard Crossman remark that in his constituency the Labour manifesto was usually delivered the day after the election, and that the only people who read it were newly appointed Cabinet ministers who wanted to find out what they were supposed to do.) Yet they are a reasonable proxy for the whole range of signals that parties give out at the time of an election, and in support of this claim I shall note that the content analysis of election manifestos during the twentieth century provides a good account of the underlying dimensions of political conflict (Robertson, 1976). If we can take manifestos as proxy evidence in this sense, it is clear that the process of party competition does not present the electorate with an accurate perception of the policy choices that have to be made in providing public services. Priorities in policy are not presented with an account of the options that must be forgone if they are to be achieved. Any bias within the system must be in the direction of inflating expectations about the quality and nature of public services.

The electoral process within the UK does not therefore satisfy one of the main and obvious conditions for any public choice mechanism properly to respond to citizen preferences, namely that it provide a clear statement of the social alternatives that confront a society. Responsiveness to citizen preferences will be low. The congruence of attitudes and policy provision that we find in the welfare state can be interpreted, I conjecture, not as a process by which policy makers respond to citizen preferences, but more as a process by which citizen preferences are shaped by policy makers. (The exception to this generalization occurs with special interest groups, promoting the preferences of a particular set of people in society. The role of these special interests probably accounts both for the tendency of political parties to make election promises to particular groups and for much redistribution of the welfare state to take place in particularized form, e.g. special arrangements for house-purchasers, rather than in the generalized form of cash. Such particularized redistribution has, of course, perverse effects from the egalitarian viewpoint, as Le Grand (1982) has shown.)

WHAT IS TO BE DONE?

It should be clear from the foregoing account that we cannot eliminate some forms of unresponsiveness without creating others. If we make policy makers more responsive to the preferences of citizens at large, we shall make them less responsive to the preferences of special interest groups. If we make services more responsive to the needs of citizens, we shall make them less responsive to the demands of professionals. And if we make public services more responsive to consumer preferences, we may make them less responsive to the needs of consumers. Consequently we cannot examine remedies for lack of responsiveness without making some sort of value judgement about the sort of responsiveness that should be promoted.

In making this judgement I should like to propose two principles that should guide our thinking. Neither, I hope, is particularly heavy in the demands it makes on our consciences, and I am far from thinking that separately or in combination they are comprehensive. However, they can guide our understanding when searching for developments that should be encouraged. The two principles are:

1   Where consumer preferences do not conflict with consumer needs, then public services should be responsive to preferences.
2   Public services should be responsive to the preferences of citizens when this does not conflict with the needs of consumers.

The sort of responsiveness that would fall under the first principle includes the following: responding to a preference for home over hospital deliveries of babies; providing for flexible visiting hours for those in hospital; and respecting local authority tenants' wishes about house decorations. The sort of responsiveness that would fall under the second principle includes: adapting the school curriculum in response to the public concern over literacy and numeracy or adapting income support so that it is more finely adjusted to need.

Although these principles are rather mild, they do nevertheless carry some force. For example, it might well be argued that meeting the demand for home deliveries is not costless. Valuable resources are taken away from maternity hospitals when used in domiciliary care, and this may stretch services for high-risk needy groups. However, to say this is to say no more than that the principles in question have weight and force when taken on their own. There is no point in even discussing a principle that is so weak it never conflicts with other desirable goals.

What devices are open to us to promote responsiveness consistent with these two principles? There are four that I shall consider: an increase in democratic control; more extensive use of the price mechanism; the development of organizational incentives within the public services; and promotion of advocacy and counter-bureaucratic services. I take each in turn.

Democratic Control

There is a long tradition of social thought, most vigorously expressed by the guild socialists (Cole, 1920), that democratic control would counter the alienating effects of large-scale public bureaucracies. This concern has been variously expressed in relation to the public services, including proposals to involve the general population in land-use planning, the debates about democratic control at the time of NHS reorganization, and the Taylor report on school governing bodies. What might we expect of democratic control as a method to encourage responsiveness?

The first and most obvious point is that the effects of democratic control will depend on how the relevant constituencies from which democratic representatives are to come are constructed. It is simply silly to advocate an increase in producer and consumer control of the public services without specifying the relative proportions of the two groups. The second point is that there is every reason to expect democratically elected representatives not to reflect the characteristics of their constituencies. The persistent findings of studies on participatory bodies are that the elected are disproportionately male, middle class and middle aged – and white where this is relevant. This does not mean that the socially unrepresentative necessarily do worse as political representatives than the socially representative, but it does caution against being sanguine. Finally, attempts to develop maximum feasible participation typically run into the problem that there is no obvious way of identifying which of the competing organizations that purport to represent minority or disadvantaged groups actually do so. The experience of health systems agencies in the United States highlights this last difficulty in particular.[5]

Participation is a time-intensive activity. ('The trouble with socialism' said Oscar Wilde, 'is that it takes too many evenings.') Although participation is more prevalent among the higher-income and better-educated groups, we would not necessarily expect a secular effect in the form of higher general levels of education and income leading to an increased desire for participation in the population at large. Indeed if Hirsch (1977) is right about patterns of modern consumption, namely that they are biased against the time-intensive, then we should expect democratic participation to be a less attractive proposition. Certainly empirical evidence of popular participation in the US is that it is higher in relation to specific neighbourhood services than more general controlling bodies (Yates, 1973).

The above are, in a sense, contingent features of democratic participation. We could imagine a world, not so *very* different from our own, in which the young, the working class and the female participated more. However, there are some intrinsic features of democratic decision-making which make it an unsatisfactory instrument for increasing the responsiveness of the public services. Put oversimply, the problem is that as soon as a democratic body has to vote on a reasonably large number of alternatives, it is more than probable that no one alternative will command majority support. The result is more likely to be determined by those who set the agenda for the voting body than by any underlying consensus. When there is always a silent majority that loses the vote, the prospects for increasing responsiveness look bleak (see Riker, 1982, pp. 181 – 95).

Greater Use of the Price Mechanism

For reasons that I have already discussed, I doubt whether a general solution to the problem of responsiveness to consumer preferences will follow from greater use of the price mechanism in the supply of services. If the characteristic inefficiencies of the public sector do not stem from a misallocation of resources, but from a more pervasive failure to take up organizational slack, then there is no reason to believe that private suppliers will overcome this problem more easily than public suppliers. After all, Leibenstein's original examples of inefficiency typically come from the private manufacturing sector (1966). Moreover, the difficulty in maintaining the principle of consumer sovereignty in some of these areas means that regulation of suppliers will probably limit their responsiveness.

However, this does not necessarily mean that the price mechanism cannot be used more extensively in some areas of the public services, in particular by giving private suppliers the right to tender for the supply of certain inputs or throughputs. For example, there is no reason in principle why pharmacies in hospitals should be integrated into the public service; they might as easily and more efficiently be run by private suppliers, as they are in Sweden.[6] It could even be a goal of policy, in these cases, to build in a bias towards private firms that are run co-operatively rather than along traditional capitalist lines. Perhaps one respect in which social policy can contribute to the economy is to provide incentives for changing its antiquated organizational structure. But this is clearly a matter that would have to be judged case by case.

The Development of Organizational Incentives

I can do no more than sketch the nature of developments here. The essential problem is how to devise a scheme of incentives that breaks down the indolence that comes with professional discretionary power. Various possibilities are available in this context, ranging from more extensive and regular peer review, through greater budgetary accountability to the introduction of performance-related standards. There are several general points to be made in connection with these and similar proposals. A useful precondition for improving responsiveness is to appreciate the distinction, which Judge and Knapp emphasize, between the public financing of a service and the public provision of a service. Thus long-term residential care for the elderly or mentally ill can be financed publicly, although it may not be provided entirely by public agencies. As Judge and Knapp make clear, we can learn much about the performance of public provision by comparing it with private provision under similar financial conditions. However, a particular problem with performance assessment is that it can bias the way in which the professional task is carried out. If teachers' examination performance is monitored, then teachers will devote more of their attention to teaching those things that will make pupils more successful in examinations, possibly to the detriment of other desirable aspects of teaching. Finally, in so far as these devices promote better professional performance, they are likely to reinforce the more paternalistic aspects of welfare provision, making professionals more responsive to the preferences of citizens and to the needs, rather than the preferences, of clients.

The Development of Counter-Bureaucratic Services

One major problem with responsiveness in the public sector stems from the complexity of the issues with which bureaucrats deal. Quite often officials do not know the rules they are supposed to be applying, so it is hardly surprising that clients feel at a loss. It is unrealistic to expect individuals to be able to learn complex rules and procedures related to the particular difficulties they are having with bureaucracies. It is therefore worth seeing how far one could encourage developments in specialist and professional services that would counteract the expertise of bureaucrats.

The original intention of Beveridge was that there should be citizens' advice centres in social security offices to help individuals cope with the complexities of the modern state. What has grown up instead is an uncoordinated set of advice and welfare rights centres run by local authorities, CABs and welfare rights groups. My impression (again casual empiricism, I'm afraid; it would be nice to have a study which brought the material together) is that the ratio of service to overheads in these organizations is extremely favourable to clients. A particular feature of these organizations is that they are often able to call on the services of committed young professionals whose short-run income expectations are not high. It would be possible to foster such developments, for example, by not requiring persons who work voluntarily in these organizations to register for work while drawing supplementary benefit. Alternatively a change in the earnings disregard rules would provide an incentive for younger people to enter this field.

On the demand side there is some merit in the suggestion of Sir Idwal Pugh that fees for professional services required to sort out complex bureaucratic problems should be allowable against tax (Parliamentary Commissioner, 1979, p. 13) – and perhaps be charged to the relevant bureaucracy in government internal accounting. For example, individuals often have to use the services of a professional accountant to sort out tax difficulties, but the Inland Revenue is conventionally unwilling to grant tax concessions to individuals in this situation. There is no reason to expect that the demand for professional services would increase dramatically as a result of this measure, but it might help to tilt the balance somewhat the other way.

CONCLUSION

It is in the nature of my argument that there is no single conclusion to which we should come when considering the problem of public service unresponsiveness. Neither wholesale privatization nor wholesale nationalization will solve the problem. Instead it can only be tackled by a series of measures, none of them perhaps significant in themselves, but which cumulatively might add up to a serious approach to the problem.

NOTES

1   For a review of these arguments see Heald, 1980.
2   Compare Klein, 1984b, p.22, and Johansson, 1981, table 7.2, p. 28. (I am grateful to Stein Ringen for bringing these Swedish data to my attention, and for translating crucial parts of the text.)
3   *The Times*, Monday 25 June 1984, p. 3.
4   See the criticism of statutory services in Hadley and Hatch, 1981, especially pp. 40 – 1.
5   For a selection of the relevant literature that could be cited in connection with these points see Klein and Lewis, 1976; Morone and Marmor, 1981, pp. 431 – 50; Peterson, 1970, pp. 491 – 507; Royal Commission on Local Government, 1969, vol.3, pp. 132 – 6; and Sharpe, 1973, pp. 129 – 68.
6   A point made to me by Alan Maynard, from whom I take the example.

10

Policies for Sharing the Job Shortage: Reducing or Redistributing Unemployment?

ALAN WALKER

INTRODUCTION

By the middle of the decade the job shortage or job gap will be, on optimistic assumptions, in the region of five million. This chapter reviews the main options for sharing this shortage. How effective are they in reducing unemployment? What implications do they have for other social and economic policies? Do they entail acceptable social and economic costs? While these are the sorts of questions to which the analysis is directed, any thorough discussion of future employment policies cannot ignore the wider range of options that are open to a government genuinely seeking to reduce the overall level and effects of unemployment. Furthermore, many forms of employment – particularly those from which the majority of the unemployed are drawn (Daniel, 1974, pp. 10 – 11) – create substantial personal and social costs, such as ill-health and disability, as well as being a source of economic insecurity. This means that a policy aimed only at reducing unemployment may succeed in overcoming some of the deep poverty and deprivation experienced by unemployed people and their families, yet may, at the same time, introduce or reinforce other forms of inequality. So, the final section of this paper extends the focus to a consideration of a social policy for work and, with it, a more positive role for social policy in arguing against acquiescence in mass unemployment.

I am very grateful to Tessa Blackstone, Jonathan Bradshaw and Michael Hill for comments on the first draft of this Chapter.

THE NECESSITY FOR REDUCING UNEMPLOYMENT

On what criteria might the various proposals for closing the job gap be evaluated? The answer will depend, of course, on the social objectives underlying public policy. If the predominant political concern is with the unemployed numbers game – or, as Hill (1983, p. 254) has put it, 'a . . . cynical desire to reduce the numbers actually registered as unemployed in as inexpensive a way as possible' – the criteria are obvious and minimalist (see, for example, Burton, 1981). If, in contrast, the primary aim is a sustained real reduction in unemployment the various options will have to be subjected to far more searching examination. The starting-point of this chapter is that one of the key objectives to which social and economic policy, including the welfare state, should be directed over the next ten years is a steady reduction in unemployment and economic insecurity.

The pressing case for an employment policy geared to the diminution of unemployment derives not from alarmist fears about social unrest but, rather, from the enormous personal, social and economic costs that unemployment entails (see Jahoda, 1979; Sinfield, 1977, 1979; Showler and Sinfield, 1981; Burghes and Lister, 1981; Hakim, 1982). The main points may be summarized.

In the first place, unemployment is now a major cause of poverty and deprivation in Britain. The latest official figures show that in 1981 just over 2.6 million unemployed people and members of their families were living in poverty or on its margins – three in ten of all those under pension age. Between 1979 and 1981 the number of people in families headed by an unemployed person living *below* the supplementary benefit level increased more than three-fold to 480,000. A long history of official and independent research has revealed the considerable hardship experienced by unemployed people and in particular by those with families (see, for example, Clark, 1978; Townsend, 1979; Moylan and Davies, 1980). All studies are unanimous in the conclusion that those living on social security benefits the longest – the long-term unemployed – suffer the deepest poverty (Sinfield, 1968; MSC, 1980; Bradshaw, Cooke and Godfrey, 1983). It is worth noting too that the chain which links poverty to unemployment is much stronger and further from being broken in Britain than in other comparable EEC countries (Walker, Lawson and Townsend, 1984).

Secondly, the immediate burden of unemployment, unlike that of inflation, is concentrated on a section of the population already likely to be experiencing social disadvantage in one form or another. Those who suffer ill-health or disability, young and older workers and people from ethnic minorities are particularly vulnerable to unemployment (Walker, 1981). The main factor determining this concentration of unemployment in some groups and the wide regional disparities in the incidence of unemployment is occupational class (Moylan and Davies, 1980, p. 831; Walker, 1982a, p. 43). As a result the unemployed are likely to have experienced a range of labour market deprivations, especially low pay, but also poor working conditions, long and unsocial hours and few, if any, non-wage benefits (Townsend, 1979; Pond, 1980). An example of the potent influence of occupational class on unemployment is provided by recent ESRC-sponsored research among redundant steel workers in Sheffield. Three years after redundancy the unemployment rate among non-skilled manual workers was just over 50 per cent, compared with 20 per cent for skilled manual people and just below that for those whose pre-redundancy employment had been supervisory, managerial or technical (Westergaard, Noble and Walker, 1984).

Thirdly, unemployment entails psychological and, in all probability, physical health costs as well as financial ones. Research has clearly demonstrated, for men at least, a marked deterioration in psychological health as a result of unemployment, though the evidence for the injurious impact on physical health is, at the moment, only suggestive, as is that indicating a link between economic recession and mortality rates (for a review of recent research, see Warr, 1984).

Fourthly, there are the economic costs of unemployment. The budgetary costs – benefit payments and taxes foregone – of just under 3 million unemployed in 1981/82 were put at £13,000 million (Dilnot and Morris, 1981), a similar amount to that spent on the entirety of health and personal social services in the same financial year. The Exchequer cost of unemployment was 2.6 per cent of GDP in 1979 and 6.1 per cent in 1981. In addition, there is the loss in output resulting from unemployment which – including only those considered officially to be unemployed – may be in the region of £14,000 million currently (Tomlinson, 1983). There is also the less readily quantifiable de-skilling and waste of skilled labour that occurs when people are unemployed for long periods or are forced to withdraw from the labour market by unemployment.

Fifthly, unemployment imposes wider costs on society as a whole, although evidence here is patchy. There are clear causal links between unemployment and homelessness, family breakdown and educational disadvantage. The existence of a causal relationship between unemployment and social unrest and racial tension is, however, much less certain (Hakim, 1982, pp. 453 – 9), though recent research suggests that unemployment does *not* induce shifts in socio-political orientation, or encourage radicalism or militancy (Westergaard, Noble and Walker, 1984). There can be no doubt whatsoever about the impoverishing and disintegrating effects of unemployment and economic decline in many inner city areas (Sinfield, 1980; Crick, 1981).

Finally, the direct personal experience of worklessness extends beyond those officially recognised as unemployed. The distinction between the unemployed and the 'non-employed' – those forced to withdraw from or discouraged from entering the labour market as a result of unemployment or recession – is often blurred. Although the unemployed undoubtedly suffer the greatest hardship, the non-employed also experience economic insecurity and are deprived in relation to the employed (Westergaard, Noble and Walker, 1984). Employment and other social policies have paid very little attention to the position of the non-employed. This is due, in large measure, to the disinterest of policy-makers in reverberations of the recession which extend beyond the unemployed count, but must, in part at least, also reflect the virtual absence of research on this group, and the relationship between unemployment and non-employment and changes in the composition of the two groups (Walker, Noble and Westergaard, 1984).

For all these reasons, high unemployment makes it extremely difficult to achieve significant social progress; goals such as a major reduction in poverty and inequality and the establishment of equal citizenship depend for their realization on a substantial reduction in unemployment. But, in addition, high unemployment means that the advances that have been made by the post-war welfare state in reducing some inequalities and ensuring the maintenance of minimum standards are made more and more difficult to sustain (Sinfield, 1983). Thus, for example, measures to promote equality of employment opportunity between the sexes, to discriminate in favour of employing people with disabilities and to enforce minimum wages have all been undermined in recent years, while some benefits and services have been cutback partly as a result of the high economic cost of unemployment (Walker, Winyard and Pond, 1983).

So, the first and most important criterion by which worksharing may be evaluated is the extent to which it will contribute to a genuine reduction in unemployment. This means, effectively, an expansion in employment as opposed to a redefinition of precisely who is classified officially as unemployed combined with a concomitant expansion in non-employment, sub-employment and underemployment among those previously in employment. A second important objective is the redistribution of unemployment and especially long-term unemployment. Does worksharing result in the vertical redistribution of unemployment or is it just a matter of shuffling the pack of unemployed people? Thirdly, it may be the case that a particular method of worksharing is advantageous even though it would have little or no impact on the level and distribution of unemployment. Are there other desirable or undesirable social consequences, both short- and long-term, associated with worksharing? For example, does worksharing result in greater equality in incomes and domestic roles, or is the price to be paid for this policy a growth in economic insecurity, low incomes and poverty? Fourthly, there may be economic costs of worksharing which preclude its widespread adoption.

OPTIONS FOR SHARING THE JOB SHORTAGE

Policy-makers seeking to tackle the job shortage have three options open to them (Blyton and Hill, 1981, p. 37). First, they may increase the demand for labour by creating temporary and/or permanent jobs. This was the active approach which characterized manpower policy under both Labour and Conservative governments in the 1970s (Hill, 1981, pp. 94 – 5). Secondly, they may attempt to reduce the supply of labour by delaying entry to and/or encouraging earlier exit from the labour force. The third strategy is to limit the time spent on the job by those in employment by such means as shorter working weeks, longer holidays and job-sharing – thereby, it is argued, creating new jobs to take up the unworked hours. The major part of this paper is addressed to the second and third strategies, both of which are concerned with the reallocation of the existing supply of jobs, and may be classified as worksharing, while the first is considered in the last section. Some of the options considered have already been tried in one form or another in this country, thereby yielding some evidence on which to base an evaluation. Comments on untried options are necessarily more circumspect.

Reducing the size of the labour force: education and training

Faced with rapidly increasing youth unemployment, governments have been reluctant to extend the school leaving age in order to reduce the labour supply and have concentrated instead on special measures aimed at 16- and 17-year-olds. In recent years the emphasis has been placed more and more on training. The switch in focus of policies aimed at youth unemployment from job creation to training is one major indication of the transition from an active to a passive or minimalist manpower policy in recent years. But it also reflects a long-standing general concern about the lack of vocational preparation in this country (MSC, 1981). Thus, in the late 1970s, the proportion of school leavers entering full-time vocational education in Britain was lower than in all other EEC countries except Ireland: one in ten compared with three in ten in the Netherlands, two in five in France and one in every two in Italy (House of Lords, 1982, p. 201).

The main special training measure currently in operation is the Youth Training Scheme (YTS). YTS is open to school-leavers up to the age of 20 who have been unemployed for at least six weeks. It replaced the Youth Opportunities Programme which was phased out between September 1983 and October 1984. YTS is intended to combine training, work experience and education. It was given a flying start by the political commitment that every 16-year-old unemployed school leaver requiring a year of training would receive an offer of a place on a suitable scheme by the end of 1983. The plan for 1983/84 was 459,000 places, but at the end of 1983 one-third of places remained empty and the MSC estimated the final total to be nearer 350,000 (one half of the number leaving school each year). By the end of May 1984 some 375,000 young people had entered the YTS, but only 238,000 were still attending. This suggests that a significant proportion of school-leavers have been unwilling to join the YTS and that a substantial group of trainees have left the scheme before completion (Finn, 1984).

YTS was partly a response to criticisms of YOP and previous schemes. The two main problems identified by economists were 'deadweight' and 'displacement'. 'Deadweight' workers are those that a firm would have hired anyway and the subsidy for which therefore represents a windfall to the employer. The second problem occurs where subsidized workers displace non-subsidized ones (Metcalf, 1982, p. 9). In addition, the lack of training, the dead-end nature of many jobs and the absence of control over the development of placements were frequent criticisms of YOP (DE, 1981).

Do pre-vocational training schemes, like YTS, promote a sustained reduction in unemployment? It is too soon to judge the impact of a fully operational YTS but, obviously, the removal of a large proportion of school-leavers from the labour market will substantially reduce youth unemployment. However, with more than half a million people under 18 out of work, the scheme will not cover the whole of this group and, in fact, it looks as if there will only be half as many entrants as there were to YOP. Most importantly, the effect on unemployment of the reduction in labour supply brought about by YTS is likely to be only temporary. Therefore the key question is whether or not those involved in the scheme will be better placed to secure permanent jobs once their period of training is over? The evidence from the operation of YOP shows that very few young clients subsequently found sustained employment (Metcalf, 1982, p. 34). It may be that the increased training component in YTS will make the young people involved more attractive to potential employers. Set against this hope, however, is the danger that YTS will drastically reduce conventional trainee opportunities in the youth labour market: if employers have a ready supply of labour at little or no cost in wages, they may decide not to hire teenagers in the traditional way. This is the problem which seems to bedevil all such schemes. If only a small proportion of trainees are able to find jobs, the scheme, like its predecessors, will quickly become discredited as young people question the purpose of training or work preparation.

As well as having minimal lasting effect on unemployment, pre-vocational training is not targetted on the long-term unemployed. (The Work Experience Programme is intended for those who have been out of work for six months or more.) It is aimed at enhancing the job prospects of non-academic young people and, in the absence of a general expansion in employment opportunities, this is likely to be at the expense of either older workers or other young people. There is no indication that this sort of training scheme will improve the relative employment prospects of the most disadvantaged groups of school-leavers without accompanying measures to ensure that they gain a fair share of available employment (Walker, 1982a). For example, very few people with disabilities on YTS schemes have managed to secure places with employers: the majority are engaged on college-based schemes.

One of the most important wider social consequences of the introduction of pre-vocational training for school leavers is the problem of the payment of trainees. YTS trainees receive a flat rate of £25 per week (to be increased by 5 per cent in 1985), although employers are free to top this up. A person aged 16 – 17 not on a scheme but claiming benefit would receive £19.60 (assuming the young person lives with his/her parents). Someone of the same age remaining in full-time education normally receives no state benefit at all. The disparity between young people doing similar jobs, but as trainees as opposed to workers, raises the question of the relatively low allowances paid to trainees. The disparity in income between those in full-time education and others raises the issue of whether there should be a general benefit for 16- to 18-year-olds regardless of whether they are in education or training.

Questions about the level of pay for trainees hark back to the earlier discussion of the purposes of policy. If one of the main intentions of pre-vocational training is to depress the wage levels of young people, as the following quotation from the famous unpublished CPRS report suggests, then a low level of pay for trainees is essential.

> The essence of the proposal is to reduce the size of the labour force by raising to 17 the age of entry to the normal labour market. . . . young people would receive a modest allowance well below the normal wage. It would be possible, in time, to prescribe a lower training wage for those being trained by their employer (including apprentices) . . . a particularly desirable objective which is unlikely to be achieved voluntarily.

If, on the other hand, the income needs of young people and their families are taken into account, the levels of pay to trainees would undoubtedly be higher and an allowance would be paid to those remaining in education.

With respect to the economic effects of pre-vocational training, YTS is actually cheaper than YOP per place provided – £2,174 compared with £2,359 (Youthaid, 1984, p. 6). Its total budget is £1,000 million. If this results in a permanent reduction in unemployment of 150,000 (the House of Lords Select Committee on Unemployment's estimate of the long-term impact of spending a similar sum on job creation), it would be a relatively efficient way of cutting unemployment, but considerably more expensive than the budget costs of keeping that number of people unemployed. In the light of the experience of YOP, however, the best that can be hoped for is placements (not all permanent) for about 100,000 people leaving YTS. This suggests that resources might be more productively spent on creating employment for young people to enter. On the other hand, the long-term economic benefit of better-trained school-leavers should undoubtedly be taken into account. Unfortunately, many of the training and education packages do not inspire confidence that they will produce this outcome (Ryan, 1984, p. 40). Moreover, even if young people are better trained for a rapidly changing workplace, unless they succeed in getting into jobs quickly after the scheme finishes, they are likely to remain unemployed for extended periods and consequently to lose the benefit of their training (Walker, 1982a, p. 90).

There are worries about both the intention and implications of pre-vocational training as the only or major response of government to mass unemployment. As Hill (1983, p. 250) points out, this suggests that it is the educational system and, in part, young people themselves that are at fault for the high level of youth unemployment and amounts to 'blaming the victim' (Ryan, 1971). Without an expansion in employment opportunities, efforts to enhance the job prospects of some young people will, at best, only succeed in redistributing unemployment among young people and, at worst, will reduce real job opportunities and reinforce the disadvantages experienced by those entering the labour market with the lowest qualifications.

Undoubtedly, there is a need for more and better training, in line with other EEC countries, and for this to be targeted on the most disadvantaged school leavers. A government serious about training as well as about tackling youth unemployment might follow the West German model of apprenticeships and pre-vocational training in schools (House of Lords, 1982, p. 110). At the moment training is concentrated on young people and in a changing labour market this should be extended to all age groups (MSC, 1983). Employers might be obliged to provide workers with both on- and off-the-job training, subsidized by the state (Layard, 1982). But this sort of option would be expensive, would not reduce unemployment by much on its own and would require a political commitment to improving the quality of the labour force.

There has not been any sustained call during the current recession for an extension of the school-leaving age. The idea was most recently and summarily rejected by the House of Lords Select Committee on Unemployment (1982, p. 89) as being too expensive (£700 million in recurrent costs alone in 1981) as well as being unpopular with a large number of young people and their parents. Unless it is coupled with educational maintenance grants and a major overhaul of the curriculum for non-academic young people, both of which are unlikely, it is a non-starter.

Reducing the size of the labour force: early retirement

The second method of cutting the supply of labour tried in this country in recent years – encouraging older workers to withdraw prematurely from the labour market – is undoubtedly the most popular option with the general public for reducing unemployment. Thus, in a Marplan poll conducted at the end of 1982, four out of five people interviewed said that early retirement was a good idea to reduce unemployment. It is also a policy which unites both Left and Right of the political spectrum. This consensus derives in large measure from the political acceptability of adding encouragement at minimal extra cost to a trend already underway, as well as from the readiness of many older workers to leave the labour force prematurely and the complete absence of information about the long-term consequences of early retirement.

Since the mid-1970s there has been a rapidly accelerating increase in the number of older workers withdrawing from the labour force. Between 1975 and 1982 the economic activity rate of men aged 60 – 64 fell from 84 per cent to 64 per cent. Among women there is also a tendency towards earlier retirement but it is less clear cut and to some extent countered by the increase in employment of middle-aged women. At present only two-fifths of males aged 60 – 64 are in full-time jobs and it is the rise of unemployment among this group which explains much of the recent growth in early retirement. For many older workers unemployment has come to mean effective retirement, but with incomes significantly lower than retirement pensions, and they are inclined, therefore, to adopt the less stigmatizing status of being early retired, particularly if extra income is available if they do so (Walker, 1982b; Walker, Noble and Westergaard, 1984). A similar relationship between unemployment and early retirement has been observed in France and Sweden (Laczko and Walker, 1985).

A universal lowering of the retirement age for men, either on its own or coupled with an increase in the retirement age for women (House of Commons, 1982) has been rejected primarily on grounds of cost (DHSS, 1984). Instead, policy has concentrated on facilitating the selective withdrawal of older workers from the labour market, subsidizing early retirement where employees are replaced and bolstering the incomes of unemployed men of 60 years and over.

The most important labour market policy is the Job Release Scheme (JRS), introduced in 1977 as a temporary measure to create vacancies for unemployed people by encouraging men aged 64 and women aged 59 to leave their jobs, and extended by the current government to cover men aged 62 and older (ostensibly to bring forward the retirement age of the large number of men born after the First World War who would reach the age of 65 in 1984/85). Between 1977 and 1981 the number of men participating in the scheme increased from 10,000 to 50,000, accounting for roughly one-third of the estimated 120,000 men aged 60 – 64 who left the labour force in that period. By the end of January 1984, 90,000 people were receiving a full-time job release allowance. The proposal of the House of Lords Select Committee on Unemployment for part-time job release was introduced in October 1983 and will last until March 1985.

Does early retirement result in a sustained reduction in

unemployment? Undoubtedly it consists of permanent withdrawal from the labour market (Parker, 1980; McGoldrick and Cooper, 1980; Walker, Noble and Westergaard, 1984). But whether or not early retirement reduces unemployment depends on the rate of replacement from among the unemployed of jobs vacated by older workers. Evidence on this is sparse (Metcalf, 1982, p. 41) and what little there is shows that early retirement is used to reduce overall manpower. For example, in the survey of 400 manufacturing establishments by White (1980) over half of those shedding labour had used early retirement as one method of doing so. Even under JRS the replacement of each leaver by a person from the unemployment register is not complete. Non-replacement has been estimated to be in the region of 15 per cent and deadweight 10 per cent (Makeham and Morgan, 1980). So the impact of JRS has been reduced by 25 per cent, which means that the total of 250,000 who have left employment under JRS since 1977 have probably been replaced by some 187,000 unemployed people. The scheme has had a small, but significant, impact on unemployment.

Selective early retirement is not aimed at easing the burden of the long-term unemployed. However, because of the level of allowances those entering the JRS tend to be low paid. Also disproportionately represented are those with long-standing illnesses or disabilities. It therefore seems to provide an escape route for some of those disadvantaged in the labour market. But since the replacement of workers leaving through early retirement is at the discretion of employers and there is evidence of discrimination by employers against the long-term unemployed (White, 1983), they are unlikely to benefit much from any job vacated. Indeed, the most important social security measure in encouraging early retirement, the extension of the long-term rate of supplementary benefit to men aged 60 – 65, recognizes the extremely poor current employment prospects of this group and their disproportionate representation among the long-term unemployed.

The main doubts about both selective and general early retirement as a method for reducing unemployment, apart from its small scale, arise from its adverse social consequences, which are rarely considered in public debate (for one exception, see House of Commons Social Services Committee, 1982). The factor which makes early retirement so attractive to politicians – its concentration on a relatively small and powerless group nearing the end of their working lives – is also the source of its main social drawbacks.

In the first place, without major changes in pensions policy, premature retirement for many older workers and their families means premature poverty (Walker, 1982b, p. 66). The policy of encouraging selective withdrawal from the labour market on low incomes advances inequalities that would have been formed on retirement and falls on those already disadvantaged in the labour market: the unskilled and people with disabilities in particular. Thus early retirement, when it comes as a rationalization of unemployment, impending redundancy or an escape from work due to ill-health, rather than as an option freely chosen and planned on the basis of financial security, is likely to result in poverty and deprivation. Policy has been formed on the basis of a rosy view of early retirement, encouraged in part by research among those able to make a free choice about taking it (McGoldrick and Cooper, 1980). But the main reason for the recent increase in early retirement is the collapse of aggregate demand and the consequent economic insecurity among older workers (Walker, Noble and Westergaard, 1984) which has effectively forced many older people into early retirement; for example, the low level of allowances paid under JRS made it an unattractive option and led to a low take-up rate until unemployment increased dramatically in 1980-82 and job prospects for older people declined steeply.

Secondly, early retirement focuses on one age group in the labour force and in doing so reinforces an ageist bias in the operation of the labour market. The JRS was introduced to alleviate youth unemployment at the expense of older workers. The effects of this require further study but an impression of the pressures which older workers are under to vacate jobs may be gained from individual expressions of guilt at holding jobs when so many young people are out of work (McGoldrick and Cooper, 1980; Walker, Noble and Westergaard, 1984). This amounts to blaming older workers for occupying jobs and, in turn, tends to reinforce fatalism about the lack of employment opportunities.

Apart from the political acceptability of selectively ending labour force participation among older workers, the main feature in its favour is its relatively low cost. Largely because of the low level of its allowances, JRS is three times more cost effective in reducing unemployment than a general lowering of the retirement age (Metcalf, 1982, p. 48). The award of the long-term rate of supplementary benefit to men over 60 can be viewed in part as a relatively cheap way of cutting the numbers officially classified as unemployed.

Despite its attractions, early retirement must be viewed with caution as a means of reducing unemployment. Research is required into its longer-term consequences. In the absence of enhanced pension provision and substantially higher JRS allowances, the disadvantages appear to outweigh the small improvement in unemployment. The alternative of partial pensions – along the lines of the successful Swedish scheme (Walker and Laczko, 1982, pp. 216 – 221) – would best fit the expressed desire of the majority of older workers for gradual withdrawal from the labour market. But this measure is intended to ease the problems of the transition from work to retirement rather than to alleviate unemployment.

Redistributing work: reducing the working week

Alongside the special measures introduced to reduce the size of the labour force, interest has been growing in the idea of redistributing work within the labour force (see, for example, CBI, 1980; TUC, 1981). Various methods have been proposed: reducing weekly working hours, promoting part-time in place of full-time work, restricting overtime, longer holidays, sabbaticals and additional shift work. The first two are considered here in order to illustrate the advantages and disadvantages of job-sharing.

The average number of hours worked by manual workers is considerably higher in Britain than in other EEC countries: 1932 annually in manufacturing compared with 1831 in France, 1671 in West Germany and 1545 in Belgium. The proportion working 48 hours or more a week in Britain (20 per cent) is three times that in France and West Germany (Hill, 1984, p. 7). In recent years a number of national agreements have introduced shorter working hours (White, 1980, 1981). The TUC has called for a 35 hour week and this is now a negotiating goal for many unions.

Estimates of the possible effect of a 35-hour week on unemployment vary widely, from an *increase* of 100,000 (CBI, on the questionable assumption that British industry is already as efficient as possible) to a fall of 600,000 (trade union research unit). The Department of Employment, hedging its bets, has made four estimates of falls ranging from 100,000 to 480,000. Whether or not reductions in normal working hours will generate employment and, if so, how much, depends crucially on what happens to overtime and wage costs. If overtime increases then the potential impact on unemployment would be reduced. Recent estimates by the Treasury suggest that about 40 per cent of the potential loss in output following a cut in hours would be made up by overtime (Allen, 1980). This implies that a shorter working week could still contribute significantly to reducing unemployment.

Turning to wage costs, the trade union position is that there should be no loss of pay. This means that if new employment is generated by a reduction in the working week, wage costs will increase. Even so, the Department of Employment has calculated that if weekly hours fall from 40 to 35 without a corresponding drop in weekly pay, and output was increased by 20 per cent, a reduction in unemployment of 350,000 would follow. Unfortunately, it also suggests that the consequent rise in unit labour costs and attendant price rises would wipe out one-third of this reduction in unemployment within two years. At best, therefore, the gains from reducing the working week would be modest. Others have questioned the assumption that this form of work-sharing would increase unit costs (see, for example, Hill, 1984). However, it must be pointed out that, against these hypothetical arguments, one of the few empirical studies of the effects of the introduction of a shorter working week found no direct increase in recruitment resulting from it (White, 1981). There are other difficulties with lowering working hours as a mechanism for cutting unemployment (Metcalf, 1982, p. 53). If demand for labour increases, the reduction is not easily reversible and there is also the considerable problem of matching jobs freed with the availability of local unemployed people with the necessary skills. Also a large proportion of employment is generated by small firms and a reduction in working hours by them would not necessarily leave enough unworked hours to justify taking on more workers.

It is when we consider the distributional impact of a reduction in working hours that the main problems become apparent. The success of this policy depends on constraining wage costs. So, as Metcalf (1982, p. 56) has argued, 'work-sharing is about income-sharing'. This is an outcome that is likely to prove unacceptable to those in jobs. What is more, since it is low-paid workers who work the longest hours and who are hourly paid (Townsend, 1979, p. 636; House of Lords, 1982, p. 95), a policy limited to reducing hours worked will increase earnings inequalities. A similar difficulty applies to the argument for a reduction in overtime as a way of bringing down unemployment (it is estimated that stopping overtime would result in an increase of over 500,000 low-paid men).

Despite its economic disadvantages as a means of reducing unemployment, since many people work long hours a reduction might help to create a healthier and more productive work force. Moreover, it must be emphasized that many of Britain's competitors sustain considerably greater affluence on shorter working hours. It would seem that most scope for introducing shorter hours while not cutting pay exists in areas employing new technology. Where new jobs are introduced, for example, extra people could be employed to work four six hour shifts instead of the traditional three of eight hours, with new technology maintaining sufficiently high levels of productivity for wage levels to be sustained.

Redistributing work: job-sharing

Job-splitting schemes have been proposed by the TUC and House of Lords Select Committee on Unemployment. A scheme was introduced in January 1983 which allows firms to split a full-time job into two part-time jobs and receive a grant to offset the transitional costs. From October 1983, a part-time Job Release Scheme has also been available, though very few have taken it up.

Job-sharing seems to present considerable advantages to employers, particularly those requiring flexibility in their workforce. Moreover, with the transitional costs met by the state, the costs to the employer are minimal, apart perhaps from a more complex administration. From the perspective of employees, however, there may be considerable disadvantages.

First, the potential of job-splitting as a method of reducing unemployment is severely restricted by the same cloud which hangs over reductions in the working week: job-sharing means income-sharing. It is only likely to appeal, therefore, to a second wage earner in a couple where the other partner is in full-time work. This means that it would be likely to draw into the labour force many of the 'hidden unemployed', or non-employed, especially married women; a not undesirable outcome, but one that will not reduce the numbers counted officially as unemployed. The two other main groups likely to be interested in job-splitting are older workers looking to withdraw partly from employment and those threatened with redundancy, as under the Temporary Short-Time Working Compensation Scheme. Secondly, since much part-time work is unskilled and in occupations requiring shift work, unsocial hours and part-day working (nurses, cleaners, school helpers), jobs would be concentrated in the service sector rather than manufacturing, where many of the unemployed are drawn from. Thirdly, part-time workers are a notoriously abused group, with little or no protection under employment laws. A policy which encourages the spread of part-time work, without introducing protection in relation to wages, conditions and dismissal, would reinforce and extend the disadvantages experienced by this group. Moreover, because the vast majority of part-time workers are women, this policy would exacerbate gender inequality in the labour market.

Most forms of redistributing work, including the two reviewed here, suffer from the same objections, primarily their adverse impact on labour costs and, therefore, competitiveness (House of Lords, 1982, p. 100). With cost-efficiency dominant this effectively rules out all forms of work redistribution except half-time working. Furthermore it is by no means clear that measures such as a shorter working week would provide extra jobs; they might further reduce labour demand.

REDUCING UNEMPLOYMENT: A SOCIAL POLICY FOR WORK

The previous section makes depressing reading for those who believe that the present job shortage can be shared more evenly without major social and economic changes. Leaving aside their disadvantages, the practicable measures considered would together permanently reduce unemployment by, at most, 200,000, the majority being young people entering employment after pre-vocational training, a large proportion of whom would have got jobs anyway, and older workers encouraged into early retirement. But the picture is not a wholly black one. Worksharing can have some impact on unemployment – sufficient, for example, for studies to be conducted of the experience of worksharing in other countries – but on its own, it is not going to make much of an impression on the problem. The need for better training opportunities, covering the whole of the working age-range, has been emphasized already. However, as experience under the American War on Poverty showed, all special programmes designed to increase the employability of individuals will have only a marginal effect unless jobs are created: 'However resourceful the projects' employment programmes, they could do little to influence the economy which determined how many usable skills were in demand' (Marris and Rein, 1967, p. 91).

This brings us to a crossroads in the consideration of the future of welfare. Those who set the limits of policy at the redistribution of existing jobs, for that is what all of the different forms of worksharing amount to, must accept that the job gap will remain at least at its current level for the forseeable future, with all the consequent costs of large scale unemployment. The implications of this position for social policy are momentous: acceptance of mass unemployment undermines the welfare state. Because it was built in part on the assumption of full employment, or sustained low unemployment, the goals of the welfare state – social integration, reductions in inequality, equal citizenship, removal of the barriers of disadvantage – either become unachievable in the face of mass unemployment or the mechanisms for achieving them require radical overhaul.

The problem, as Sinfield (1983, p. 67) points out, arises from the conflict between two separate and insulated issues in the debate about the future of welfare. On the one hand, there is concern about the scale of unemployment and how the job shortage may best be shared. On the other, there is the issue of the scale of poverty and current need among those outside of the labour force and the fundamental importance of employment in providing adequate resources. So, the acceptance of 'realism' on the former without action on the latter is likely to increase poverty and economic insecurity. In other words, full-scale worksharing would require radical changes in *both* employment and social security, including perhaps the introduction of some form of basic income (Roberts, 1983; and see Bradshaw's chapter for a discussion of this). In those circumstances worksharing becomes a different proposition. Caution is required, therefore, in repeating the frequent assertion that we will have to learn to live with unemployment and redistribute jobs – because the effort required to do this properly may be more extensive and radical than anything contemplated by those arguing for a return to full employment. To attempt worksharing, or any similar reorganization of work, on its own, will increase those problems that the welfare state is intended, in part at least, to tackle.

There are other good reasons for changing the pattern of employment, for example, to cope with the introduction of new technology or to provide some people with more pleasant, less arduous and physically and mentally damaging work routines. But those looking seriously for ways of reducing unemployment substantially, without major adverse social consequences, will have to look elsewhere. This leaves the first of the three strategies outlined earlier: increasing the demand for labour, 'by far the most effective means of combatting unemployment' (Metcalf, 1982, p. 61). Unfortunately there is no sign to date of the government accepting the need for direct stimulation of the economy even to the extent of the very modest public investment suggested by the House of Lords Select Committee on Unemployment (1982).

Policy-makers, social policy analysts and other social scientists who choose not to accept mass unemployment reject those assumptions underlining current policies which put the welfare of unemployed people and their families second to the interests of economic policy and management, and, at the same time, they refuse to accept the wholly subordinate position of social policy to the economy. This secondary position of public welfare policies to economic policies has been amply demonstrated by the remorseless rise in unemployment over the last five years (Walker, Winyard and Pond, 1983). The economic policies which have contributed to this rise also revealed the interrelationship between economic and social policy, because they are so obviously based on assumptions about the sort of society that the government is attempting to create and about which groups' living standards will prosper and which will decline (for a full account of this relationship, see Walker, 1984, pp. 45 – 69). It was the recognition of the social costs of unemployment that led Beveridge to argue for full employment and for an economic policy which embodied this social objective. It might be that, some 40 years later and again in response to mass unemployment, social policy will be reasserted and as a result social and economic objectives will be realigned. It is only from this quarter that questions are likely to be raised about the development of the economy: should social progress be subordinate to economic management? Should high productivity and profits be tempered by employment needs? Should decisions about who and how many of the unemployed are to be given a share in employment be dictated solely by economic managers?

The construction of an employment policy geared to reducing unemployment requires the reconstitution of the relationship between social welfare goals and economic policy (Walker, 1984). In particular it means a change in the narrow micro-economic theories of employment determination which underpin present policies (Adam Smith Institute, 1983), as well as most of the measures designed to redistribute unemployment, and a greater recognition of the *social* foundations of work and employment, including the economic, social and psychological importance of employment in a modern industrial society. This is undoubtedly a tall order in the face of a constant barrage of opinion asserting that there is no alternative. One way to begin to overcome the current fatalism about unemployment and the belief that there is a limited supply of work to go around, is to conduct comparative studies of employment policy in different countries. What for one country is regarded as surplus labour is for others, or for the same country at different stages in its history, treated as scarce labour (Showler and Sinfield, 1981).

A comparison of recent responses to unemployment in West Germany and Sweden, for example, shows how these two countries responded to unemployment differently with different results. Not only is unemployment in Sweden less than half the rate it is in West Germany, but it is distributed much more evenly according to gender and among disadvantaged groups. How did Sweden do it? Not by excluding people from the workforce, more rapid economic growth or greater trade union restraint, but, primarily, by the scale of its positive labour market policies, augmented by an expansion in public sector employment and underpinned by a political commitment to full employment (Webber, 1983).

Caution is required in translating the experience of other countries into policy, but the message for the discussion of the future of the welfare state is clear. If its role is to be restricted only to providing social security benefits for an ever-increasing number of unemployed, it will either encounter a crisis of funding or pauperize its claimants, or both. If, in contrast, it is directed at reducing unemployment it can achieve a substantial measure of success.

What form might a positive employment policy take? First of all it must be recognized that there is no easy solution to unemployment. To bring it down to 500,000 by the end of the decade will require the creation of 2,500 jobs per day. Because of changes in the world economy, the development of new technology and the growth of the potential labour force, the problem is likely to become even more difficult to overcome. So, a long-term perspective is required – at least ten years.

Secondly, there is a need to re-establish employment policy at the centre of social policy by allocating a positive role for the welfare state in enabling people to become independent and self-sufficient through employment. It is through the welfare state that increased employment can be combined with other social objectives, such as meeting the needs of elderly people for carers (see Bosanquet's chapter for a discussion of this issue) or, more radically, promoting gender equality in child care by means of parental leave. The creation of jobs in the public sector also helps to minimize substitution effects (Hill, 1983, p. 251).

Thirdly, economic policy needs to be addressed more often to job creation. The concept of 'employment-centred growth' (Jenkins and Miller, 1983, p. 26) is helpful. This seeks to stimulate and support, for example by means of tax incentives, industries and services providing employment opportunities, particularly for low skilled workers.

Fourthly, a combination of *both* job creation and worksharing measures are required. The programme proposed by the House of Lords Select Committee on Unemployment (1982, p. 162) is a reasonable starting point. Long-term job creation in the public and voluntary sectors and investment-led job creation, coupled with job-splitting for older workers nearing retirement and the award of the higher rate of supplementary benefit for those over 55, would reduce unemployment by more than 500,000 at a gross cost of some £3,000 million. As well as making social objectives easier to achieve, the growth of demand would also make worksharing a more viable prospect (Blyton and Hill, 1981, p. 42). A policy aimed at stimulating demand would need to be combined with policies on wages and income distribution (Meade, 1984).

Finally, as well as job creation and redistribution there are other aspects of work which require attention: the quality of working life as well as the quantity is a matter for social policy. This might include the provision of increased opportunities for leisure, less arduous and disabling working conditions and more flexible working hours, without reducing security, and thereby also contribute to increasing welfare.

CONCLUSION

Worksharing by itself is an inadequate response to the major personal, social and economic problems created by unemployment. Policy-makers serious about reducing unemployment must embark on some form of job creation. Without a positive policy to reduce unemployment of all of the other progressive objectives of social policy are called into question, not least by the demands on resources to pay even basic subsistence benefits. In other words, without an employment policy the future for welfare is very bleak indeed.

11

Welfare Needs, Welfare Jobs and Efficiency

NICK BOSANQUET

INTRODUCTION

This chapter examines the proposal that the caring services could make a substantial contribution to reducing unemployment by creating jobs. It is often said that this could be done with little cost to the Exchequer because of savings in unemployment and supplementary benefit. The main conclusion of the chapter is that such calculations are far too optimistic. There will probably be some future growth in employment but on a more modest scale than is sometimes suggested. The services are currently faced with major problems in terms of flexibility, productivity and getting the balance of staffing which would best serve clients' needs. Until these problems are resolved there is little chance of their responding strongly in terms of policies which are altruistic from the point of view of the individual manager. Sustainable jobs are more likely to be created by those who have a clear set of employment philosophies and policies – not by those who face management problems of great severity.

The caring services are often discussed as if they had a very general role in society; but they are also carrying out some highly specific tasks, often as public monopolies. They can be set aims relating to the wider problems in society – but they should also be serving their clients' interests. We could define the staffing policies which would serve the general social aim of reducing unemployment: it would be convenient if these were also the policies which best fitted the needs of actual or potential clients. But there may well be conflicts between the general interest and the interests of particular client groups.

Proposals for changing employment in the caring services have to be service led. They have to start from questions about effectiveness. What patterns of 'caring' would make a real difference to clients in terms of opportunities and quality of life? Once these questions have been answered there can be detailed proposals for the kind of staff required to provide the services. This chapter, therefore, reviews the various caring services, in order to identify the manpower requirements specific to each of them. However, before embarking on this detailed analysis, four general points need to be noted.

First, the aim of all the caring services is to strengthen opportunities for normal life in the community. This would indicate large scope for the use of volunteers to support informal carers. But the difficult questions start with the appropriate balance between paid staff and volunteer effort. A service which is developing informal help and volunteer support may need a rather larger proportion of qualified full-time staff than one in which unqualified full-time employees are giving direct services to clients: in short, the opportunities for creating jobs for unskilled unemployed men or women may be limited.

Second, if the caring services are seeking to enlarge opportunities for clients – as they frequently profess – then this, too, has implications for staffing. To achieve this aim means active management and this, in turn, means a very different staffing structure from a service where aspirations are lower. The paradox, again, is that employment opportunities for less qualified staff would be fewer in the kind of services that we are trying to bring into being than they are at present.

Third, the caring services face some special problems in providing better opportunities for training and career development for women workers who are in the great majority. They often have poor access to training and to promotion, and a very considerable investment and change in attitude will be required to alter this pattern. Here there could be a possible conflict between the investment and management effort required to move towards equal opportunities and that required by immediate priorities in employment creation.

Fourth, and perhaps most crucially, any policy decisions about using the caring services to expand job opportunities are likely to be taken against a background of intense competition for public spending. New, and more revealing, forms of accounting might reduce the net cost to the Exchequer of creating extra jobs, particularly for the unskilled or semi-skilled unemployed. But such new forms of accounting can be applied to other types of public spending as well. In practice, therefore, they are not likely to reduce the competition very much. In any case, given conventional public expenditure accounting, any additional resources to the caring services are likely to be small. Any proposal for using the caring services to generate extra employment must therefore be balanced against the need to make the most effective use of the available resources.

THE 'CARING' WORKFORCE AND ITS PAST DEVELOPMENT

The size of the current 'caring' workforce (in whole time equivalents) in 1980 in England can be summarized as follows:

Staff working with the elderly	202,500
Staff working with the mentally handicapped	44,500
Staff working with the mentally ill	49,000
Staff working with children	35,000
	331,000

(Detailed estimates are set out in the tables).

The part-time contribution is important so the total number of people doing some paid caring is about 500,000.

It may be useful to move away from the numbers and to ask who are the carers at present and what are the main management problems being faced. In the care of the elderly there are three main groups: those working in social services departments, those working in hospitals, and those working in private homes. Most of the staff are middle-aged women and they are very likely to work part time, especially in the local authority day services. Turnover from social service departments has been low as the level of pay compares favourably with those found for jobs in private services and there has been little recruitment in the recent past. These are long-service workforces with enormous experience and in the case of home helps the ability to work with minimal supervision. Within residential care the main difficulty has been adjusting to the care of people who are more physically dependent and also more likely to be mentally confused. Local authority homes have in effect become nursing homes through the increase in age and dependency of the residents and the difficulty of gaining admission to hospital. There is little on-the-job training and any qualified staff in supervisory positions are more likely to have qualified as nurses.

Within the community social services the main problems are those of making more intensive use of resources so as to help more dependent and handicapped people. This problem has been most acute for day centres which have been badly affected by transport difficulties, but it has also affected the home help service. Such adjustments have been made mainly as part of the general process of rationing by which help has had to be concentrated on the more dependent. Long service and continued contact between home help and client are very important assets of this service, and any increased staffing would have to maintain this continuity of contact.

Private and voluntary homes have larger numbers of staff who would be resident. Little is known about the staffing problems here or how they are resolved. In terms of pay voluntary homes generally follow local authority scales but not their other conditions such as superannuation. Private homes are likely to pay somewhat less, reflecting the labour markets in retirement areas. Few have pension schemes for their staff, which add about 15 per cent to the salary cost of staff in local authority homes.

The pattern of this workforce has shown little change over the last 25 years. Residential staff, home helps, and nursing staff in long-stay geriatric wards are all familiar figures. Nor have they increased in numbers recently as much as is sometimes thought. The main story has been that of how these traditional roles adjusted to the care of more dependent people and how time was rationed. Outside the nursing field the degree of active or effective management of 'caring' time is small. Staff carry out tasks to well understood routines. The main question is about whether more help might not have been given to the informal carers. There has been much more change in the kind of people involved in the care of mentally handicapped people. Within hospitals there has been a change in numbers; within the community new services have grown both in hostels and in ordinary housing. In the voluntary sector there is a new workforce made up often of young graduates. Pay and especially fringe benefits have been rather less than in local authorities. The main 'management' problem here has been in finding ways of transferring money and staff posts from the hospital to the community services. Within the voluntary sector there is a new workforce composed of young workers who turn over quite rapidly, which reflects their age, the relatively low levels of pay and the fact that better jobs are to be gained by moving between projects rather than staying within the same internal labour market. But the numbers in this new workforce are still quite small.

THE SCOPE FOR JOB CREATION IN THE CARING SERVICES

The macro-economic argument is that jobs could be created at a low net cost to the Exchequer because of savings in the payment of unemployment and supplementary benefit. But there are certain major difficulties about putting too much weight on this kind of accounting. It must be accepted that the decision to take a 'caring' job must be a voluntary one related to some long-term interest and commitment in the field. We are not talking here about short-term and temporary jobs, or about placements similar to those found on the Youth Training Scheme. Certainly some unemployed people may be interested in such permanent jobs. But the argument about low net cost has to show that most of the jobs would be filled by those who are or would be long-term unemployed. Most people in this high-risk group are male manual workers in high unemployment regions or inner cities. Most of the caring jobs are currently being done by part-time married women. While sex stereotypes may be changing they are not changing to the extent that it would be possible to redeploy many redundant shipyard workers as home helps; there are also some geographical difficulties. There would certainly be a demand for subsidized carers in voluntary and private old peoples homes: but most of these jobs would be in retirement areas in the south-west and on the south coast, again remote from those parts of the country where there are large numbers of long-term unemployed. Most of the jobs in residential care involve shift work and weekend working.

Within the newer community services the requirement for staff is being filled by staff who are certainly highly motivated and often quite highly educated as well. Now it might be possible to extend the search process to include some long-term unemployed people: but they would have to have strong motivation and they would lack the experience that most applicants for better-paid jobs in this field already have. Any new jobs for carers that were well paid would be filled by those who are already in this labour queue rather than those from outside the field. If the field were limited to those with high exchequer costs, this would also be unfair to the young single sub-employed who form the current labour supply.

I have suggested that proposals for changing employment in the caring services should be led by the requirements of the service. It is only in the services for the elderly that any real priority could be given to the employment of unqualified carers. For the other client groups the first priorities are to extend services for more severely handicapped people in the community. This requires people with strong vocational commitment and in many cases with a good deal of training. Even in the services for the elderly the limits in the number of carers who could be effectively managed would soon be reached.

None of this is to underestimate the importance of giving more support to informal carers; but even here the opportunity costs of increased staffing have to be weighed up. There is a real choice to be made between support in cash and support in care. Certainly there is also a case for special programmes to help the long-term unemployed: but such programmes should spread their incentives across the labour market and open up the widest possible field of potential employers. The creation of jobs in caring must follow from the redirection and management of services and it would be unwise to concentrate too much on services which currently face such major problems in rationing time and in effective management. The caring workforce is quite large as it is, and in terms of really effective care already suffers from severe productivity problems. In the past growth was used to make up for inflexibility. But in an era of low growth the management problems of transfer from hospital to the community, of effective management in the community and of negotiation with unions have become more important.

Productivity Trends in the Caring Services

Within the social services these choices have to be looked at against a background of recent large increases in the real costs of providing a given quantity of service, as Table 11.1 shows. Costs may rise in response to an increase in dependency: alternatively they may simply rise without much change in service pressure. One clear conclusion is that the rise in costs over this period is a fairly general one except for the home help and the meals services. Within residential care the rise in cost has affected both services where clients have become more dependent, as in the case of residential care for elderly people, and services where the balance of evidence does not show any major increase in dependency – as with services for mentally handicapped people. The causes of this rise in residential care cost need further and detailed investigation in the field. [1]

It is unlikely that such cost increases will have continued at the same

TABLE 11.1   % CHANGE IN SOCIAL SERVICES ACTIVITY
(OUTPUTS) AND EXPENDITURE 1975/76 TO 1980/81 IN ENGLAND

	Activity	*Real Expenditure*
Residential care		
elderly	2	19
mentally ill	10	58
mentally handicapped		
adults	41	87
children	13	91
Day care		
elderly	37	55
mentally ill	44	64
mentally handicapped	19	26
Social workers	11	33
home helps	10	9
boarding out	12	63
meals	2	2

Source: Webb and Wistow, 1982, p. 176

rate in the early 1980s. The earlier period was one in which public sector pay was rising relatively rapidly, especially in 1979 – 80. Caring may not become relatively more expensive – but it has ceased to be cheap. There were some increases in expenditure over the five years – at an average rate of about 2 per cent a year. Most of the increase went towards the rising costs of the service. The level of outputs was maintained – but against a background of demographic change which suggested rising need.

There were also significant increases in cost within the National Health Service. Over the period 1976 – 81 costs per day rose by 10 per cent in geriatric hospitals, by 24 per cent in hospitals for mental illness and by 20 per cent for places in mental handicap hospitals (DHSS, 1983b, p. 7). There was a general recognition of the need to improve staffing levels, in these hospitals, which contributed to this increase in cost. The NHS held down spending per place on the priority hospital services, partly to provide for an increase in spending on district nursing at 5 per cent a year.

Services for the Elderly

What did the general changes in cost mean in terms of changing labour demands within each service? How did the balance of recruitment change under these pressures? Most of the staff working in these services – with the exception of nurses -- have no formal training (Table 11.2). About two-thirds of the total staff across all services are in grades for which no special qualification is required. Part-time working is very important in this field: most home helps work part time rather than full time (Table 11.5).

TABLE 11.2   SOCIAL SERVICES, NHS AND OTHER STAFF (WHOLE-TIME EQUIVALENTS) WORKING WHOLLY OR MAINLY WITH ELDERLY PEOPLE

Social services staff	1974	1982	*change (%)*
Staff in residential homes	45,000	53,000	19
of which care assistants	21,000	26,000	24
Day centre staff	3,000	6,000	100
Home helps	42,500	49,500	16
Sub total	90,500	108,500	20
NHS Staff		1980	
District nursing staff		17,000	
Staff qualifying for the geriatric lead			
SRNs		9,000	
SENs		8,500	
Nursing auxiliaries		19,500	
Staff in the voluntary and private sector		1980	
Staff in voluntary and private homes		15,000	
Staff in nursing homes		20,000	
Staff in voluntary day care		5,000	
Total		202,500	

This workforce has been facing major problems in giving a service to increasing numbers of frail elderly people. More of the weight of care has been shifted back onto relatives, and such paid time as was available has been concentrated on fewer people. For this client group there would certainly be scope for increasing the numbers of staff involved in the home help service. However within the residential services the main staffing requirement is for people who can contribute actively to rehabilitation. The residential services have already made a considerable commitment in terms of staffing cost to unqualified staff, and this would not be the obvious priority for any marginal expenditure.

Services for Mentally Handicapped People

The major underlying problem here is that of raising the ability of the services in the community to look after more dependent people. This has to be resolved against a background of disappointing lack of progress towards reducing numbers in the large hospitals. In manpower terms the sign of this failure is that much of the investment in extra staffing has been in unqualified nursing staff, who now account for 39 per cent of all the manpower currently employed (Table 11.3). There is also evidence that most hostel staff are untrained. Within the Adult Training Centres the main requirement is for trained instructors rather than for unqualified helpers. The development of staffing locally has been detrimentally affected by the failure to resolve problems

TABLE 11.3   SOCIAL SERVICES, NHS AND OTHER STAFF WORKING WHOLLY OR MAINLY WITH MENTALLY HANDICAPPED PEOPLE

	1974	1982
Social services staff		
staff in hostels	3,000	4,500
staff in ACTs	5,000	7,500
	1969	1981
NHS Staff		
Qualified nurses	8,500	12,000
Unqualified nurses	6,000	17,500
Occupational therapists and helpers	300	750
Physiotherapists and helpers	37	225
Speech therapists	18	32
Staff in the voluntary and private sectors		2,000
Total		44,500

nationally about the future balance between staff with 'social' and 'nursing' training.

The most successful programme has been that for group homes. Estimates in 1980 were that about 2,000 places had been created over the previous ten years by the use of housing associates and funds and voluntary help. A recent study of their finances suggests that the current revenue costs which these schemes involved for organizers were quite low, at about £300 a year per resident, and could be contained within the ordinary supplementary benefit allowances (Ritchie, Keegan and Bosanquet, 1983, p.85). The dependency levels of residents varied but the range was roughly comparable to that of residents in local authority hostels.

The hostel programme has been criticized for producing hostels which are too large and where residents are mainly looked after by unqualified staff (DHSS, 1980, p. 51). The hospitals are also frequently criticized for retaining too many patients who ought to be elsewhere and for their lack of effective rehabilitation. The general picture is one of acute difficulty in providing a better balance of services and in getting more appropriate patterns of training. Within the social services there are some more minor problems of flexibility between day care and residential staff. The residential staff are often underused during the day. There can also be demarcation problems. In local authorities most residential homes employ both domestic and care staff while in voluntary homes the roles are combined. Voluntary homes can therefore run with lower levels of cost and of staffing.

From the client's point of view that has all meant unsatisfactory results in terms of services available. The numbers of mentally handicapped people in residential care have risen in the past ten years, taking hospitals and hostels together, and most of the new hostel residents have come from the community rather than from the hospitals. The level of support to mentally handicapped people and their families who are still living in the community remains very poor. The lack of effective help to school leavers and to young adults is only the most obvious problem.

All this comes about in a service which has had priority in terms of funding and staffing over the last ten years and which has seen growth in spending. The continued imbalance of spending towards residential care and the lack of effective community services for more severely handicapped people stand out as the most glaring defects. The priorities for extra spending at the margin would be for staff in community handicap teams: for physiotherapists and others concerned with the active rehabilitation of more severely handicaped people and in training for social models of care. In the case of services for the elderly a strong case can be made for recruiting staff in the less qualified groups: but in the case of services for mentally handicapped people the main priority is for people who could begin to establish new patterns of community service. Further recruitment of unqualified staff at present without such changes could not be seen as being a high priority in terms of client interest. These services do present in a particularly acute form a conflict between the general interest and the particular interest of clients.

Services for Mentally Ill People

The hospital contribution is still the overwhelming one. There are about 35,000 nursing staff working in psychiatric hospitals as compared to 5000 people in local authority day centres and hostels (Table 11.4). The voluntary contribution is particularly important in this field. The Richmond Fellowship and MIND have made some of the most important contributions both in terms of services and of staff training: however they employ in total not more than a few thousand. Within the health service there have been increases in the numbers of community nursing staff: the grade did not exist ten years ago and there are now about 2,000 people working as community psychiatric nurses. Within these services the main priority is now to increase the ability of community services to give more effective help to people with a long history of recurrent mental illness.

TABLE 11.4   SOCIAL SERVICE NHS AND OTHER STAFF (WTE) WORKING WHOLLY OR MAINLY WITH MENTALLY ILL PEOPLE (WTE)

	1982
Social service staff in hostels and day centres	5,000
NHS staff in hospitals	40,000
NHS community psychiatric nurses	2,000
Staff in the voluntary and private sectors	2,000
Total	49,000

WTE means whole-time equivalent.

TABLE 11.5   THE IMPORTANCE OF PART-TIMERS IN THE SOCIAL
SERVICES, 1980

Types of staff	(1) Numbers	(2) WTE	Ratio 1/2
Staff in residential homes for the elderly	71,185	52,535	1.35
Staff in day centres	6,742	5,170	1.30
Home helps	92,898	48,809	1.90
Staff in ATCs	8,234	6,910	1.19
Staff in homes and hostels for the mentally ill/ handicapped	9,189	6,827	1.34
Staff in community homes for children	26,912	22,069	1.22
Totals	215,160	142,320	1.5

Within the NHS staff are more likely to be full time. For example, among nursing staff
working with the mentally ill and mentally handicapped there were 72,797 people
employed contributing 67,230 WTEs in 1980.

The Private and Voluntary Sectors

The role of the private profit-making sector is greatest in the care of the
elderly. It is estimated that there are about 3,000 private and voluntary
homes for the elderly. Many of these are run by proprietors who are self-
employed, as shown in the chapter by Judge and Knapp. The data
suggest that there were in 1979 about 26,000 residents in voluntary
homes and 21,000 in private ones for elderly people (DHSS, 1981b,
Annex B). In addition there are about 30,000 residents in private
nursing homes. Thus the number of places is substantial in relation to
the total of about 150,000 residents in long-stay care provided by the
NHS and local authorities. Little is known about staffing levels in these
homes, but given the presence of working proprietors the level of
employee staffing is likely to be lower than in local authority homes. If
the same staffing ratios did apply this would suggest a total of about

40,000 staff in homes and nursing homes taken together; but this is likely to be an overestimate. A very rough estimate would be that 25,000 – 30,000 staff are involved in residential care of the elderly in private and voluntary homes.

There are also places in voluntary homes and hostels for mentally ill and mentally handicapped people. The recent survey for the Department of the Environment suggests that staffing levels are fairly low: in 29 projects looked at in detail nine employed full-time staff. In the whole sample of 662 schemes for mentally ill people providing 3,000 places, 5 per cent of schemes had resident staff: of 355 schemes for 2,000 mentally handicapped people 18 per cent had resident staff. To these would have to be added people in village communities, Richmond Fellowship homes and other projects which would not be counted as housing projects. The overall total of staff in all these kinds of projects certainly cannot be more than 2,000.

The contribution of voluntary and private efforts today and of community care is not documented. Overall there are 90,000 – 100,000 people employed by voluntary organizations in Great Britain. This includes organizations such as the Boy Scouts and there is no available breakdown of this employment by client group. A generous estimate for the total numbers employed by Age Concern, the WVS and others working with the elderly would be 5,000.

The Children's Services

There are about 20,500 people employed in local authority community homes and 9,000 employed in day nurseries. There are possibly 5,000 – 8,000 people employed by voluntary groups such as the NSPCC and Dr Barnardo's. In addition there is the important contribution made by foster parents, and any new resources should surely be concentrated on recruiting and supporting more foster parents. The average payment made to foster parents has risen as social workers have tried to foster older or more difficult children. The number of staff in community homes has shown a sharp fall over the past two years.

Informal Caring and the Volunteer Contribution

The contribution of relatives is both large and has been of increasing importance in the past ten years. For example there are now many fewer mentally handicapped children (although more adults) in long-term residential care. Almost half of people over 85 live with younger relatives. It is generally agreed that there is far too little support for these informal carers in terms of respite care and access to day centres. The Wolfenden Committee estimated that about 16 million hours were worked each week by volunteers in social fields. Two-thirds of these were in fields related to the personal social services. By comparison the local authorities employed about 200,000 staff in the social services. Thus the contribution of volunteers is already a very important one although such calculations may rather exaggerate their effective contribution. The obvious priority here is for the kind of support which would be given highest priority by informal carers. There might well be a role here for an enlarged home help service and for more help with day and respite care.

ANOTHER APPROACH TO EMPLOYMENT IN THE CARING SERVICES

Any decisions about expanding employment in the caring services must be taken in the context of a much wider set of problems to do with making more effective use of people's time in the NHS[2] and the social services. Some of the current difficulties of the NHS may be taken as an example.

1   There is too much emphasis on numbers, as opposed to 'output'.
2   The employer interest in productivity is fitful. The fits usually occur when bureaucratic norms are not being met.
3   Training is not often an activity which is under the manager's direct control and which can be related to the needs of the job. Training tends to be something imposed on the service by professional bodies from outside. This can lead to an underevaluation of the importance of on-the-job training and of the investment required to produce it.
4   Decisions about capital investment and about the use of manpower are made separately. Only rarely have there been attempts to see whether capital could be used to save manpower, or how different mixes of capital and labour could affect the service. Yet it is dificult to see how there can be efficiency unless such choices are well to the fore. There are many pressures to take the line of least resistance, rather than to develop a coherent strategy. The line may in fact be very different. Sometimes the line of least resistance will be towards hiring untrained staff, as has happened in the case of nursing staff in hospitals for mentally handicapped people. In other cases there may be great pressure

to over-qualification. For example, it is now very difficult to employ less qualified people trained on-the-job to do tasks such as mixing media in hospitals and laboratories. All the pressures have been towards raising entry standards and qualification levels. This has meant that costs are higher than might be, and that opportunities for on-the-job training for people without formal qualifications have been reduced.

5   The dynamic changes over time are rarely met through changes in on-the-job training, but most commonly through changes in formal qualifications. This means that the balance of the health workforce tends to be influenced by the play of professional power and by the accident of the labour market, rather than by employer intention or the needs of the service.

Any proposal for more effective local employment policies has to start by asking about benefits. What would be the gains to the NHS and to patient care? The main aim of policy should be seen in terms of raising productivity rather than that of reducing numbers. The central question for the NHS is how to meet an increasing – and changing – pattern of need with staff numbers which are bound to grow more slowly, if at all. If total numbers grow more slowly this will in fact raise the need for flexibility. The strategic plans now being suggested for the Oxford region imply, for example, that many more staff will have to transfer from hospital to community care or from in-patient care to day surgery than would be the case if total numbers grew rapidly. The benefits in terms of more effective and available care from such a pattern of change would be great, but would not show up quickly.

Such a policy has to begin by accepting the basic NHS framework of a service funded by central goverment. Within this constraint, how could we move towards a system which increases the incentives to productivity and flexibility? It is useful to look at what employers elsewhere in the economy have been doing. The NHS may be able to discover a better approach to being an employer than everyone else, but this hardly seems likely, given that its main pre-occupations are elsewhere. There have been certain common themes for the better employers whether in the public or the private sector.

First, they have been moving away from industry-wide agreements towards trying to concentrate decisions on pay and manpower at the plant and company level. The trend in industrial relations has been towards decentralization. Even though the NHS is nominally one service, the Whitley Council agreements in their present form look very like the kind of industry-wide agreements that the Donovan

Commission complained about. They have the effect of stifling initiative by local managers.

Second, there has been a move towards much greater use of study of work measurement and of job evaluation. Employers are now giving much more thought to where people are working and what they are doing. Within the NHS the position is very different. It is only the change at the margin or the change which threatens cash limits and manpower targets which is contested. As long as the bureaucratic standards are met, staff time is a kind of free good.

Third, employers have been putting much more emphasis on training on the job for the primary core of their workforce. They have been developing their internal labour market so as to offer better career prospects and to have a more flexible and committed workforce. Fourth, employers have been trying to reduce the size of the 'primary' team to which they are fully committed and to deal with fluctuations in workload through more use of sub-contracting. The costs of the primary commitment have risen and future investment and 'product' development cannot be financed except by producing current outputs at a lower cost. Fifth, employers have been trying to build new local relationships with unions in search of higher productivity.[3]

All this has implications for the NHS. Ideally, there should be a much more decentralized approach with District Health Authorities functioning as employers with some sense of their own identity. The key change would be towards a more 'economic' approach to the use of staff time and to the longer-term development of manpower. Gains in cost savings would be shared with staff, so this approach would imply that the more efficient employers would be able to pay more. The ritual headcounts would cease to be the main 'manpower' policy in the NHS. Instead, there would be a greater day-to-day interest in efficiency – in producing a certain quality of service at least cost.

Of course, the difficulties in the way of this NPP, or New Plan for Productivity, would be enormous. There would be various kinds of group interest; there would be anxiety about anomalies and about widening differences in pay between DHAs. There would be questions about national labour markets and about the need for consistent pay structures across the country and there would be further worries about possible reductions in pay and standards. Realistically, it would be better to start with groups other than doctors and nurses, and it would be necessary to retain Whitley Council agreements as a framework, although one that would increasingly serve a function of setting minimum standards.

In spite of all the difficulties, there are also some incentives. One is that the smaller committed workforce could, on average, earn more. Another is that a more flexible system could deliver greater long-term job security. It would be possible to retain some of the good things about the NHS's approach to manpower, such as the wide spread of formal qualifications, while dealing with some of the weak points, such as the lack of drive in on-the-job training. It is difficult to see how health authorities could show greater drive as employers and make more effective use of staff time, without changes of this kind. The essential steps would be to give DHAs much greater freedom to use savings from better use of manpower to improve services and to give them much greater freedom to share cost savings with employees in higher pay.

CONCLUSIONS

Employers in the caring services are trying to make adjustments and to introduce greater flexibility into services so as to provide a more helpful pattern of care to their clients. There are difficult decisions about how to use limited resources most effectively in pursuit of this aim. On one service model the main emphasis in any new spending could be on informal carers and on a greater use of volunteer staff. This would imply that new paid staff would be mainly people who would organize and recruit for this new kind of service. In the other model there could be expansion of services in the current pattern without much change. In both services there would be some role for creating jobs for less qualified staff in the care of elderly people but the role would be greater in the second model. But in either case the numbers of new jobs involved would not make very much impact on the overall level of unemployment. There is a considerable inconsistency between the general aspiration and the staffing pattern suggested by a service-centred approach. The best approach is probably to develop and expand the more appropriate service model and then to let the employment patterns take their course.

It is the essence of these new types of service that client need should set staffing patterns, and client need will change. There is a danger of imposing certain norms, however benevolently intentioned, from the centre. The problem of unemployment is best handled through incentives to employers of all kinds throughout the economy. People in the caring services are now raising their aspirations: there may well be a very strong case for expanding activity – but the direction should be set by client interest.

NOTES

1   In one outer London borough, the cost of an hour's work by a care assistant
    in an old people's home rose by 270% between 1974 and 1984 from £0.78
    to £2.89 per hour. An increase in labour overheads from 10.5% to 15.7%
    of total cost contributed to this as did regrading from Care Assistant 1 to
    Care Assistant 2 – but most of the increase came about because of
    increase in the basic rates. Average weekly earnings of female manual
    workers rose by 272% from 1974 to 1983.

2   There are also good points about the way the NHS uses its manpower. It
    has lower levels of staffing per capita for the main health professions than
    do other health systems. The doctor population ratios and the nurse
    population ratios are lower for Britain than for most other developed
    countries. The NHS makes more use of people with 'intermediate' levels
    of skill than do other health systems. The NHS has benefited from the
    strong role of the nursing profession and from its ability to adapt to
    changing requirements. There are also more developed career structures
    for a range of technician skills than in most health systems. The work force
    shows a balance between primary and hospital care which is much better
    balanced than elsewhere. The system of training and qualifications adjusts
    quite well to the changing patterns of need; for all the weaknesses of
    training for work with priority groups, such training does exist in the UK.
    Finally there has been considerable improvements in productivity of staff
    working in support functions, and staff retention has improved.

3   See Atkinson (1984) and Bain (1983) for good discussions of these issues.

12

Social Security Policy and Assumptions about Patterns of Work

JONATHAN BRADSHAW

INTRODUCTION

The social security system established in Britain after the Second World War was designed primarily for those not in work, whether because of retirement, sickness, or unemployment. Those in work were not provided for, except through relatively low family allowances payable in respect of second and subsequent children. Although the purity of this design has since been diluted by the introduction of benefits payable to supplement work income the essential logic of the system is still based on a distinction between working and not working – a distinction which does not recognize the existence of part-time work as a normal form of economic activity. For example, the Social Security Advisory Committee (SSAC) recently rejected the idea that income support for disabled workers should be based on the supplementary benefits scheme because 'supplementary benefits are essentially for people who are not employed' (SSAC, 1983, para. 5.22). This is not an inevitable characteristic of social assistance schemes: many countries pay benefits on a test of income regardless of the source of that income (Kahn and Kamerman, 1983).

Since the Second World War, part-time employment has become much more common, as Ermisch's chapter demonstrates, which suggests that it may be appropriate to reconsider the relationship between work income and the social security system, and in particular the question of whether this system should more explicitly recognize – or even favour – the existence of part-time work. This impetus for rethinking is given added weight by the arguments that the availability, nature and distribution of work will change radically over the next two decades. Handy (1984), for example, has claimed that full employment as we knew it in the post-war era will never return, and Gershuny and Pahl (1979) have argued that the most urgent priority for research in the social sciences is to gain an understanding of how work can be reorientated. The continuation or exacerbation of current levels of unemployment would also raise further questions about the appropriate response of social security policy. If people were encouraged to supplement their benefit incomes with occasional or part-time earnings, would this reduce the supply of full-time workers and enable more people to work part time? Would it be a cheap means of boosting the incomes of long-term claimants? Would it increase the demand for labour by enabling more employers to create more part-time jobs? Might it even increase the supply of labour by encouraging those currently outside the labour market to seek part-time employment?

Alan Walker's chapter discusses the wider social policy implications of some of these questions; this chapter focuses on the issues they raise for social security policy. It begins by summarizing and discussing the nature and purpose of the various elements whereby current policy 'disregards' certain earnings when calculating benefit entitlement and goes on to examine what we know about labour market participation by benefit recipients. It then sets out the policy choices available in relation to 'disregards' and considers the evidence about their likely effects.

BENEFITS AND EARNINGS: CURRENT POLICIES AND PURPOSES

The Social Security Advisory Committee has produced an excellent review of current policy towards occasional earnings (SSAC, 1983). In general, the level of earnings disregarded in the social security system is very low. There is only one benefit, widows' benefit, with no limit on earnings. Retirement pensioners have a relatively generous disregard of £65 per week, but this compares with £2 per day for a person receiving unemployment benefit, £4 per week for most claimants of supplementary benefit and no disregard for family income supplement (FIS). The maternity allowance cannot be claimed if there are any earnings.

The way earnings are calculated varies from one benefit to another: for most benefits they are net of work-related expenses and child care costs, but income tax and social insurance costs are also deducted in the case of supplementary benefits. For FIS and housing benefit, gross income with no allowances of any kind is taken into account. There are differences within and between benefits in the way the earnings of the claimant and those of other adults in the family are treated, as well as differences according to whether the other adult is a man or a woman. The equal treatment between men and women introduced into some areas of social security in November 1983 has led to considerable improvements in the treatment of male dependency disregards. Within the supplementary benefit scheme there are also differences in the way single parents' and couples' earnings are disregarded.

There is no reason why benefits serving different purposes should have identical earnings disregards. Earnings disregards can serve a variety of purposes within a single benefit and different purposes for different benefits. For those social security benefits designed to substitute for earnings, disregards may be intended to increase economic welfare, to increase income (not necessarily the same thing), to save the administrative hassle associated with taking account of minor variations in small earnings and to avoid having to police trivial fraud in undeclared pin money. But their primary purpose is often to keep the claimant in touch with the world of work so that they may retain self-reliance and skills and thus return to work as soon as possible. Certainly, this is the view of the SSAC: 'We believe earnings limits to be an important factor in developing incentives to work and particularly in encouraging claimants to keep some contact with the labour market' (1983, para. 7.1). Weale et al. (1984) in their study of the tapered earnings disregard, introduced in 1970 for single parents on supplementary benefits, also distinguish the objectives of increasing the extensiveness of labour market participation and increasing the intensiveness – that is, disregards may be designed to encourage more people to participate or to encourage people to participate more.

So earnings disregards can and do serve a variety of purposes but as with much social security policy these purposes are rarely made explicit. Indeed, disregards are generally a neglected topic. They have always been low, and they have not usually been increased in line with inflation. The unemployment benefit disregard was increased in 1982 for the first time in 10 years and the supplementary benefit disregard has, with the exception of the introduction of the tapered earnings disregard (TED) for single parents, remained unchanged since 1975.

Apart from the SSAC, the most recent systematic discussion of disregards took place in the context of the Supplementary Benefits Review. The review's conclusion in respect of the unemployed was clearly based on the assumption that enough full-time employment was or could be made available to provide for those out of work:

Part-time working by men, who are the majority of unemployed claimants, is rare. There is no evidence that an increase in the disregard would induce any change in their behaviour, but there is some danger that any increase in the total income from benefit and part-time work might discourage claimants from moving back into full-time work because the net gain from doing so would be reduced. We do not therefore think a significant increase in the disregard for the unemployed can be justified on its merits. (DHSS, 1978, para. 8.19)

Whilst they were prepared to countenance an increase in the disregard for lone parents, the sick and disabled and spouses 'to encourage them to continue in employment, to raise the family's living standards, to maintain their link with the employment field and to encourage their self-reliance', the cost of a higher disregard and the extra administrative complications led the review eventually to recommend only the introduction of the tapered disregard for single parents (which now exists).

CLAIMANTS AND EMPLOYMENT

Data on the labour market participation of social security claimants and their spouses are sparse. However, the general conclusions from the evidence about the use of disregards is that 'very few claimants avail themselves of the easements which already exist' (SSAC, 1983, para. 7.10). In December 1982, only 4.2 per cent of non-pensioner recipients of supplementary benefits reported earnings. When this group is broken down further, about 8 per cent of those who were sick and over 13 per cent of single parents had earnings, compared to less than 2 per cent of the unemployed.[1] We know very little about the earnings of recipients of insurance benefits, but one might expect them to be higher because the disregards for most of these benefits are more generous.

The participation rates of the dependent adult or spouse of a claimant are generally higher than those of the claimants, and DHSS data show that 12 per cent of the wives of the unemployed were working outside the home in December 1982; about two-thirds earned more than £20 per week. There is, however, evidence that the wives of unemployed men are less likely to work than the wives of employed men: the DHSS Cohort Study of the unemployed concluded that the wives of the unemployed were both less likely to work and more likely to leave the labour force after their husband became unemployed. It also found that the wives of men on unemployment benefit were less likely to give up work than the wives of men on supplementary benefit. (Moylan, Millar and Davis, 1984). Warr and Jackson (1984) have recently reported similar results from a cross-sectional study of the unemployed. On average 33 per cent of a sample of unemployed married men had wives who were working, but the proportion with working wives fell from 39 per cent for those unemployed for less than a month to 19 per cent for those unemployed for over a year.

The reasons why partners of social security claimants do not participate in work, or withdraw from the world of work when spouses become unemployed, are likely to be very complex but the evidence of the pattern of participation over time is consistent with the view that wives are influenced by their understanding of current disregards policy. For the first 12 months of unemployment a wife's earnings only mean that the man receives the benefit rate appropriate for a single person rather than that for a couple with a non-working wife. After a year, eligibility for unemployment benefit runs out and earnings in excess of £4 are then fully deducted from the supplementary benefit received by the household, leaving less reason to work. Warr and Jackson (1984) concluded that the speculation that wives give up a job as part of a household strategy only arises because of the nature of financial benefits paid to the unemployed in the UK. It would be valuable to discover whether in other countries with different arrangements there are different patterns of family employment.

What impact do wives' earnings have on family living standards? We know that without wives' earnings, the number of families and children living below 140 per cent of supplementary benefit level would increase threefold (Layard, Piachaud and Stewart, 1978). Similarly, recent work by Cooke (1984) on the living standards of the unemployed found that the most important reason for families with an employed and unemployed head moving out of poverty was the increased labour market participation of the spouse.

POLICY CHOICES AND ARGUMENTS

There are broadly two schools of thought about the future of social security policy on earnings disregards – the incrementalists and the radicals. The incrementalists are epitomized by the Social Security Advisory Committee. The SSAC accepts that there is no reason for uniformity in disregards policy but nevertheless argues that there must be room for some rationalization of the present diverse ways in which earnings are treated in social security provision. It also sees no justification in failing to uprate disregards in line with inflation and therefore recommends 'that the supplementary benefit disregard should be increased, by stages as necessary, so as to approach its real 1975 value' (SSAC, 1983, para. 7.11). It also recommends that the earnings disregards for the unemployed should be harmonized and increased to £9 per week.

What objections might there be to these proposals? Any increase in disregards has costs both in staff and money arising from the people who are brought into benefit eligibility or whose benefit increases as a result of the change. The SSAC proposals would cost about £40 million, and arguably it would improve the incomes of a group of people who are not necessarily most in need – those who are able to work or who are already working and may be benefiting from the existing disregard. Pahl (1984) has concluded from research in the Isle of Sheppey that opportunities in the informal economy are exploited most by those already participating in the formal economy – they already have the skill, capital resources and contacts. In the same way, increasing disregards may only provide additional help to those already cushioned to some extent from the hardships of unemployment. Other objections to increasing disregards are that they might undermine work incentives by increasing the reservation wage and, far from encouraging people to come off benefits, they would actually make a combination of benefits and disregarded part-time earnings a viable long-term income.[2]

However, the SSAC argued that the guiding principle with disregards policy 'should be the need to keep claimants of working age in touch with the labour market, in which it is hoped they will again be able to take part', and that:

> This low level of use, and probably awareness of the existing provisions permitting claimants to do some work and receive some earnings indicates there there is little danger of a modest increase in them leading to a situation where claimants subsist partly on benefit and partly on earnings, in preference to full-time work. (1983, para. 7.11)

This is where the radicals differ fundamentally from the incrementalists. Far from it being a danger, the radicals see a reduction in the supply of labour as a major purpose of the changes they advocate. They subscribe to one or other type of social dividend scheme, which propose that every member of society will be entitled to a basic income payable regardless of income or employment status. Thus, the work test in social security would be effectively abolished. Different people advocating a social dividend express this advantage in different ways. Thus Jordan stresses the freedom it will give 'from subordination to capital and freedom from the state':

> A social dividend would for the first time take away this coercive obligation on the working class. Unlike the social security system, which forces claimants to be idle while dependent on the state but obliges them to work as soon as paid employment – however unpleasant – becomes available, it would give wage workers the same right as those with property incomes: the right not to work (1984)

Roberts, in contrast, advocates a 'National Dividend' as a means of coping with automation, providing labour at lower cost to industry, and increasing the flexibility of wages:

> If the provision of basic subsistence income can be made independent of employment, then the equilibrium wage should be able to free itself from its historic connection with the subsistence level, and to rise or fall as the demand for labour changes without causing serious distress. (1982, p. 20).

By removing the link between a minimum wage and subsistence level, market forces will operate freely and jobs would be created. There would be no need for a retirement age. Employers' national insurance contributions would no longer exist. Distinctions between part-time and full-time work would no longer exist. Women with young children would withdraw from the labour force and job security and redundancy payments could be abolished (Roberts, 1982).

Miller (1983) has investigated the likely impact of a social dividend scheme on work incentives and labour supply. She concludes that the factors that affect incentives to work will change in different directions, and that it is impossible to forecast whether the aggregate supply of labour will rise or fall if a social dividend scheme were introduced. She believes it to be probable that there would be a fairness-increasing redistribution of work and that the demand for labour would increase with the end of taxes on employment. All the advocates of social dividend from their different ideological perspectives see the advantage of the scheme to be that people would be left free to choose whether or by how much they wished to enhance their income by earnings. They believe that with the support of the dividend, people could work for lower earnings and more jobs would be created. Many, including those with domestic responsibilities, would decide not to enter the labour force at all, whilst others would look for only part time work.

Although these objectives may be desirable, we cannot be confident that they will be achieved by a social dividend scheme. Furthermore, what are the implications of the state assuming such an important role in determining peoples' incomes? Will a social dividend scheme have a Speenhamland effect, shifting power away from workers and towards employers? There is no society in the world in which the able-bodied have a right to an income without being required to work, unless they are very rich. Even the possibility of continued high unemployment – of a permanent jobs shortage – seems unlikely to lead to such a radical change. What is much more likely, certainly in the short-term, are the kind of incremental changes to disregards policy proposed by the SSAC. What effects can we expect them to have?

THE EFFECTS OF INCREMENTAL CHANGE

Three factors, apart from the level of the disregard, are likely to play a part in determining the amount of labour market participation by social security recipients.

1   Awareness of disregards rules. One of the main findings of a study of the tapered earnings disregard for single parents was that most did not know about it. Only nine claimants out of a sample of 473 knew about the four main elements of the disregard, and most of those who gave financial reasons for not working or not working longer were substantially misinformed about the consequences of earning more. However, the study also found that there was no increase in participation following an injection of information (Weale et al., 1984).

2   Availability of jobs. It is inevitable that the decline in demand for labour in recent years has affected the opportunities of social security claimants. Certainly, the absence of suitable opportunities was given by many single parents in the tapered earnings disregard study as a reason for not working or not working more. There is evidence that while female labour participation has continued to rise, the level of participation of single parents (on benefit) has levelled off.

3   Other constraints. The other constraints on working are likely to

differ according to the type of claimant. Thus, the disabled are likely to face problems transporting themselves to work. For the unemployed, part-time work may conflict with their job search activity. For single parent families, the most important constraint on part-time work is the availability and/or cost of child care facilities.

Given these other factors, what impact does changing the level of disregards have? Most of the available empirical evidence is American and can be summarized briefly. Kiefer and Newman (1979) found significant differences in the supply of part-time workers in four states. Part-time work was higher in states with a high earnings disregard. There were only minor differences between states using disregards and those using tapered tax rates – a 75 per cent tax rate was on average equivalent to a disregard of about one-third of the weekly benefit amount. The Seattle-Denver income maintenance experiment sought to measure the effects of reducing tax rates in transfer programmes. The early results suggested that reduced tax rates which allowed working beneficiaries to keep a greater percentage of their welfare benefits increased the amount of paid work they did. However, this increase was more than offset by the reduction in labour supply of those who became eligible for benefits for the first time as a result of reductions in the tax rate. The increase in taxes needed to pay for the more generous tax rates also led to the wives of higher income earners increasing their labour supply to maintain their incomes and the overall change increased total output (Danziger, Garfinkel and Haveman, 1983). Similar results have been found in earlier studies of AFDC recipients. Levy (1979) found that liberalizing earnings disregards encouraged current recipients to increase their labour supply but these increases were more than offset by the reduction in the work of former non-recipients attracted onto AFDC. Barr and Hall (1981) found that increasing the tax rate on earnings drove some families off AFDC altogether, but their likely wage rate was a much more important determinant of dependence. Munts (1970) investigated the effects on labour participation of tax rates on earnings in partial unemployment benefit schemes. He found that marginal tax rates did shape work behaviour and that 100 per cent marginal tax rates, abrupt cancellations of benefit and switch-backed rates between zero and infinity were all undesirable.

These studies help to confirm conclusions that would be derived from the economic theory of labour supply, but they tend to focus on the extent to which disregards provide financial incentives for participation in work. Only indirectly and in passing do they assess the extent to which improvements in disregards *reduce* labour supply. In the present employment situation this might be the primary objective of changing disregards policy. Nevertheless, there is evidence from these studies that there will be a diminution of the intensiveness of labour supply and an increase in its extensiveness if disregards are increased.

The only recent evaluation of a change in disregards in the UK has been the study of the effects of the tapered earnings disregard on single parents. The DHSS carried out their own analysis of the effects of the change using the Annual Statistical Enquiries for 1980 and 1981 and reached four main conclusions.

1 Between November 1978 and December 1982 there was a small decline in the proportion of lone parents on SB with part-time earnings. This was probably due to declining job opportunities.
2 There was no increase in the proportion of SB recipients taking up part-time work following the reform.
3 Although fewer earners gave up SB in the year following the change in policy, this was no different from an overall tendency for fewer on SB to leave the books.
4 There was no tendency for those earning between £4 and £20 (those who might have benefitted) to increase their earnings following the introduction of the tapered disregard.

It may be that a more dramatic change in disregards policy would have had a larger effect, but it seems that the main effect of the introduction of the tapered earnings disregard was to increase the incomes of lone parents already in work. Single parents are, however, unlikely to be typical; as Weale et al. concluded:

> For lone mothers, the decision to take paid work depends upon a complex interaction of preferences, child care constraints, job opportunities and financial returns. Only the last was directly affected by the introduction of TED. (1984)

Even if the levels of disregards do not have a major impact on the participation rates of single parents, would they affect the participation of the unemployed or their spouses? It is clear from the data cited earlier that existing disregards are not encouraging much participation by the unemployed or their spouses. However, there has been a remarkable increase in the numbers receiving FIS during the period of rapid increase in unemployment. The number of recipients increased from 78,000 in April 1979 to 186,000 in April 1983. There has also been an increase in the proportion of FIS recipients who are self-employed from 7 per cent in 1979 to 10 per cent in 1982 (DHSS, 1983). There has been no systematic explanation for this growth in FIS recipients. It is likely to be explained by a combination of factors – declining working hours, short-time working, increasing numbers of one earner families, and perhaps increased take-up by the self-employed due to increased awareness of the benefit among their professional advisers.

However, the point in this context is that FIS is playing the part of a generous disregard of earnings and more people are utilizing it. Without FIS, a proportion of self-employed businesses and some firms subsidizing wages via FIS might no longer be viable, and, in addition, many workers would not be able to afford to work part time for the wages that they do. Thus, FIS is acting as a modest mechanism for maintaining the supply and demand of jobs at the same time as encouraging worksharing. We may, therefore, be developing a benefit to complement part-time earnings – but it is an unforeseen policy development.

CONCLUSIONS

Social security provision in Britain draws a rigid line between income from work and income from benefits. Disregards of earnings are generally low, and have deteriorated in value over the last ten years. Very few households attempt to combine work and dependence on social security. Yet there may be a case for a totally new approach to this issue. Far from encouraging people to work rather than exist on social security, we may want to discourage people from attempting to work full time or assist them to work part time – so that what jobs are available can be shared by more people, and to enable those who are unable to work full time to boost their living standards by part-time work.

If patterns of work are indeed changing permanently, as Handy (1984) argues, these issues can only become more urgent, as we seek to reduce the supply of and increase the demand for labour. Social security policy inevitably interacts with employment policy. Can we now begin to plan the interaction in order to maximize their combined contribution to improving social welfare?

NOTES

1   These data were provided by the DHSS and are drawn from their annual Statistical Inquiry.
2   This view was a major factor in the decision of the first Reagan administration in the USA to cut back sharply on such 'workfare' provisions; see Bernstein, 1984, for a fuller discussion.

13

Work, Women and Welfare

JANE LEWIS

INTRODUCTION

This volume identifies and focuses on two major challenges to social policy in the future: constraints on resources (and in particular on public spending) and the changing nature of employment. These issues have particular salience both for the supply and quality of jobs to women and for the constraints on their ability to participate in employment. In order to consider these implications, this analysis first examines both recent changes in women's employment and the main explanations for their labour market position. It then outlines the emerging factors which may shape and constrain women's employment before considering the policy issues and choices to which these give rise.

RECENT DEVELOPMENTS IN WOMEN'S EMPLOYMENT

The main characteristics of women's increasing labour market participation are well known and can be quickly summarized. Between 1961 and 1980 the proportion of the workforce that is female increased from 35 to 40 per cent. The increase was most spectacular for married women aged 15-59, whose economic activity rate rose from 7 per cent to 16 per cent. This means that above the age of 34 married women are as likely to work as single women. Since 1960, women entering employment have demonstrated an attachment to the labour force equal to that of men, and it appears that they will work for as many years as men, other than for breaks for childbearing (Bruegel, 1983).

There is however little evidence of any concomitant improvement in female career paths. Indeed, the net increase in women's jobs since 1961 is entirely account for by part-time employment, and while there is no intrinsic reason why part-time jobs should be low status and low paid, this is usual in Britain today. Hakim (1979, 1981) showed that in 1971 no fewer than 84 per cent of women were in occupations *dominated* by women, twice as many as could be expected if women were to be spread in the same way as all workers across all occupations in the economy. The latest survey of horizontal occupational segregation at the workplace level has found that two-thirds of women are in jobs *only* done by women (Martin and Roberts, 1984). Women also experience vertical segregation and within particular occupations are concentrated in junior and intermediate non-manual work and in semi-skilled and unskilled manual work. There is no evidence of any easing in either horizontal or vertical segregation despite the passing of the 1975 Sex Discrimination Act, nor of any lasting improvement in women's pay since the full implementation of the Equal Pay Act in 1975. Indeed, the tendency for women to be concentrated in occupations which pay both men and women poorly increased during the 1970s.

Furthermore, it is likely that the expectations of young women are substantially in conflict with the realities of women's position in the workforce. The percentage of girls aged 16 – 19 in full time education is greater than that of boys, and girls now equal boys in the number of 'A' level passes they achieve. The recent women and employment survey found that women under 30 were least likely to find their work stimulating or worthwhile. In addition, a surprisingly large minority (37 per cent) expressed their intention of continuing to work throughout the childbearing period, taking only maternity leave (Martin and Roberts, 1984, pp. 203-4). This probably reflects not only the greater attachment of young women to the workforce but also their hope for a fulfilling career. For while it is clear that at the moment the presence of children is an accurate predictor of women's labour force participation (Joshi, 1984), it is by no means clear that this reflects their wishes: it seems likely that more women would work if day care were available.

The extent to which this conflict between future expectations and present realities will become an actual source of frustration for women depends on future developments in the female job market, developments which can be understood only in the light of theories and beliefs about how women have come to occupy their current position in the labour market (see Amsden 1980, Bruegel 1983). The most influential explanation for women's marginal position in the workforce focuses upon the 'essential incompatibility' between productive and reproductive work: as long as women choose to have children and therefore leave the workforce for varying periods of time, they will *choose* to invest less in job training and employers will also behave circumspectly with regard to selecting female workers for training and advancement. If, as seems to be the case, women are showing greater attachment to the labour force, then this theory of women's employment would predict that the position of women in the labour market would very gradually improve.

In reality, however, the position women find themselves in as members of the labour force is the result of a much more complicated set of negotiations between the employer (who may also act as husband and father), the woman worker (who may also be a wife and mother), the male worker (also a husband, father and trade unionist), and the state, which has historically intervened to control the terms and conditions of women's employment much more than those of men. These negotiations are carried out in relation to the changing nature and structure of jobs, which is in turn dependent on the scale and technique of production and methods of work.

Historically, there has always been a notion of a woman's job and a woman's rate. Women have entered a particular field, such as engineering, when processes have been subdivided or diluted; or as a result of technological innovation (the typewriter being the classic example), or when the service offered is new and allied to women's traditional work in the home, such as state elementary school teaching. Occupations have also been 'feminized', usually because technological or organizational changes have rendered them blind alley jobs, as was the case in the late nineteenth-century retailing trade.

The important point is that there has always been sexual division of labour even though its boundaries have shifted between countries, between regions within countries, and over time. Not that the process of negotiations has been smooth: middle-class men, for example, may experience tensions between their self-interest as employers and their idea as husbands as to an appropriate role for their wives. But the strength of the sexual division of labour as a normative, shared concept is such that women have never in fact acted as a genuine reserve army of labour (*pace* Walker's chapter) other than in time of war. During the 1950s, for instance, male immigrant labour was preferred for stereotypically male jobs to that of married women. This more sophisticated understanding of the persistence of the sexual division of labour and the complicated ideological and material constraints on women's choices suggests that it is unlikely that sexual divisions will completely disappear or even significantly diminish in the absence of radical positive action programmes.

FACTORS SHAPING WOMEN'S WORK IN THE FUTURE

Just as it is impossible to explain women's historical position in the labour force in terms of simple choice theory, so it is impossible to predict future developments on any simple basis. The hours and kinds of work women undertake will depend on a wide variety of variables, including technological change, changes in the cycle of unpaid caring work (which women currently tend to accept as their responsibility in the final event), and the possibility of change in the sexual divison of labour inside as well as outside the home.

To take first the issue of part time work, the expansion of which has been so crucially connected to the increase in women's employment in Britain, it is not necessarily the case that married women want to work part time: why, for example, do so few US women (22 per cent as opposed to 42 per cent in Britain) 'choose' to work part-time? It may be, as Ermisch's chapter suggests, that in the Britain of the 1960s the shortage of unmarried women and young male workers forced employers to make more use of part-time married women workers, in which case the 1990s may see a similar pattern. Certainly national insurance benefit structures make part-time work an attractive alternative to employers. The future of part-time work is ultimately linked to the kinds of work women may expect to do in the future. However, the recent expansion of part-time work took place largely in service jobs, many of them in the public sector, where the work done by home helps and school dinner ladies, for example, has historically moved between the unpaid, informal (part-time) and formal labour markets, always being performed by women. The location of such work in the future is not certain. While there is evidence that the sexual segregation of labour protected women as a group from unemployment in the recession of the mid-1970s (Bruegel, 1979, and Walby, 1983), more recent cuts in public services have adversely affected women in welfare sector jobs. Indeed, since 1979 the boundaries have been more tightly drawn around the formal labour market, forcing women (as well as the young and the old) into either the informal or the unpaid sectors.

Even if full- and part-time work in the welfare sector declines, it is possible that new technology will create new types of part-time jobs for women: one recent analysis predicts that 70 per cent of the new jobs likely to be created between 1983 and 1990 will go to women (IER, 1983). However these jobs both will displace full-time clerical workers (Rimmer and Popay, 1982) and may often be located in the home. This new class of homeworker may not be prey to the problems of extreme low pay experienced by the traditional homeworker (Employment Committee, 1982), but may nevertheless share the problems of isolation, poor unionization and lack of entitlement to social benefits.

Women's need and desire to work outside the home for wages is also likely to be increasingly adversely affected by the burden of caring for the increasing numbers of very elderly people. As Lesley Rimmer has pointed out, increasingly women are caught in a 'caring cycle', consisting of first children, then elderly kin and finally husbands, especially if it is the husband's second marriage, and to a younger woman (1983). Just as the presence of children reduces the likelihood of married women participating in the labour force, so does the presence of an elderly person (Greenhalgh, 1980). In a recent study of 22 married couples caring for dependent relatives, nine wives had given up work to care with an average loss of income of £4,500 (Nissel and Bonnerjea, 1982). At the least, women's work opportunities become restricted to whatever part-time work they can find locally. Whether or not women *want* part-time work in the areas and on the conditions it is presently offered, it is often the only option many women have because of the unequal sexual division of labour in the home (Land, 1981).

POLICY IMPLICATIONS

During the last ten years feminists have propounded a two fold strategy designed first to secure greater recognition of the contribution women already make to the family economy and second to improve women's position in the labour market. Neither the tax nor social security systems were intended to deal with the phenomenon of the two-earner family which now accounts for about three-fifths of all couples. Moreover, between 1968 and 1977, the proportion of women who earned as much or more than their husbands rose from 3.6 per cent to 8 per cent, and if the analysis is confined to women working full time whose husbands are employed, from 5 per cent to 14.5 per cent (Rimmer, 1983).

A full policy of disaggregation throughout the social security tax system, favoured by feminists in the late 1970s, may be no more feasible in terms of practical politics than a social dividend scheme, but an individually based earnings-related system of unemployment benefit would serve both two-earner families and part-time workers better than the present system. The other alternative of making unemployment benefit 'family' based would in all probability do nothing to recognize the specific contribution made by the wife to the family income and continues to assume, against weighty evidence (Pahl, 1980, 1983), that resources within the family are shared equally.

To improve women's position in the labour market, feminist analysis has urged the adoption of positive action programmes including affirmative hiring and education policies and an increase in the social wage (in the form of increased day care provision and child benefit) as a means to undercut the idea of the husband as *the* breadwinner and to ease the burden of unpaid domestic work that falls on women. While affirmative hiring policies are probably the only means of correcting the historical burden of discrimination against women (Radcliffe Richards, 1980), they have met with hostility and suspicion in Britain and are in any case virtually impossible to implement during a period of high unemployment.

The major impediments which women face as workers stem from the unequal division of labour in the home. This is not the inevitable result of their continued desire to bear children. Much more could be done to ensure that child bearing *per se* does not deskill women, for example, recent amendments to the Canadian Labour Code provide for 41 weeks maternity leave and require that the employee must now be reinstated in the position she held prior to the leave. Moreover, 24 weeks of leave is to be available to both parents (as in Sweden) in the hope that it will encourage a more equal division of domestic work.

The two-fold problem of unemployment and the rapidly increasing burden of caring raise in an acute form the issue of how work is defined in our society. As Groves and Finch have pointed out, the invalid care allowance is the only benefit that recognizes the financial relationship between paid work and the unpaid work of caring (1983). Of course this benefit is not available to married or cohabiting women on the assumption that such work is part of the 'natural' duties of women. Arguably it should be extended to these women, but this runs the risk of reinforcing their isolation and the idea that caring is natural work for women without doing anything to meet their psychological need for paid employment. Ideally, as Baldwin and Glendinning have suggested, the possibility for husbands and wives to care should be opened out so that both spouses may choose the mix of caring work and paid employment that suits them best (1983). Any encouragement that might be given to parents to invest greater amounts of non-market time in caring for children or the elderly, as suggested by Ermisch, must ensure that equal incentive is given to men and women.

Sharing what is presently unpaid work has a natural corollary in sharing paid work. The possibilities of genuine job sharing (i.e. part-time work with full-time conditions and entitlements) have in practice yet to be explored. Undoubtedly it would be easier to job share in some occupations than others, for example in sixth form teaching and further education. The risk of sharing poverty is also real, as Walker argues, though less so if job sharing is floated on a voluntary basis as part of a household strategy. It may be more utopian still to talk as Walker's chapter does of a shorter working week, but if this idea is to emerge on the policy agenda, it is worthwhile thinking in terms of a shorter working *day* as a means to promoting the sharing of domestic labour.

Only if more incentive is given to men to share in what is now unpaid work will sexual divisions in the workplace be broken down. Shared domestic obligations will enable women to start equal in the workplace and will also undermine the job stereotyping that results in sexual segregation. At the moment it is, as Bosanquet's chapter argues, undoubtedly ridiculous, both in terms of practical politics and NHS personnel needs, to suggest that an unemployed shipbuilder become a home help. Nevertheless, until the idea that it is preposterous for men to engage in the work of caring changes, there is little hope of significant change in the position of women in the labour market.

Conclusions

Social Policy after Incrementalism

RUDOLF KLEIN and MICHAEL O'HIGGINS

The conclusions that emerge from this book are, paradoxically, both reassuring and unsettling. They are reassuring to the extent that the analysis offered suggests that there is no 'crisis' of the welfare state or of welfare provision in the simplistic sense of impending bankruptcy. They are unsettling to the extent that the evidence suggests that the future cannot sensibly be viewed as an extrapolation of the past. In a sense, this book is therefore about the problems of social policy in an age of uncertainty. There is uncertainty about economic prospects. There is uncertainty about the demands that will be made on the welfare state. There is uncertainty about the appropriate boundary between the public and private roles, and the extent to which the traditional objectives encapsulated in the institution of the welfare state can be met in different ways. There is uncertainty about the shifting domains of economic and social policy.

If this analysis is accepted, it follows that the challenge now is to devise an intellectual style or approach to social policy suited to the post-incrementalist era. In other words, social policy can no longer be planned on the assumption that the dividends of growth (even if reduced) should finance continued expansion along the same lines as in the past. For this is to ignore, as suggested in the introduction, problems of discontinuity: the fact that a new environment may throw up new issues in ways we cannot hope fully to anticipate or predict. In these circumstances to commit future dividends of growth to the preservation of existing programmes is also to exclude, by implication, the scope or the need to address such new issues.

In this final chapter, we therefore attempt to sketch out a possible conceptual framework for social policy analysis and planning in the age of uncertainty. In doing so, our starting point is that policy must be guided by two main concerns. The first is, as already stressed, the *management of uncertainty* (MU). The second is *catastrophe avoidance* (CA): i.e. policy must be concerned to avoid long-term commitments based on over-hopeful assumptions about the willingness or ability of future generations to meet the bill. After discussing the implications of both slow growth and uncertainty, this paper therefore outlines the characteristics of a policy approach – what we term *purposeful opportunism* (PO) – which would seem to be able to cope with both catastrophe avoidance and the management of uncertainty.

COPING WITH UNCERTAINTY

Any attempt to look into the future, whether five or 15 years ahead, is rather like filling in a football pools coupon. It involves permutating a variety of factors. These range from assumptions about demographic trends to assumptions about the international trade situation. They must, furthermore, include assumptions about the effects of different economic strategies – about which economists tend to differ sharply – and about the social impact, notably on unemployment, of different growth and productivity rates. Finally, compounding the perils of prediction, we have to reckon with a further variable: the way in which future governments may define any given situation politically, and the priorities (as between cutting public expenditure or cutting taxes, for example) they may choose to pursue.

In this situation, the only certainty is uncertainty, increasingly so, self-evidently, the further we look into the future. Crisis becomes one scenario, among many others. The range of possibilities, on a pessimism/optimism scale, is enormous. It follows that the planning and management of social policy – and indeed of public policy generally – is about planning for, and the management of, uncertainty and change in a turbulent environment.

Obviously not every factor is entirely uncertain; we can extrapolate the cost of meeting existing commitments, and this is what our exercise in scenario-generation does. We can attach probabilities to some outcomes. But this is simply to narrow the range of uncertainty, not to eliminate it. Moreover, uncertainty about trends is reinforced by uncertainty about likely variations around those trends. Governments have to shape their policies in the light of what may well be manic-depressive growth patterns, which in the past led also to manic-depressive patterns of public expenditure policy-making.

It was precisely this pattern of policy making which led to the demand for a more rational machinery of public expenditure planning. This demand found its classic exposition in the Plowden Report (Plowden, 1961) and the subsequent development of the PESC system of public expenditure control with its five-year planning horizon. In the event, however, this exercise in planning rationality led to precisely those irrational consequences which it was designed to prevent: a succession of public expenditure crises, in which spending was cut in order to achieve instant savings irrespective of the long-term effects on the programmes concerned. For what characterized public expenditure planning throughout the sixties, and well into the seventies, was over-optimism about the prospects of economic growth. The public expenditure plans had to be cut because the dividends of economic growth, which were supposed to finance it, did not materialize.

In all this, then, there is a paradox. If governments cannot realistically hope to *plan* future public expenditure – in the way it is possible to design a railway timetable in the expectation that the trains will more or less run on time and arrive at the right destinations – they must none the less have a framework of assumptions about the implications of present policies for the future, if only to avoid storing up unpleasant surprises for themselves or taking on commitments which they cannot hope to meet, i.e. catastrophe avoidance. This is, of course, why the Conservative government's 1984 Green Paper (Treasury, 1984b) takes a longer look into the future than any previous document published by the Treasury.

On the one hand, therefore, the need to look into the future when framing social policies is unavoidable. On the other hand, it is clear that planning social policies in the traditional sense of making precise commitments is likely to be shipwrecked on the rocks of uncertainty.

LOW GROWTH AND RIGIDITY

Whilst uncertainty is one inevitable feature of planning for the future, one of the more certain aspects is that the share of social expenditure in public expenditure, and in national income, is likely at best to grow only slowly. Even assuming that the need for social expenditure – an ambiguous concept in any case – is not itself rising, such slow growth creates problems both because of changes in the composition of need and because of organizational factors.

The first point may be illustrated by examination of demographic patterns over the next 15 years. The number of five- to 15-year-old children in England is expected to decline by 16 per cent – almost one million individuals – between 1981 and 1989. This is likely to be followed, however, by a rise of almost a million in the following decade, so this population group is expected to be only half a per cent larger in 2001 than in 1981 (Ermisch, 1983). The most likely policy response is one which, because of institutional inertia and rigidities, is out of phase with demands: a gradually diminishing 'excess' supply of teachers and classrooms during the first period followed by a gradual shortage in the second decade. Yet such fluctuations are not uncommon. Can we plan a more effective response?

Similarly, the data on the impact of demographic changes on the need for health and personal social services (HPSS) spending cited in O'Higgins and Patterson's chapter show that for most years during the 1990s overall HPSS spending need changes very little. This aggregate calm conceals considerable variations in the changes in the needs of the major components of HPSS – hospital services, general practitioners and personal social services. Moreover, the organization and technology of service delivery may well change over the next couple of decades. For example, the diffusion of a new information technology may transform the relationship between service providers and consumers, by giving the latter direct access to information. We need, therefore, to consider how to accommodate, manage and encourage flexibility and change within any given budget if organizations are to be able to adapt to changing pressures and tasks effectively. Equally, we have to consider whether the traditional definition of tasks and problems by professional service providers is appropriate: to put on the agenda options which at present are excluded from analysis because they affront professional paradigms and interests.

This conclusion is further reinforced if we consider the internal dynamics of organizations. Even making the unlikely assumption that organizational tasks will remain unchanged, we have to find a substitute for expansion as an instrument for fostering creativity and avoiding stagnation: the problem currently faced by universities, among other organizations. Within constrained budgets or fixed employment totals, this implies deliberately making space for experiment and innovation by eliminating a proportion of previous activities. Programme euthanasia may be just as important as policy birth control in an era of slow growth.

PLANNING FOR SURPRISES

How then do we plan in the face of uncertainty and low growth-scope? We would suggest that the planning and management of social policies, subject to uncertainty and low growth, requires purposeful opportunism (PO) and the institutionalization of capacities for adaptibility, flexibility and change.

What we mean by this is that governments should be clear as to where they want to go, but flexible about how to get there. They should be ready to adapt their policies in the light of changing circumstances, but prepared in advance to adapt them in ways consistent with their long-term objectives. In other words, the acceptance of uncertainty – the recognition of surprises lying in wait for us – should be built into our way of thinking about the development of social policies. In one sense this is trite: we all acknowledge it to be true. But we have failed to incorporate this awareness in our institutions and practices. We do not prepare the possible adaptations in advance. We do not have routines for change.

Our advocacy of a strategy of purposeful opportunism rests both on description and on a prescription. Opportunism is, in fact, what distinguishes all governments, of whatever party, and is at least as helpful in characterizing their behaviour as that familiar, and by now somewhat jaded warhorse of policy explanation – incrementalism. Governments react and adapt to events. What we are suggesting, however, is that the inevitability of such opportunistic adaptations to the environment should be accepted, anticipated and institutionalized into policy thinking. It is at least as 'rational' as a system of long-term planning which regularly comes unstuck. Prescriptively, therefore, we would argue that creating a long-term framework of social policy should be less about programme *planning* (inputs) than about setting policy *objectives* (outcomes), and thinking in advance about developing a range of *instruments* which may be adapted or substituted for each other as the policy environment changes – so as to avoid the often perverse and damaging effects of *ad hoc*, hurried adaptations.

One implication of this is that programmes may have to be designed with reversibility and termination in mind. We should, in other words, be evolving options which are consistent with our objectives but which do not necessarily involve long-term commitments. Social policy, in short, does not necessarily have to be about institution-building. It can also be about time-limited programmes, targeted towards achieving specific aims, which do not necessarily involve the creation of a self-perpetuating interest group of service producers.

A strategy of purposeful opportunism would therefore suggest building up a reserve bank of reversible or automatically terminating policy options. So if more resources than expected become available (whether for economic or political reasons), short-term schemes, consistent with long-term aims and with a limited life expectancy, would be available. An obvious example here would be an energy conservation programme targeted at low-income population groups. This is a limited commitment, would improve the living conditions of low-income households and might even reduce long-term social security expenditure on fuel cost supplements and debt difficulties among the poor. The regular use of such self-terminating programmes would further provide the space for adaptation and change which was earlier identified as necessary.

More important and also more radically, putting the emphasis on consistent *objectives* while allowing for opportunism in the choice of *instruments* underlines the need to redefine what we mean by social policies. In the past, there has been a tendency to define social policies in terms of specific instruments: the programmes and services of what is known as the welfare state. But if we define social policies in terms of a particular set of objectives or desired outcomes (the promotion of equity in health status or the maintenance of minimum incomes, for example), we then have far greater freedom to use whatever instruments may be indicated by a PO strategy in any given situation.

Thus we might decide that health is best promoted not by putting more money into the National Health Service, but by spending more on housing, or that the most effective way to help maintain minimum incomes is by creating temporary jobs in a national energy preservation programme. Such a PO strategy would recognize not only economic but also political constraints: a government which would recoil at the prospect of creating more jobs in the public sector might well rejoice at the stimulus to small businesses offered by such an energy conservation programme. Again, if a government is committed to giving priority to tax reduction – rather than increasing public expenditure – then a PO strategy would suggest examining the extent to which such cuts can be made compatible with, or supportive of, social policy objectives, for example as part of a more wide-ranging reform of taxation and social security.

TOWARDS THE NEW STRATEGY

In making the case for a strategy of purposeful opportunism, we do not claim to have discovered anything new. Our underlying theory of policy-making rests, to summarize our argument, on the recognition that all governments *are* opportunists – as they have to be. A new economic environment has simply strengthened the case for recognizing this explicitly, and incorporating the inevitability of opportunism into the way we think about social policy. For what has been lacking too often in the past, and what is now more necessary than ever in an era of uncertainty, is the framework of purposefulness which alone can help to prevent opportunism from being random, inconsistent and sometimes destructive. In thinking about the future of social policy, it is therefore crucial both to develop the framework of purposefulness – by setting objectives – and to identify a range of opportunistic options for moving towards the achievement of our aims. The former is needed to maintain a thread of consistency and a sense of direction; the latter is needed to provide the flexibility and adaptibility essential for the management of uncertainty.

Such a strategy would furthermore involve not just reversing the incremental upward creep that characterized the development of social policy programmes in the past but adopting a very different stance. In other words, decrementalism is not the answer to uncertainty and pessimism about economic growth. For decrementalism, in the sense of either reduced growth rates or creeping cuts, is likely to reinforce precisely those institutional rigidities which we have identified as one of the problems that needs to be overcome. It would mean an acceptance of the traditional means for achieving policy objectives, when the need is to devise new and more flexible instruments.

The thesis of this chapter, building on many of the arguments in this book, therefore suggests a new set of concerns for the agenda of social policy analysis. It underlines the importance of deepening our understanding of how short-life, self-liquidating programmes (whether public or private) can contribute to long-term policy objectives. It emphasizes the need to examine how best to overcome organizational rigidities which may impede adaptation. It brings out the importance of establishing the costs and benefits of regulatory strategies as a substitute for institution building. Finally, it indicates the need to devise incentives for promoting the adaptability and creativity which will be essential in an era when rapid changes in the economic and social structure of our society are generating new demands. The present welfare state is, in a sense, a monument to the first Industrial Revolution: to the problems it created and to the values which shaped it. Future social policies will, however, have to cope with the consequences of the second Industrial Revolution: this will, almost inevitably, mean responding to a new set of problems and perhaps a new set of values.

Bibliography

Adam Smith Institute, (1983) *Omega Report: Employment Policy*, London: Adam Smith Institute.

Allen, R. (1980) *The Economic Effects of a Shorter Working Week*, London: HM Treasury.

Alt, J. (1979) *The Politics of Economic Decline*, Cambridge University Press.

Amsden, A. (1980) *The Economics of Women's Work*, Harmondsworth: Penguin.

Atkinson, J. (1984) *Manning for Uncertainty: Some Emerging UK Work Patterns*, Institute for Manpower Studies, University of Sussex.

Bain, G. S. (ed.) (1983) *Industrial Relations in Britain*, Oxford: Basil Blackwell.

Balbo, L. (1981) 'Crazy Quilts: Rethinking the Welfare State Debate from a Woman's Perspective', mimeo.

Baldwin, S. and Glendinning, C. (1983) 'Employment, Women and the Disabled Child', in J. Finch and D. Groves (eds), *A Labour of Love: Women, Work and Caring*, London: Routledge and Kegan Paul.

Barr, N.A. and Hall, R.E. (1981) 'The Probability of Dependence on Public Assistance', *Economica*, May.

Bebbington, A. and Davies, B. (1983) 'Equity and Efficiency in the Allocation of the Personal Social Services', *Journal of Social Policy*, 12,3.

Bernstein, B. (1984) 'Welfare Dependency' in D. L. Bawden (ed.) *The Social Contract Revisited*, Washington DC: Urban Institute Press.

Beveridge, W. (1944) *Full Employment in a Free Society*, London: Allen & Unwin.

Birch, A. (1975) 'Economic Models of Political Behaviour', *British Journal of Political Science*, 5, 2.

Birnbaum, H., Bishop, C., Lee, A. J. and Jensen G. (1981) 'Why Do Nursing Home Costs Vary? The Determinants of Nursing Home Costs', *Medical Care*, XIX,11.

Blyton, P. and Hill, S. (1981) 'The Economics of Worksharing', *National Westminster Bank Quarterly Review*, November 1981, pp. 37 – 45.

Bolton Report (1971) *Report of the Committee of Inquiry on Small Firms*, Cmnd 4811, HMSO, London.

Bradshaw, J., Cooke, K. and Godfrey, C. (1983) 'The Impact of Unemployment on the Living Standards of Families', *Journal of Social Policy*, vol. 12, part 4, pp. 433-52.

Bruegel, Irene (1979) 'Women as a Reserve Army of Labour', *Feminist Review* 3.

Bruegel, Irene (1983) 'Women's Employment, Legislation and the Labour Market', in Jane Lewis (ed.), *Women's Welfare/Women's Rights*, London: Croom Helm.

Burghes, L. and Lister, R. (1981) (eds) *Unemployment: Who Pays the Price?*, London: CPAG.

Burton, J. (1981) 'Reflation Will Not Cure Unemployment', *Journal of Economic Affairs*, vol. 1, 2, pp. 84 – 8.

Cameron, David R. (1978) 'The Expansion of the Public Economy: A Comparative Analysis', *American Political Science Review*, 72.

Cameron, David R. (1982) 'On the Limits of the Public Economy', *The Annals*, 4.

Cameron, David R. (1984) 'Social Democracy, Corporatism, Labour Quiescence, and the Representation of Economic Interest in Advanced Capitalist Society', in John H. Goldthorpe (ed.), *Order and Conflict in Contemporary Capitalism*, Oxford University Press.

CBI (1980) *Jobs – Facing the Future*, London, CBI.

Challis, D. and Davies B. (1984) *Matching Needs to Resources in Community Care*, mimeo, Personal Social Services Research Unit, University of Kent.

Chancellor of the Exchequer (1961) *Control of Public Expenditure*, Cmnd 1432, London: HMSO.

Clark, M. (1978) 'The Unemployed on Supplementary Benefit', *Journal of Social Policy*, vol. 7, part 4, pp. 385 – 410.

Cole, G. D. H. (1920) *Guild Socialism Re-Stated*, London: Leonard Parsons.

Cooke, K. (1984) 'Incomes In and Out of Work: A Longtitudinal Analysis of the Family Finances and Family Resources Surveys', *SPRU Working Paper 186*, Social Policy Research Unit, University of York.

Courtenay, G. and Jowell, R. (1981) 'Referenda', *Public Money*, December.

Crewe, I. (1983) 'Post-Mortem', *Guardian*, 13 and 14 June.

Crick, B. (1981) (ed.) *Unemployment*, London: Methuen.

Daniel, W. W. (1974) *A National Survey of the Unemployed*, London: PEP.

Danziger, S., Garfinkel, I. and Haveman, R. (1983) 'Poverty, Welfare and Earnings: a New Approach', *Challenge*, 22, 4.

Darton, R. (1984) 'Residential Accommodation for the Elderly, 1970 – 81', in S. Hatch (ed.), *Residential Care for the Elderly*, London: Policy Studies Institute.

Darton, R. and Knapp M. (1984) 'The Cost of Residential Care for the Elderly: the Effects of Dependency, Design and Social Environment', *Ageing and Society*, 4, 2.

Davies, B. and Knapp M. (1981) *Old People's Homes and the Production of Welfare*, London: Routledge and Kegan Paul.

DE (1981) *A New Training Initiative: A Programme for Action*, Cmnd. 8455, London: HMSO.

DE (1984) 'Labour Force Outlook for Great Britain', *Employment Gazette*, February.

DHSS (1978) *Social Assistance: A Review of the Supplementary Benefits Scheme in Great Britain*, London: Department of Health and Social Security.

DHSS (1979) *Residential Care for the Elderly in London*, London: Department of Health and Social Security.

DHSS (1980) *Mental Handicap: Progress, Problems and Priorities*, London: HMSO.

DHSS (1981a) *A Study of Boarding-Out of Children*, London: Department of Health & Social Security.

DHSS (1981b) *Growing Older*, Cmnd. 8173, London: HMSO.

DHSS (1981c) *Community Care*, London: HMSO.

DHSS (1983a) *Social Security Statistics 1982*, London: HMSO.

DHSS (1983b) *Health Care and Its Costs*, London: HMSO.

DHSS (1983c) *Reply to the Third Report from the Social Services Committee 1981-82 on the Age of Retirement*, Cmnd. 9095, London: HMSO.

Dilnot, A. and Morris, C. (1981) 'The Exchequer Costs of Unemployment', *Fiscal Studies*, vol. 2, 2, pp. 15 – 17.

Duke, V. and Edgell, S. (1981) *The Politics of the Cuts*, University of Salford.

Dunleavy, P. (1979) 'The Urban Bases of Political Alignment', *British Journal of Political Science*, 9, 2.

Dunleavy, P. (1980) 'The Political Implications of Sectoral Changes', *Political Studies*, 28, I and II.

Employment Committee, (1982) *Report of the Employment Committee of the House of Commons on Home Working*, HC 39, London: HMSO.

Ermisch, J. F. (1983) *The Political Economy of Demographic Change* London: Heinemann.

Ermisch, J. F. (1984) 'British Labour Market Responses to Age Distribution Changes', *PSI Research Paper*, London: Policy Studies Institute.

Finch, J. and Groves, D. (eds) (1983) *A Labour of Love: Women, Work and Caring*, London: Routledge and Kegan Paul.

Finn, D. (1984) *The Employment Effects of the New Technologies*, London: Unemployment Unit.

Fishbein, M. (1967) *Readings in Attitude Theory*, New York: Wiley.

Forsyth, G. (1966) *Doctors and State Medicine*, London: Pitman.

Free, L. and Cantril, H. (1968) *The Political Beliefs of Americans*, New York: Simon and Shuster.

Gershuny J. and Pahl, R. (1979) 'Work Outside Employment: Some Preliminary Speculations', *New Universities Quarterly*, Winter.

Gilbert, Neil (1984) 'Welfare for Profit: Moral, Empiricial and Theoretical Perspectives', *Journal of Social Policy*, 13, 1.

234 Bibliography

Golby, C. W. and Johns G. (1971) 'Attitude and Motivation', *Committee of Inquiry on Small Firms*, research report no. 7, London: HMSO.

Golding, P. and Middleton, S. (1982) *Images of Welfare*, Oxford: Basil Blackwell.

Goldthorpe, J., Lockwood, D., Bechofer, F. and Platt, J. (1968) *The Affluent Worker*, Cambridge University Press.

Gough, I. (1980) 'Thatcherism and the Welfare State', *Marxism Today*, 24, 7.

Greenhalgh, C. (1980) 'Participation and Hours of Work for Married Women in Great Britain', *Oxford Economic Papers*, 32, 2.

Groves, D. and Finch, J. (1983) 'Natural Selection: Perspectives on Entitlement to the Invalid Care Allowance', in J. Finch and D. Groves (eds), *A Labour of Love: Women, Work and Caring*, London: Routledge and Kegan Paul.

Hadley, Roger and Stephen Hatch, (1981) *Social Welfare and the Failure of the State* London: George Allen & Unwin.

Hague, D. (1980) 'The Central Problem of Public Expenditure', *Manchester Business School Review*, Autumn.

Hakim, C. (1979) *Occupational Segregation*, DE research paper no. 9, London: Department of Employment.

Hakim, C. (1981) 'Job Segregation: Trends in the 1970s', *Employment Gazette*, December.

Hakim, C. (1982) 'The Social Consequences of High Unemployment', *Journal of Social Policy*, vol. 11, part 4, pp. 433 – 468.

Handy, C. (1984) *The Future of Work*, Oxford: Basil Blackwell.

Harris, R. and Seldon, A. (1979) *Over-Ruled on Welfare*, London: Institute of Economic Affairs.

Heald, David (1980) 'The Rehabilitation of the Market in Social Policy' in Noel Timms (ed.), *Social Welfare: Why and How?* London: Routledge and Kegan Paul.

Heclo, Hugh (1974) *Modern Social Politics in Britain and Sweden*, New Haven: Yale University Press.

Heidenheimer, Arnold, Heclo, Hugh and Adams, Carolyn T. (1983) *Comparative Public Policy*, 2nd edition, New York: St Martin's Press.

Hill, M. (1981) 'Unemployment and Government Manpower Policy', in B. Showler and A. Sinfield (eds), pp. 89 – 121.

Hill, M. (1983) 'Government Responses to Unemployment' in M. Loney, D. Boswell and J. Clarke (eds) *Social Policy and Social Welfare*, Milton Keynes, Open University Press, pp. 241 – 254.

Hill, S. (1984) 'Can Worksharing Reduce Unemployment?', *Unemployment Unit Bulletin*, No. 12, March, pp. 6 – 8.

Hirsch, Fred and Goldthorpe John H. (eds) (1978) *The Political Economy of Inflation*, Oxford: Martin Robertson and .Cambridge, Mass.: Harvard University Press.

Hirsch, Fred (1977) *Social Limits to Growth*, London: Routledge and Kegan Paul.

Hirschman, A. (1970) *Exit, Voice and Loyalty*, Cambridge, Mass.: Harvard University Press.

Hockley, G. and Harbour, G. (1982) 'The People's Choice', *Public Money*, March.

House of Commons Social Services Committee (1982) *Age of Retirement*, Session 1981 – 82, HC 26 – 1, London: HMSO.

House of Lords Select Committee on Unemployment (1982) *Report*, vol. 1, HL 142, London: HMSO.

IER (1983) *Review of the Economy and Employment*, Summer, Institute for Employment Research, University of Warwick.

Jahoda, M. (1979) 'The Psychological Meanings of Unemployment', *New Society*, 6 September, pp. 492 – 5.

Jenkins, M. C. and Miller, S. M. (1983) 'The Next American Welfare State', paper presented to the European Centre for Social Welfare Training and Research Conference: Can There Be A New Welfare State, September 1983.

Jenkins, S. (1985) 'Reforming the Social Security System: a Critique of the IFS Proposals', *Political Quarterly*, 56, 1.

Johansson, Sten, (1981) *Valfardsforandringar vid Sidan av Inkomster* Stockholm: Swedish Institute for Social Research.

Jordan, B. (1984) 'The Social Wage: a Right for All', *New Society*, 26 April.

Joshi, H. (1984) 'Unfair Shares', *Guardian*, 8 May.

Joshi, H. and Owen, S. (1981) *Demographic Predictors of Women's Work Participation in Post-War Britain*, Centre for Population Studies working paper no. 81 – 3, London School of Hygiene, University of London.

Joshi, H. and Owen S. (1983) *How Many Pensionable Years? The Lifetime Earnings History of Men and Women*, Government Economic Service Working Paper no. 65, London: HM Treasury.

Judge, Ken (1982) 'Is There a Crisis in the Welfare State?', *International Journal of Sociology and Social Policy*, 2, 1.

Judge, Ken (1984) 'The Establishment of Family Enterprises', discussion paper 311, Personal Social Services Research Unit, University of Kent at Canterbury.

Judge, Ken and Darton, Robin (1985) *Caring for Profit*, forthcoming.

Judge, Ken, Knapp, Martin and Smith, Jillian (1983) 'The Comparative Costs of Public and Private Residential Homes for the Elderly', Discussion Paper 289, Personal Social Services Research Unit, University of Kent at Canterbury.

Judge, K., Smith, J. and Taylor-Gooby, P. (1983) 'Public Opinion and Privatisation of Welfare', *Journal of Social Policy*, 12, 4.

Kahn, A. J. and Kamerman, S. B. (1983) *Income Transfers for Families with Children*, Philadelphia: Temple University Press.

Kavanagh, D. (1983) *Political Science and Political Behaviour*, London: George Allen & Unwin.

Key, V. O. (1961) *Public Opinion and American Democracy*, New York: Alfred Knopf.

Kiefer, N. and Newman, G. R. (1979) *The Effect of Alternative Partial Benefits Formulae on Beneficiary Part-Time Work Behaviour*, Report to the US Department of Labor.

Klein, Rudolf (1974) 'The Case for Elitism: Public Opinion and Public Policy', *Political Quarterly* 45, 4.

Klein, Rudolf (1976) 'The Politics of Public Expenditure: American Theory and British Practice', *British Journal of Political Science*, 6.

Klein, Rudolf (1982) *Public Expenditure in an Inflationary World*, mimeo, Brookings Institution Project on Inflation.

Klein, Rudolf, (1983) *The Politics of the National Health Service*, London and New York: Longman.

Klein, Rudolf (1984a) 'Privatization and the Welfare State', *Lloyds Bank Review*, January.

Klein, Rudolf, (1984b) 'The Politics of Participation' in Robert Maxwell and Nigel Weaver (eds), *Public Participation in Health*, London: King Edward's Hospital Fund.

Klein, Rudolf and Lewis, Janet (1976) *The Politics of Consumer Representation: A Study of Community Health Councils* London: Centre for Studies in Social Policy.

Knapp, Martin (1984) *The Economics of Social Care*, London: Macmillan.

Knapp, Martin and Missiakoulis, Spyros (1982) 'Inter-Sectoral Cost Comparisons: Day Care for the Elderly', *Journal of Social Policy*, 11, 2.

Koetting, M. (1980) *Nursing Home Organisation and Efficiency*, Lexington, Mass.: Lexington Books.

Korpi, Walter (1983) *The Democratic Class Struggle*, London: Macmillan.

Kramer, Ralph M. (1981) *Voluntary Agencies in the Welfare State*, Berkeley: University of California Press.

Laczko, F. and Walker, A. (1985) 'Excluding Older Workers From the Labour Market: Early Retirement Policies in Britain, France and Sweden' in C. Jones and M. Brenton (eds) *The Yearbook of Social Policy in Britain 1984*, London, Routledge and Kegan Paul.

Land, H. (1981) *Parity Begins at Home*, London: Equal Opportunities Commission/Social Science Research Council.

Land, H. and Parker, R. (1978) 'United Kingdom', in A. J. Kahn and S. B. Kamerman (eds), *Family Policy*, New York: Columbia University Press.

Lansley, S. and Gosschalk, B. (1984) 'Tax Cuts Welcome, But Not at Any Price', *Guardian*, 8 February.

Lansley, S. and Weir, S. (1983) 'Towards a Popular View of Poverty', *New Society*, 25 August.

Layard, R. (1982) *Youth Employment and Training*, London: Centre for Labour Economics, LSE.

Layard, R., Piachaud, D. and Stewart, M. (1978) *The Causes of Poverty*, London: HMSO.

Le Grand, J. (1982) *The Strategy of Equality*, London: George Allen and Unwin.

Levy, F. (1979) 'The Labor Supply of Female Household Heads – AFDC Work Incentives Don't Work Too Well', *Journal of Human Resources*, XIV, 1.

Lewis, A. (1980) 'Attitudes to Public Expenditure', *Political Studies*, 28, 2.

Leibenstein, Harvey, (1966) 'Allocative Efficiency versus X-Efficiency' *American Economic Review* 56.

McGoldrick, A. and Cooper, C. (1980), 'Voluntary Early Retirement – Taking the Decision', *Employment Gazette*, August, pp. 859 – 64.

Makeham, P. and Morgan, P., (1980) *Evaluation of the Job Release Scheme*, London: Department of Employment.

Marris, P. and Rein, M., (1967) *Dilemmas of Social Reform*, London: Routledge and Kegan Paul.

Marshall, G. (1984) 'Some Remarks on the Study of Working-Class Consciousness', *Politics and Society*, 12, 3.

Marsland, D. (1984) 'Attitudes to Welfare', *Sociology*, 18, 1.

Martin, J. and Roberts, C. (1984) 'Women's Employment in the 1980s. Evidence from the Women and Employment Survey', *Employment Gazette*, May.

Meade, J., (1984) 'Full Employment, New Technologies and the Distribution of Income', *Journal of Social Policy*, vol. 13, 2, pp. 129 – 46.

Metcalf, D. (1982) *Alternatives to Unemployment*, London: PSI.

Middlemass, K. (1979) *Politics in Industrial Society*, London: André Deutsch.

Millar, J. (1984) 'Lone Mothers' Labour Participation: Evidence from the Family Finances and Family Resources Surveys', SPRU working paper no. 182, Social Policy Research Unit, University of York.

Miller, A. (1983) 'In Praise of Social Dividend', *Heriot-Watt Working Paper in Economics*.

Millward, Robert, (1982) 'The Comparative Performance of Public and Private Ownership', in Lord Roll (ed), *The Mixed Economy*, London: Macmillan.

Minford, Patrick, (1984) 'State Expenditure: a Study in Waste', *Economic Affairs*, Supplement (April – June).

Mishra, Ramesh (1984) *The Welfare State in Crisis*, Brighton: Harvester Press; and New York: St. Martin's Press.

Morone, J. A. and Marmor, T.R. (1981) 'Representing Consumer Interests: the Case of American Health Planning', *Ethics* 91, 3.

Moylan, S. and Davies, B. (1980) 'The Disadvantages of the Unemployed', *Employment Gazette*, August, pp. 830 – 3.

Moylan, S., Millar, J. and Davis, R. (1984) *Report of the DHSS Cohort Study of Unemployed Men*, London: Department of Health and Social Security.

MSC (1980) *A Study of the Long-Term Unemployed*, London: MSC.

MSC (1981) *A New Training Initiative*, Consultative Document, London: MSC.

MSC (1983) *Towards an Adult Training Strategy*, London: MSC.

Munts, R. (1970) 'Partial Benefit Schedules in Unemployment Insurance: their Effect on Work Incentives', *Journal of Human Resources*, v, 2.

NCCOP (1965) *Private Homes for Old People*, London: National Corporation for the Care of Old People.

Nissel, M. and Bonnerjea, L. (1982) *Family Care of the Handicapped Elderly: Who Pays?*, London: Policy Studies Institute.

O'Brien, J., Saxberg B. and Smith H. L. (1983) 'For-Profit or Not-For-Profit Nursing Homes: Does it Matter?', *Gerontologist*, 23, 4.

OECD (1981) *The Welfare State in Crisis*, Paris: Organization for Economic Co-operation and Development.

OECD (1984) 'The Future of the Welfare State', *OECD Observer*, January.

OECD (1985) *The Growth and Control of Social Expenditure, 1960 – 1990*, OECD Studies in Social Policy, Paris: Organization for Economic Co-operation and Development.

O'Higgins, Michael (1985) 'Public-Private Interaction in Social Policy: A Comparative Study of Pensions Provision in Sweden, West Germany and the United Kingdom' in L. Rainwater and M. Rein (eds), *The Public-Private Interplay in Social Welfare*, Armonk, New York: M. E. Sharpe.

O'Higgins, Michael and Ruggles, Patricia (1985) 'Retrenchment and the New Right: a Comparative Analysis of the Thatcher and Reagan Administrations' in G. Esping-Andersen, M. Rein and L. Rainwater (eds) *Stagnation and Renewal: Social Policy in Recession*, Armonk, New York: M. E. Sharpe.

Oxford RHA (1983) *The Region's Health: a New Way Forward*, Oxford Regional Health Authority.

Pahl, Jan (1980) 'Patterns of Money Management within Marriage', *Journal of Social Policy*, 9.

Pahl, Jan (1983) 'The Allocation of Money and the Structuring of Inequality within Marriage', *Sociological Review*, 31.

Pahl, R. (1984) *Divisions of Labour*, Oxford: Basil Blackwell.

Pahl, R. and Wallace, C. (1984) *Household Work Strategies in Economic Recession*, mimeo, University of Kent at Canterbury.

Parker, S. (1980) *Older Workers and Retirement*, London: HMSO.

Parliamentary Commissioner for Administration (1979) *Annual Report for 1978*, London: HMSO.

Peacock, Alan and Wiseman, Jack (1967) *The Growth of Public Expenditure in the United Kingdom*, 2nd edition, London: Allen and Unwin.

Peterson, Paul E. (1970) 'Forms of Representation: Participation of the Poor in the Community Action Program', *American Political Science Review*, 64, 2.

Piachaud, D. (1974) 'Attitudes to Pensions', *Journal of Social Policy*, 3, 2.

Pinker, R. (1971) *Social Theory and Social Policy*, London: Heinemann.

Pissarides, C. (1981) 'Staying on at School in England and Wales', *Economica*, 48.

Plowden (1961) *Control of Public Expenditure* (The Plowden Report), Cmnd 1432, London: HMSO.

Pond, C. (1980) 'Low Pay and Unemployment', *Low Pay Review*, August, pp. 1-5.

Radcliffe Richards, J. (1980) *The Sceptical Feminist*, London: Routledge and Kegan Paul.

Rainwater, L. and Rein, M. (eds) (1985) *The Public-Private Interplay in Social Welfare*, Armonk, New York: M. E. Sharpe.

Richardson, J. and Moon, J. (1984) 'The Politics of Unemployment in Britain', *Political Quarterly*, 55, 1.

Riker, William H. (1982) *Liberalism Against Populism*, San Francisco: W. H. Freeman and Company.

Rimmer, L. (1983) 'The Economics of Work and Caring', in J. Finch and D. Groves (eds), *A Labour of Love: Women, Work and Caring*, London: Routledge and Kegan Paul.

Rimmer, L. and Popay, J. (1982) *Employment Trends and the Family*, London: Study Commission on the Family.

Ritchie, J., Keegan J. and Bosanquet, N. (1983) *Housing for Mentally Ill and Mentally Handicapped People*, London: HMSO.

Roberts, K. (1982) *Automation, Unemployment and the Distribution of Income*, Maastricht: European Centre for Work and Society.

Roberts, K. (1983) 'Could a Basic Income be the Answer to Unemployment?', *Initiatives*, no. 7, pp. 3 – 5.

Robertson, David (1976) *A Theory of Party Competition* London: Wiley.

Rose, D., Vogler, C., Marshall, G. and Newby, H. (1984) 'Economic Restructuring: the British Experience', *Annals of the American Academy of Political and Social Science*, September.

Rose, R. (1980) *Class does not Equal Party*, Centre for the Study of Public Policy, University of Strathclyde.

Rose, R. (1983a) 'Two and One-Half Cheers for the Market in Britain', *Public Opinion*, June/July.

Rose, R. (1983b) *Getting by in Three Economies*, Centre for the Study of Public Policy, University of Strathclyde.

Rosser, Rachel (1983) 'Issues of Measurement in the Design of Health Indicators: a Review', in A. J. Culyer (ed.) *Health Indicators*, Oxford: Martin Robertson.

Royal Commission on Local Government in England and Wales (1969) *Report*, London: HMSO.

Royal Commission on the National Health Service, (1979) *Report*, Cmnd 7615, London: HMSO.

Runciman, W. (1971) *Relative Deprivation and Social Justice*, Harmondsworth: Penguin.

Ryan, P. (1984) 'The New Training Initiative After Two Years', *Lloyds Bank Review*, no. 152, April, pp. 31 – 45.

Ryan, W. (1971) *Blaming the Victim*, New York: Orbach and Chambers.

Sarlvik, B. and Crewe, I. (1983) *Decade of Dealignment*, Cambridge University Press.

Savas, E. S., (1977) *Alternatives for Delivering Public Services*, Boulder, Colorado: Westview Press..

Scase, R. and Goffee R. (1982) *The Entrepreneurial Middle Class*, London: Croom Helm.

Schlackmann (1978) *Report on Research on Public Attitudes Towards the S. B. Scheme*, mimeo, London: Schlackmann Organization.

Schmitter, P. (ed.) (1977) 'Corporatism and Policy-Making in Western Europe', *Comparative Political Studies*, 10, 1.

Sharpe, L. J. (1973) 'American Democracy Reconsidered. Part II', *British Journal of Political Science*, 3, 2.

Shonfield, Andrew (1969) *Modern Capitalism*, Oxford University Press.

Showler, B. and Sinfield, A. (1981) (eds) *The Workless State*, Oxford: Martin Robertson.

Sinfield, A. (1968) *The Long-Term Unemployed*, Paris, OECD.

Sinfield, A. (1977) 'The Social Costs of Unemployment' in K. Jones et al. (eds) *The Year Book of Social Policy in Britain 1976*, London: Routledge & Kegan Paul.

Sinfield, A. (1979) *What Unemployment Means*, Oxford, Martin Robertson.

Sinfield, A. (1980) 'The Blunt Facts of Unemployment', *New Universities Quarterly*, Winter.

Sinfield, A. (1983) *The Necessity for Full Employment* in H. Glennerster (ed.), *The Future of the Welfare State*, London, Heinemann, pp. 61 – 73.

Smith, Jillian (1984) 'PSSRU Survey of Residential Homes for the elderly 1981: Representativeness of Samples in the Private Sector', discussion paper 307, Personal Social Services Research Unit, University of Kent at Canterbury.

SSAC (1983) *Second report of the Social Security Advisory Committee 1982/83*, London: HMSO.

Taylor-Gooby, P. (1976) 'Rent Benefits and Tenants' Attitudes', *Journal of Social Policy*, 5, 1.

Taylor-Gooby, P. (1982) 'Two Cheers for the Welfare State', *Journal of Public Policy*, 2, 4.

Taylor-Gooby, P. (1983) 'The Welfare State and Individual Freedom', *Political Studies*, 31, 2.

Taylor-Gooby, P. (1985) *Public Opinion, Ideology and State Welfare*, London: Routledge and Kegan Paul.

Thevenot, L. (1979) 'Evolution du Personelle Dissente 1968 – 1971', Paris: INSEE.

Tomlinson, J. (1983) 'Does Mass Unemployment Matter?', *National Westminster Bank Quarterly Review*, February, pp. 35 – 45.

Townsend, P. (1979) *Poverty in the United Kingdom*, Harmondsworth: Penguin.

Treasury (1984a) *The Government's Expenditure Plans 1984 – 85 to 1986 – 87*, Cmnd 9143, London: HMSO.

Treasury (1984b) *The Next Ten Years: Public Expenditure and Taxation into the 1990s*, Cmnd 9189, London: HMSO.

TUC (1981) *Unemployment: the Fight for TUC Alternatives*, London: TUC.

Walby, Sylvia (1973) 'Patriarchal Structures: the Case of Unemployment', in Eva Gmarnikow, David Morgan, June Putrvis and Daphne Taylorson (eds) *Gender, Class and Work*, London: Heinemann.

Walker, A. (1981) 'The Level and Distribution of Unemployment' in L. Burghes and R. Lister (1981), pp. 7 – 30.

Walker, A. (1982a) *Unqualified and Underemployed*, London: Macmillan.

Walker, A. (1982b) 'The Social Consequences of Early Retirement', *Political Quarterly*, vol. 53, no. 1, pp. 61 – 72.

Walker, A. (1984) *Social Planning*, Oxford: Blackwell/Robertson.

Walker, A. and Laczko, F. (1982) 'Early Retirement and Flexible Retirement' in House of Commons Social Services Committee (1982), vol. II, HC 26 – II, pp. 211 – 22.

Walker, A., Winyard, S. and Pond, C. (1983) 'Conservative Economic Policy: the Social Consequences' in D. Bull and P. Wilding (eds) *Thatcherism and the Poor*, London, CPAG, pp. 13 – 26.

Walker, A., Noble, I. and Westergaard, J. (1985) 'From Secure Employment to Labour Market Insecurity: the Impact of Redundancy on Older Workers' in B. Roberts, R. Finnegan and D. Gallie (eds) *New Approaches to Economic Life: Economic Restructuring, Unemployment and the Social Division of Labour*, Manchester University Press.

Walker, R., Lawson, R. and Townsend, P. (1984) *Responses to Poverty: Lessons From Europe*, London: Heinemann.

Warr, P. (1984) 'Economic Recession and Mental Health: A Review of Research', Sheffield, MRC/ESRC Applied Psychology Unit.

Warr, P. and Jackson, P. (1984) 'Men Without Jobs: Some Correlates of Age and Length of Unemployment', *Journal of Occupational psychology*, 57.

Watson, David (1984) 'Moral Objections to Welfare for Profit', *Journal of Social Policy*, 13, 3.

Weale, A., Bradshaw, J., Piachaud D. and Maynard, A. (1984) *Women, Work and Social Security*, London: Bedford Square Press.

Webb, A, and Wistow, G. (1982) 'The Personal Social Services Trends in Expenditure and Provision', in House of Commons Social Services Committee, *Second Report, 1981 – 2: Public Expenditure on the Social Services*, vol. 2, London: HMSO.

Webber, D. (1983) 'Combating and Acquiescing in Unemployment: Crisis Management in Sweden and West Germany', *West European Politics*, vol. 6, no. 1, pp. 23 – 43.

West, P., Illsley, R. and Kelman, H. (1984) 'Public Preferences for the Care of Dependency Groups', *Social Science and Medicine*, 18, 4.

West, P. (1984) *The Family, the Welfare State and Community Care*, mimeo, University of Aberdeen.

Westergaard, J., Noble, I. and Walker, A. (1984) *After Redundancy: Final Report to the ESRC*, London: ESRC.

White, J. (1980) *Shorter Working Time*, London: PSI.

White, M. (1981) *Case Studies of Shorter Working Time*, London: PSI.

White, M. (1983) *Long-Term Unemployment and Labour Markets*, London: PSI.

Whiteley, P. (1981) 'Public Opinion and the Demand for Welfare in Britain', *Journal of Social Policy*, 10, 4.

Wilensky, Harold (1976) *The Welfare State and Equality*, Berkeley: University of California Press.

Willcocks, D., Peace, S., and Kellaher L., with Ring J. (1982) *The Residential Life of Old People: a Study in 100 Local Authority Old People's Homes*, volumes I and II, Survey Research Unit, North London Polytechnic.

Wilson Report (1979) *The Financing of Small Firms: Interim Report of the Committee to Review the Functioning of Financial Institutions*, Cmnd 7503, London: HMSO.

Yates, D. (1973) *Neighbourhood Democracy*, Lexington, Mass.: D. C. Heath.

Youthaid (1984) *The Youth Training Scheme*, Briefing Paper, London: Youthaid.

Notes on Contributors

NICK BOSANQUET is a Senior Research Fellow, Centre for Health Economics, University of York. He is the author of *After the New Right*, (Heinemann, 1983) and is currently researching into the economics of the family doctor service. His other recent research has been into the recruitment and training of young workers in the NHS.

JONATHAN BRADSHAW is Professor of Social Policy and Director of the Social Policy Research Unit at the University of York. SPRU is engaged on a programme of research on benefits and services for disabled people, social security policy and the social aspects of energy policy funded by the DHSS. He has authored or co-authored a number of books, including *Reserved for the Poor* (Martin Robertson 1983), *Energy and Social Policy* (Routledge 1983), *Issues in Social Policy* (Routledge and Kegan Paul 1982), *Child Support in the European Community* (Bedford Square Press 1980) and *The Family Fund* (Routledge and Kegan Paul 1980).

DAVID CAMERON is an associate professor of political science at Yale University. He did graduate work at the London School of Economics and received his Ph.D. from the University of Michigan. He has published several articles and chapters in edited volumes on various topics of comparative political economy.

GAVYN DAVIES is Chief Economist at Simon and Coates. He was a member of the Prime Minister's Policy Unit from 1974 to 1979.

JOHN ERMISCH is a Senior Research Fellow at the Policy Studies Institute. Previously, he lectured in Economics and Statistics at the

University of Kansas and at Chicago State University and was a research economist at the US Department of Housing and Urban Development, Washington DC. He is author of *The Political Economy of Demographic Change* (1983), *Housing Finance: Who Gains?* (1984) and articles in demographic and economics journals. His main interests are in economic aspects of the causes and implications of demographic change and the economics of housing.

COLIN GILLION, originally an econometrician and macro-economist specialising in input-output studies, joined the Country Studies Division of the OECD in 1977 and became Head of the Social Affairs Division in 1983. Recent studies undertaken by this Division include work in the areas of health care policies, social security pension schemes and the problems of ageing societies, as well as current work on social expenditures.

RICHARD HEMMING was a Senior Research Officer at the Institute for Fiscal Studies before joining the OECD in 1983, where he worked the areas of social security and taxation. He is the author of *Poverty and Incentives: The Economics of Social Security*, Oxford University Press 1984. At the OECD his work has been in the area of social expenditure. He has recently moved to the IMF in Washington DC.

KEN JUDGE is Deputy Director of the Personal Social Services Research Unit at the University of Kent, and the editor of the *Journal of Social Policy*. He was previously a lecturer in social policy at the University of Bristol and was educated at Cambridge and LSE. He has written three books and numerous articles on economic and financial aspects of social policy. He is currently directing a research team which is promoting and evaluating the Government's 'Care in the Community' initiative.

RUDOLF KLEIN is Professor of Social Policy and Director of the Centre for the Analysis of Social Policy at the University of Bath, and co-editor of Political Quarterly. He has published extensively on both health care policy-making (his most recent book being *The Politics of the National Health Service*, Longman, 1983) and on public expenditure and social policy.

MARTIN KNAPP is a Senior Research Fellow in the Personal Social Services Research Unit and Lecturer in Economics at the University of Kent at Canterbury. His research interests are mainly in the economics of social policy, with particular concentration on the personal social services. His textbook, *The Economics of Social Care* was recently published by Macmillan (1984) and he is co-author of *Old People's Homes and the Production of Welfare* (1981). His is currently conducting further research on child care services, and particularly intermediate treatment.

JANE LEWIS teaches in the Department of Social Science and Administration at the LSE. She is the author of *The Politics of Motherhood* (Croom Helm, 1980) and *Women in England 1870-1950: Sexual Divisions and Social Changes* (Harvester and Indiana UP, 1984) and the editor of *Women's Welfare Women's Rights* (Croom Helm, 1983). She has also written numerous articles on women's history and women and social policy.

MICHAEL O'HIGGINS is a Reader in Social Policy at the University of Bath and during 1984/85 a Visiting Scholar at Harvard University. From 1980 to 1984 he acted as a Specialist Adviser to the Social Services Committee of the House of Commons. He has published, in both British and international contexts, on income distribution and redistribution, social security policy analysis, public expenditure and social policy and the hidden economy.

ALAN PATTERSON worked for the National Coal Board before taking a degree in environmental sciences at the University of East Anglia. During 1984 he was a Research Associate in the Centre for the Analysis of Social Policy at the University of Bath, and he is currently undertaking post-graduate research at the University of Sussex.

DAVID PIACHAUD is a Reader in Social Administration at the London School of Economics and was a member of the Prime Minister's Policy Unit between 1974 and 1979. He is the author or co-author of a wide range of books and papers, including *The Causes of Poverty* (HMSO, 1978), *Child Support in the European Community* (Bedford Square Press, 1980) and *The Distribution and Redistribution of Incomes* (Bedford Square Press, 1982).

MARTIN REIN is Professor of Social Policy in the Department of Urban Studies and Planning at Massachusetts Institute of Technology. Recently published books include: *Social Science and Public Policy*, *From Policy to Practice* and *Women's Claims* (with Lisa Peattie).

PETER TAYLOR-GOOBY teaches social policy at the University of Kent. He studied philosophy at the University of Bristol and social policy at the University of York, and has also worked as a school-teacher and social security counter clerk in Newcastle. He has carried out research on public attitudes to state and private welfare provision financed by the Economic and Social Research Council. He is author of *Public Opinion, Ideology and State Welfare* (Routledge and Kegan Paul, 1985); and co-author of *Social Theory and Social Welfare* (Edward Arnold, 1981) and *Political Philosophy and Social Welfare* (Routledge and Kegan Paul, 1980).

ALAN WALKER is a Reader in Social Policy at the University of Sheffield. He has carried out research on the distribution of unemployment, the employment experiences of educationally handicapped school leavers, employment and disability, early retirement and the impact of redundancy in the steel industry. He is author of *Unqualified and Underemployed* (Macmillan, 1981) and *Social Planning* (Basil Blackwell/Martin Robertson, 1984), editor of *Public Expenditure and Social Policy* (Heinemann, 1982), *Community Care* (Blackwell/Robertson, 1982) and co-editor of *Disability in Britain* (Martin Robertson, 1981).

ALBERT WEALE is Lecturer in Politics and Assistant Director of the Institute for Research in the Social Sciences at the University of York. He is the author of a number of works on social policy, including *Political Theory and Social Policy* (Macmillan, 1983) as well as specialist articles. His chapter in this volume was completed while he was a Visiting Fellow in the Social Justice Project at the Australian National University.

Index